PRISONS, PRISONERS AND PAROLE

Carolyn Leckie

Bruce Short Solicitors
3 Rattray Street
Dundee
DD1 1NA
LP44 Dundee

AUSTRALIA
Law Book Co.
Sydney

CANADA and USA
Carswell
Toronto

HONG KONG
Sweet & Maxwell Asia

NEW ZEALAND
Brookers
Wellington

SINGAPORE and MALAYSIA
Sweet & Maxwell Asia
Singapore and Kuala Lumpur

PRISONS, PRISONERS AND PAROLE

First Edition

Douglas Thomson
Solicitor Advocate

THOMSON

W. GREEN

Published in 2007 by
W. Green & Son Ltd
21 Alva Street
Edinburgh EH2 4PS

www.wgreen.thomson.com

Typeset by YHT Ltd, London
Printed and bound in Great Britain by Athenaeum Press Ltd,
Gateshead, Tyne and Wear

No natural forests were destroyed to make this product;
only farmed timber was used and replanted

A CIP catalogue record for this book is available from
the British Library.

ISBN   978-0-414-01692-7

FOREWORD

This book fills a long standing gap in Scottish legal writing.

Deprivation of liberty is the harshest punishment which can be passed in a Scottish court. It should only be imposed when the severity of the crime that has been committed or the safety of the public leaves the court with no other possible disposal.

For many years the court and the legal system regarded its task as completed once the prison gates clanged shut. What happened thereafter was a matter for the prison administration. Over the last twenty years or so it has been increasingly understood that this position is no longer tenable. The law does not end at the prison gate. Rather, it must shine into the deepest recesses of the prison. This is in the interests of prisoners, prison staff and the public.

Douglas Thomson has written a much needed book which is legally sound and eminently readable. It places Scottish prisons in their historical context and describes their daily reality from the perspective of the applicable law and regulations. It is also a useful reference point for the relevant case law.

Prisoners, Prisons and Parole is likely to become required reading for those involved in prisons, from whichever perspective.

Andrew Coyle CMG
Professor of Prison Studies
King's College
University of London

PREFACE

In the 13 years since Dr (as he then was) Jim McManus wrote the
first ever book on prisons law in Scotland, the entire legislative and
political landscape has been changed out of all recognition. Scotland was still many years from having its own legislature, the
European Convention on Human Rights was not incorporated into
UK Law, and only a tiny percentage of life prisoners knew when
they were due to be considered for parole. Litigation by prisoners in
the Scottish courts was rare in the extreme (fewer than 10 cases in
the index of *Prisons, Prisoners and the Law* involved actions raised
by serving Scottish prisoners), and perhaps most notably, the
average daily prison population was causing concern, as it regularly
exceeded 5,500.

The two most striking developments are the huge changes in
prisons law and practice necessitated by the coming into force of the
Human Rights Act 1998, and the vast amount of new legislation
that emanates from the Scottish Parliament. Without the ECHR, it
is unlikely that every life prisoner would know the date upon which
his case will first be considered by the Parole Board, or have the
case considered by a Tribunal, nor would prisoners find it quite so
easy to obtain a hearing in court in respect of any grievance they
may perceive. On the other hand, the Scottish Parliament has found
legislative time to bring in measures that increase the level of
supervision upon some offenders, and legislation recently passed is
expected by all to increase the number of persons incarcerated by a
significant percentage. The press and public retain their traditional
interest in crime and punishment, although whether their percep-
tions are always founded in objective reality may be debatable.

There can be no doubt that the whole issue of the use of imprisonment as a sanction, and of whether imprisonment yields practical social benefits will continue to be debated as long as society has
a concept of crime. This book is designed to inform those at all
levels who come into contact with the Scottish prison system; it is
not designed solely for lawyers and prison professionals.

All errors and omissions from the text are the sole responsibility
of the author, who wishes to express his thanks, in no particular
order, to: the partners and staff of McArthur Stanton, and those
members of the Dumbarton bar who have tolerated me as I prepared the text; the membership and the Secretariat of the Parole

Board for Scotland, whose helpful suggestions and encouragement are much appreciated, those at SPS who answered my repeated enquiries, and of course the production and editing staff at W. Green, without whom ... *takes out onion*

March 2007

CONTENTS

TABLE OF CASES

TABLE OF STATUTES

TABLE OF STATUTORY INSTRUMENTS

CHAPTER 1

THE DEVELOPMENT OF IMPRISONMENT IN SCOTLAND

Introduction

While the central role of the deprivation of liberty within our **1–01** penal system is now universally taken for granted, the sanction of imprisonment as a punishment in itself is, in fact, a relatively recent development. Rather than arising out of a deeply held philosophical belief in the importance of the deprivation of liberty as a sanction appropriate to a democratic society, the central position of imprisonment within our criminal justice system appears to owe as much to a pragmatic approach to events as they occur, as to any more theoretical concerns.

Indeed, if you were to tell the average burgess of a moderately sized Scottish town of the early eighteenth century that two centuries later the average daily population of persons held in custody in Scotland maintained at the expense of every single tax payer within the county would exceed 7,000, with the public seeming to present itself as more than happy for a significant increase in that number of persons, he would clearly wonder as to the type of society we have become.

For as long as there has been a recognised system of justice in Scotland, there has been a need for places within which offenders can be detained. However, prior to the nineteenth century, such establishments could scarcely be described as "prisons" in the sense that we would understand them today.

The early development of imprisonment

Until the nineteenth century, it was the obligation of every burgh **1–02** in Scotland to provide a place of confinement for prisoners, with the obligation to maintain the cost of a prison resting upon the burgesses themselves. At this time, the concept of deprivation of liberty as a sanction in its own right was relatively unknown to our jurisprudence, and therefore the purpose of detention in such establishments was, in general, reserved for those awaiting trial, awaiting sentence, or those who were incarcerated in respect of unpaid debts. In the average Scottish burgh, the number of persons incarcerated at any one time would rarely reach double figures. In terms of the Prisons Act 1597, burghs were placed under an obligation to provide prisons for the entire Kingdom, in which were to be detained both civil debtors and those facing criminal charges. In the event of a civil debtor absconding during his time of incarceration, responsibility for payment of his debts to his creditors fell upon the burgh itself. As the obligation to aliment criminal prisoners after conviction fell upon the burghs, the sanction of imprisonment was, understandably, unpopular amongst the burgesses. The obligation to aliment the prisoners whilst awaiting trial, however, rested with the counties.

In this era, it may therefore be concluded that the sanction of imprisonment itself as a punishment would be rarely used. It must be borne in mind that the entire population of Scotland as at 1700 is estimated to be of the order of 1,200,000 (the first census of the Scottish population was not carried out until 1750) and the population of Scotland had only risen to 1,608,000 by the time of the census of 1881. In the eighteenth century, serious crime seems to have been a comparative rarity within Scotland. Levels of capital punishment in the latter half of the eighteenth century were far below the levels found in England. The average number of executions carried out in Scotland annually in the latter part of the eighteenth century was of the order of five per year, at a time when London and the County of Middlesex, (an area with a population substantially less than 1,000,000) would regularly execute over 40 offenders per year. In addition, the sanction of transportation, much used in England throughout the eighteenth and early nineteenth century, was considerably less popular in Scotland.

Against this background, it seems reasonable to conclude that the successful prosecution of serious crime in Scotland in the late eighteenth and early nineteenth centuries was not a matter of particularly pressing social concern. As in the present day, the overwhelming majority of offending was of a relatively minor nature, the vast bulk of which was drink-related. These minor offences would tend to be dealt with by the imposition of financial penalties or some form of corporal punishment, such as a public flogging, or placement in the stocks, where the miscreant's visible turmoil at his public fettering would provide hours of amusement in the locality.

1–03   At a time two centuries before the existence of a properly constituted police force, when the fastest form of transportation of information was by horseback, it might be reasonable to conclude that that the local citizenry in the more rural parts of Scotland would be prepared to consider more expeditious means of dealing with local miscreants than by way of travelling on horseback for a day or so to the local sheriff to report their concerns as to the misdeeds of a local offender.

It should also perhaps be noted that in the eighteenth century, accused persons appearing before the High Court of Justiciary enjoyed the right to Petition for Banishment before their cases came to trial. If the victims of the alleged offences were in agreement with the petition, then the courts would customarily grant such petitions although it should be noted that the number of persons sentenced to transportation between 1718 and 1775 appears to have been of the order of seven hundred, the vast majority of these being transported in the aftermath of the 1745 uprising. England, of course, made a comparatively far higher use of transportation, particularly to Australia.

By the end of the eighteenth century, and with America now an independent colony, the sanction of transportation had become considerably less practicable than before. Convicted persons therefore found themselves incarcerated by necessity, pending decision being made as to their ultimate disposal. At around the same period, and particularly in the aftermath of the French Revolution and the growth in popular philosophies based around the concept of individual freedom, the sanction of deprivation of personal liberty as a punishment in itself began to increase in popularity.

It may also be of significance that a statute passed in 1819 placed **1–04** the voluntary contributions occasionally made by counties to burgh prisons upon a statutory footing for the first time. If the burghers were no longer the sole paymasters of the local "thieves' hole", they might be happier to see more miscreants detained there.

At a time when transportation was ceasing to be a viable sanction, a purely local system of prison administration created further variations in the standard of imprisonment from one part of the country to another. From contemporary records, there is little doubt that the conditions in which the average Scottish prisoner was incarcerated at that time were utterly squalid and desolate. Heat, light and ventilation were rarely provided, and privacy was utterly unknown, as prisoners were chained together to the walls of small straw-strewn hovels. In county towns, it seems that the money provided by prisoners' families for food would regularly be spent on drink, for staff and inmates alike. It might appear to modern eyes that this would do little to deter the drunken offender from resuming the same way of life on release, but this seems to have mattered little to our forbears.

A few of the older local prisons can still be seen in one form or another to this day. Stirling and Inveraray have turned theirs into tourist attractions, recreating the cramped space and implements of torture used in the eighteenth century, while a portion of the ruins of the former Dumbarton Prison is still visible immediately to the rear of the local sheriff court. The Governor's House of the former Calton Jail in Edinburgh still stands to this day, overlooking the eastern end of Waverley Station.

By the late eighteenth to early nineteenth century, the sanction of transportation had fallen into disuse. Scotland had tended to transport its felons across the Atlantic, and following the American War of Independence the number of colonies within the Caribbean willing to be recipients of our rejects dwindled rapidly. Somewhere else had to be found.

1–05   In 1798, Glasgow opened a Bridewell containing 115 cells in Duke Street. In 1824 a further 150 cells were opened. For the first time, a Scottish city had a place of some size specifically designed for the purpose of incarceration. At the start of the nineteenth century, conditions within the Bridewell remained squalid in the extreme, with as many as eight individuals crammed into filthy ill-ventilated cells, with no attempt at separation according to age or experience. Within the burghs, prisons remained small, unhygienic, and ill-managed, with counties seldom feeling the necessity to spend their funds on improving the conditions of criminals.

When English philanthropists such as John Howard and the brother and sister team of Joseph Gurney and Elizabeth Fry travelled to Scotland, they were unsurprisingly appalled at the conditions they discovered, and their concerns were influential in the findings of the House of Commons Select Committee in 1826, which reported:

> "The result of this inquiry has ... been to show, that with a few exceptions, the state of those prisons is very defective in point of security, accommodation and management, while the funds from which such prisons ought to be improved are, in most instances, inadequate to that purpose".

The only institution to receive compliments in the committee's report was the Glasgow Bridewell, which had, since 1808, been under the Governorship of William Brebner (1783–1845), a reformer and the man universally regarded as the founding father of the Scottish Prison Service. It was he who introduced the practice of separation of prisoners, more than doubling the number of cells, and he provided work for prisoners each day from 6am until 8pm.

For the first time, the notion of imprisonment became one of punishment and amelioration. It was recognised that deprivation of liberty was itself a sanction, and that prisoners should be encouraged to work positively whilst in prison. Education, at a very basic level, was introduced and prisoners were separated according to gender, with female prisoners attended by female staff.

Introduction of state control

Under the Prisons (Scotland) Act 1839, prisons came under state **1–06** control for the first time. A Board of Directors of Prisons was formed, with authority to regulate the discipline and management of all prisons throughout the country. An Inspector of Prisons was appointed, and the first set of Prison Rules was introduced in 1840. Local prisons were placed under the control of county boards, responsible for the appointment of staff and for making decisions on the day-to-day running of the prisons. It was central to this system that those employed by county boards should be employed full-time as prison officers. Previously those involved in the running of prisons were part-timers who were under no obligation to demonstrate any aptitude for the management or administration of a place of detention. Indeed in the early nineteenth century it appears that the governor of Alloa Jail combined his duties of overseeing local wrongdoers with being the local chimney sweep. It was often not merely the inmates who had spent the bulk of their waking hours in a state of intoxication. In 1845, the Board of Directors found it necessary to remind county boards that staffing a prison could not be combined with the duties of constable or sheriff officer.

The first General Prison in Scotland was opened in Perth in 1842, on a site that had previously housed prisoners of war in the Napoleonic Era. Much of the building, though much altered and improved, remains in use to this day. All prisoners serving sentences in excess of nine months, those sentenced to penal servitude, and the quaintly termed (to modern ears) "criminal lunatics", served their sentences in Perth. By 1852, it housed 431 inmates, and was the third largest penal establishment in the country, behind the Bridewells of Glasgow (651 inmates) and Edinburgh (610 inmates). These three establishments housed 57 per cent of the 2976 inmates that year. The remaining 43 per cent were spread amongst 80 local establishments, many of which admitted no inmates at all. Local prisons in Paisley, Stirling and Dundee housed over a hundred prisoners, while the entire prison population of some counties of the size of Fife and Dunbartonshire was below 50. The era of the small local prison housing a handful of inmates was coming to a close.

In terms of the Prisons (Scotland) Act 1877, ss.4 and 5, the expense of maintaining Scotland's prisons was for the first time to be met solely out of central funds, and the responsibility for prison administration was transferred to the Secretary for Scotland (as he was then called). Five Prison Commissioners were appointed, including the Sheriff Principal of Perth and the Crown Agent *ex officio*, with a duty to report to parliament on their activities. To ensure that a level of local input remained, s.16 granted authority to local sheriffs to visit prisons within their sheriffdoms, and ss.14 and 15 authorised the setting up of visiting committees, consisting of justices of the peace, magistrates and commissioners of supply, thus ensuring the continuation of a local voice, as local prisons became replaced by General Prisons. Between 1878 and 1888 the number of county prisons, already in decline, dwindled further, from 56 to 15. Barlinnie Prison in Glasgow became a general prison in 1882 (the same year that Dumfries began construction), and Peterhead was opened in 1888. Interestingly, the impetus for the construction of the prison and its adjacent harbour by prisoners' labour, came about following a recognition that Scottish prisoners had not previously contributed to the direct cost of the United Kingdom prison programme. Since the building of Peterhead, Scottish prisoners have not been sent to England except in special circumstances. Aberdeen Prison was begun in 1890, Inverness in 1901, and Edinburgh in 1914, although it was not completed until 1930 (it should be noted that the last inmates from the former Calton Jail in the city centre left there in 1925), while Polmont Borstal, a forerunner to the present day Young Offenders Institution on the same site, was purchased by the state in 1911.

The Twentieth Century

1–07   By virtue of the Reorganisation of Offices (Scotland) Act 1928, the Prison Commissioners were abolished and replaced by the Prisons Department for Scotland. This was abolished in 1939, when its functions were placed under the direct control of the Secretary of State for Scotland, where they remained until the coming into force of the Scotland Act 1998, when prisons came under the umbrella of the Justice Department. When the commissioners demitted office, there remained only 12 prisons in the whole of Scotland, a number that has remained relatively constant to the present day, when there are now 16. New establishments were opened at Glenochil in 1966, initially taking only offenders aged from 16–21, but since 1987 housing adult offenders, and since 2003 only housing convicted adult prisoners, and at Shotts in 1978. Scotland's first and only dedicated prison for female offenders was established at Cornton Vale, Stirling, in 1978, three years after it was first opened, and was substantially extended in 2005.

It may be interesting to note that, with growing centralisation into larger establishments, the number of prisoners dropped dramatically, falling from a daily average of around 3000 to 1639 by 1928, and the number of female prisoners in particular declined, and to this day remains proportionately low. In the mid-nineteenth century, around one in three inmates were female. By 1938 the proportion had dropped to ten per cent, and by 1966 to barely three per cent. While the number of women in prison has increased steadily over the past ten years, and the proportion of female inmates in the total prison population has risen somewhat, it still remains just below five per cent of the total population.

Following certain further developments after the Second World War, culminating in the Criminal Justice (Scotland) Act 1949, the legislation governing the operation and administration of prisons, and the basic principles of custody and control of prisoners, was consolidated into the Prisons (Scotland) Act 1952. This Act and the rules made thereunder, the Prisons (Scotland) Rules 1952, remained in force, subject to some minor statutory amendments, until 1989 and 1994 respectively, during periods that saw both massive changes in social attitudes and a huge increase in the prison population. The Prisons (Scotland) Act 1989, as amended, a con-solidating statute, remains the primary legislation governing imprisonment and the powers of the Secretary of State (now, of course, the Justice Minister) to regulate the administration of prisons and to issue rules in regard to the administration of prisons — as such, the salient features of the Act will be discussed in a succeeding chapter.

The Prisons (Scotland) Rules 1952

While the 1952 Rules have been repealed in their entirety, they **1–08** remain an interesting document of the era when the "treatment model" was the dominant theory in prison administration. The prevailing orthodoxy of the time was that social deviance could be equiparated with other forms of illness, and could therefore respond to treatment. Rule 5 stated "The purposes of training and treatment of convicted prisoners shall be to establish in them the will to live a good and useful life on discharge, and to fit them to do so". An identical form of wording appeared in the Young Offenders (Scotland) Rules 1965, r.3. The concept of "preventative deten-tion", whereby sentences could be extended far beyond any retri-butive element proportionate to the offence itself, by the addition of a preventative element during which the offender could be treated, had been introduced by the 1949 Act. Of course, the two most obvious difficulties in the application of a treatment model to any prison system were firstly that there remains no evidence whatso-ever of any society ever discovering a "cure" for criminality, and secondly, that not all offenders, who would be considered to be in need of treatment, were in fact caught, successfully prosecuted and imprisoned. Therefore, at best a minority of those felt to need treatment would ever even find themselves in a situation where treatment would be offered.

In terms of the 1952 rules, the only individual within any prison that was invested with any rights at all was the Governor. He, of course, was provided with a large staff to enable him to exercise his rights, but the concept that the prisoners themselves retained any rights once the gates closed upon them was utterly alien to the draftsmen of the rules. Effectively, anything given to a sentenced prisoner during his time in custody was of the nature of a privilege, the withdrawal of which gave rise to no claim on the part of the prisoner. Of course, prisoners retained their entitlement to work, exercise, and leisure time, to food and education, and to visits from friends and family, but none of these were enshrined as "rights". Should a prisoner be accused of offending against any of the rules concerning prison discipline, such as by refusing to work, using threatening and abusive language to an officer or damaging prison property, the governor would convene a hearing within the Orderly Room, at which he would hear evidence from members of his own staff, at which the prisoner had no entitlement to legal representation, and at the end of which, if guilt were established, he could order that the prisoner forfeit up to fourteen days remission, thus altering the prisoner's date of liberation. In more serious cases, the allegation would be heard by the Visiting Committee, an external body appointed by the local authority. The prisoner who was aggrieved by an unfavourable decision had no automatic right of redress.

Prisoners had no access to the telephone system, and all mail into and out of prison, including legal correspondence in respect of outstanding trials and appeals, would routinely be scrutinised by staff before being given to the prisoner. If the governor felt them not to be conducive to good order, family visits could be cancelled. As recently as 1988, it was felt appropriate in at least one mainstream Scottish prison for all visits to prisoners on one floor in one hall to be cancelled without prior notification, as a result of the disruptive behaviour of certain inmates only.

While a system of parole for those serving longer sentences had been introduced by the Criminal Justice Act 1967, the Parole Board's function was advisory, and the decision on whether to release a prisoner on parole or not rested with the Secretary of State. These decisions were made on a paper review of a dossier seen only by the Parole Board and the appropriate civil servants. The prisoner had no right to see the contents of the dossier, or to challenge or correct any errors and ambiguities. Once the decision whether or not to grant parole had been made, the prisoner would be advised of the decision itself, in the form of a brief extract from the board's minutes. If the decision was not in favour of his liberation, and the length of his sentence merited it, he would be advised in broad terms of the date by which his next review would be completed, and there the matter would rest.

Legal and political developments

In the course of the four decades between the 1952 rules and their **1–09** replacement by the Prisons and Young Offenders Institutions (Scotland) Rules 1994, attitudes to prisons and imprisonment developed in a number of ways that would not have been foreseen by the draftsmen of the earlier rules. While prisoners were not encouraged to raise actions in the Scottish courts to challenge the conditions of their detention (such actions appear unknown to the Scottish Law Reports until after a number of landmark cases had been taken to the European Court of Human Rights in the 1970s and 1980s), the few early examples of such challenges being argued in England indicate the prevailing judicial attitudes of the times as less than favourable. In *Becker v The Home Office* [1972] 2 Q.B. 407, Lord Denning famously stated "If the courts were to entertain actions by disgruntled prisoners, the Governor's life would be made intolerable".

Changing attitudes in the fields of criminology and penology, and changing social attitudes, including a growth in the use of litigation to challenge perceived injustice, began to create a shift in attitudes. The courts began to recognise the existence, albeit still with limitations, of prisoners retaining certain rights. Lord Wilberforce, issuing his judgement in *Raymond v Honey* [1983] A.C. 1, observed: "A convicted prisoner, in spite of his imprisonment, retains all rights not taken way expressly or by necessary implication". This dictum was approved by the Outer House in *Thomson v Secretary of State for Scotland*, 1989 S.C.L.R. 161.

The continuing increase in the numbers of persons sent to prison, and the fact that the majority of those imprisoned for the first time returned to prison within two years, indicated that the "treatment model" was having little success in rehabilitating offenders. Compelling a prisoner to accept treatment for his perceived deviance from social norms had required a considerable degree of intervention, and was widely resented. By the 1970s the treatment model was no longer used as official penal policy. The sanction of preventative detention fell into disuse, and was ultimately abolished in 1980.

1–10   The absence of any domestic remedies, either at common law or under statute, against perceived injustices, persuaded a number of aggrieved prisoners, particularly in the early stages Irish Republicans, to challenge the lawfulness of United Kingdom prison policy in the European Court of Human Rights. Despite the UK being one of the first signatories of the European Convention on Human Rights and Fundamental Freedoms, it took until 1998 for the Convention itself to find its way onto the statute book. However, the UK had always recognised the need to accept the jurisdiction of the court in determining whether a citizen's Convention rights had been violated, and British citizens had had the right to petition the court since 1965. Given the climate of secrecy in decision-making, and the effective recognition that rights ceased at the prison gates, it was no surprise that prisoners began to use applications to the European Court to seek to determine the lawfulness or otherwise of the conditions of their detention.

Drawing its members from a wide number of judicial systems, the European Court of Human Rights proved more receptive to a rights-based culture than the traditional common law based judiciaries of England and Scotland, and from 1984 onward, a number of decisions of that court began to be issued that were directly critical of UK prison policy, and forced those charged with the administration of prisons to think again about some long-cherished ideals. In *Campbell and Fell v United Kingdom*, 7 E.H.R.R. 165, decided in June 1984, the court held that proceedings before the Board of Visitors (the English equivalent of the Visiting Committee), in respect of alleged assaults on staff, at the end of which the applicants lost 570 days remission, were subject to Art.6.1. The government invited the court to declare that proceedings before the Board of Visitors were not subject to Art.6, seeking to draw a distinction between prisoners rights and privileges, and the court observed:

> "The Court, for its part, does not find that the distinction between privilege and right is of great assistance to it for the present purposes; what is more important is that the practice of granting remission — whereby a prisoner will be set free on the estimated date for release given to him at the outset of his sentence, unless remission has been forfeited in disciplinary proceedings ... creates in him a legitimate expectation that he will recover his liberty before the end of his term of imprisonment. Forfeiture of remission thus has the effect of causing the detention to continue beyond the period corresponding to that expectation."

In that case, the issues of the availability of legal aid, and of the legitimacy of prisons interfering with prisoners' correspondence were also raised, and the court unanimously held that, in withholding correspondence, there had been a violation of Art.8 of the Convention.

The domestic situation

At around the same time, the situation within individual prisons **1–11** in Scotland had visibly deteriorated. Unhappy, unmotivated staff, disgruntled at their pay and working conditions, were expected to maintain control of an increasing number of prisoners who resented the conditions in which they were kept. A vociferous minority, principally of long-term prisoners, many of whom were aware of recent decisions of the European courts, were no longer prepared to acquiesce silently in treatment they felt to be degrading, with their perception being that petty rules were being applied arbitrarily to maintain control. Within a few years in the mid-1980s disfiguring riots developed in Edinburgh, Perth, Glenochil, Shotts and Peterhead, causing massive damage to the prison structures, and serious physical and mental injury to a great many officers. Whatever view one took of the causes of the riots, the characters of the rioters, and the appropriateness of the damage done, it was clear to all involved in prison administration that maintaining the status quo was not an option. It was not enough simply to blame the disturbances on an "untrainable" hard core of prisoners, but to look at the entire prison management systems. By the end of the 1980s, as many as 25 per cent of hall staff in some establishments were on long-term sick leave, and the resultant staff shortages, forcing already tired officers into working additional shifts just to ensure that hall were manned, pushed the day-to-day administration of the system close to meltdown.

Throughout the final years of the 1980s and the early years of the 1990s, a wide-ranging debate as to the reasons for the disturbances and the lessons to be learned from them took place. It was clear that the reasons for disquiet were varied and complex, and that the source of the disquiet ranged far beyond a small group of troublemakers. It is perhaps fortunate that at that very time Scotland was blessed with a number of visionary figures within prison administration, able to look beyond the particular circumstances of each incident. Andrew Coyle, then Governor of HM Prison Shotts, with eighteen years service within SPS, and now Professor of Prison Studies in King's College, London University, argued in *Inside — Rethinking Scotland's Prisons* (Scottish Child, Edinburgh, 1991) that the root of our prisons' instability should be traced to the system in which they are held, which had since 1929 developed away from the criminal justice system and into an arm of the Civil Service. His conclusions were firmly in favour of the notion of "positive custody", with the prison offering opportunities to the prisoner.

The reaction of the prison service

1–12   The Scottish Prison Service published a number of important consultative documents, setting out a vision for the future of the prison system. This, in itself, represented a huge break with tradition. Prior to 1988, discussion about present and future management of prisons would take place in private, with contributors to the debate being invited to contribute. In March 1988 the SPS published its first consultation document "Custody and Care", which was followed in May 1990 by "Opportunity and Responsibility". By now, the previous approach that centred upon the notion that prisoners effectively forfeited all rights on admission, and required to earn privileges by way of good conduct and adherence to the rules, was no longer tenable, and an entirely new view of prisoners replaced it. "Opportunity and Responsibility" regarded prisoners as responsible adults, who were entitled to exercise a degree of free will in making choices about what to do with their time within prison. It was the duty of the prison service to provide a safe and secure custodial environment, in which prisoners would be encouraged to make use of the facilities provided. For the first time, prisons would regard offering prisoners the chance to undertake relevant offence-focussed coursework geared towards their particular needs as central to their role. As will be seen later, as these programmes developed, these needs would not solely relate to the nature of the index offence, but would relate to specific areas in which an inmate was felt likely to benefit from work whilst in custody.

The importance of maintaining family contact was further recognised. Attempts should be made, so far as practicable, to minimise the disruption to family life, and prisoners should be subject to the minimum amount of security and other restrictions required for safe and orderly confinement. In order to achieve these goals, it would be necessary both to bring into force an entirely new set of prison rules, and to review and amend the security classifications then in force, which had been created in 1966 following the Mountbatten Report into Prison Escapes in England and Wales. It may indicate the level of priority given to these matters to note that the Prisons and Young Offenders Institutions (Scotland) Rules were laid before parliament on July 19, 1994, and (with a few minor exceptions) came into force on November 1, 1994. It took until

April 2001, however, for the previous Security Categories to be abolished, and replaced by Supervision Categories.

The Prisoners and Young Offenders Institution (Scotland) Rules 1994

For the first time, the 1994 Rules granted certain specific rights to prisoners, for example with regard to the possession of tobacco (r.41), retention in their cells of certain items of their own property (r.44), the obtaining of books and newspapers (r.46), to correspondence by way of letters (rr.48–52) and telephone calls (r.54), and to accumulated visits (r.57). In terms of r.136, the Visiting Committee was given the power to investigate a prisoner's complaint, and intimate its findings to the Secretary of State and the governor. These rules had of course been drafted in the light of certain recent decisions of the European Court of Human Rights, and in the anticipation that the European Convention on Human Rights would become part of UK law within a relatively short period. Before the rules came into force, the notion of prisoners being granted specific entitlements was controversial, with many within the prison system predicting that exercise of these rights would lead to the governor's life being made as intolerable as Lord Denning had predicted two decades previously. Instead, after some initial difficulties, it became clear that prisoners and staff preferred the new system, as, for the first time, there was a reasonably accessible code available to all within the establishment that set out in detail the precise rights and obligations of all parties. The openness that was central to the 1994 Rules left few in any doubt where the bulk of the boundaries lay. It may or may not be coincidental, but since the coming into force of the 1994 Rules there has been no serious repetition of the disfiguring riots that blighted Scotland's prisons in the 1980s. These rules were substantially altered and amended on several occasions over the following decade, and were ultimately repealed and replaced by the Prisons and Young Offenders Institutions (Scotland) Rules 2006, with effect from March 26, 2006. These rules will be discussed in detail in the following chapters.

The 1994 Rules were not the only significant development in prison practice that year. The Criminal Justice and Public Order Act 1994 added new ss.41B and 41C into the 1989 Act, conferring powers on officers to require prisoners to provide samples for the purpose of ascertaining whether he has drugs (s.41B) or alcohol (s.41C) in his body. New rules 88A and 88B were inserted into the 1994 rules shortly thereafter, defining the procedures for compulsory testing. Following publication of a further consultation document "Right and Just" in 1993, which had recommended a

1–13

two-tier system of grievance panels, the SPS introduced a new internal complaints procedure, to be under the supervision of the first Scottish Prison Complaints Commissioner, whose remit was to respond to prisoners' complaints about any prison administrative matter, including governor's adjudications, and who took office in autumn 1994. Also, until that year, every prison (and therefore every prisoner) fell under the sole responsibility of the Secretary of State. In terms of the Criminal Justice and Public Order Act 1994, the private sector became empowered to become involved in the operation of prisons and escort services to and from prisons. The Secretary of State could thus contract out the running of a prison to a private company, who shall appoint a director, whose powers are broadly analogous to those of a governor in a state-run establishment. While the transportation of prisoners to and from the courts is now in the hands of the private sector, and while electronic monitoring in terms of ss.245A–245I of the Criminal Procedure (Scotland) Act 1995 is also in private hands, to date only one prison in Scotland (HM Prison Kilmarnock, opened in March 1999) has been opened by the private sector.

Other developments

1–14   On October 1, 1993, the provisions for sentencing convicted prisoners were substantially altered by the coming into force of the Prisoners and Criminal Proceedings (Scotland) Act 1993. Following the recommendations of the Kincraig Committee's Report "Parole and Related Issues in Scotland" (1989, Cm 598), the arrangements for release of prisoners were divided according to the length of the prisoner's sentence. Those serving less than four years *in cumulo* would be released automatically at the halfway stage of their sentences, subject to the proviso that if they re-offended before their sentence end date, they were liable to be ordered to be returned to custody for an appropriate period of the unexpired portion of their sentence, in addition to any sentence the court considered appropriate in respect of the new offence. So far as those serving four years or more were concerned, they were eligible for release on parole licence at the halfway point of their sentence if their level of risk were considered manageable within the community; otherwise, they would be released on licence at the two-thirds stage of their sentence, subject to such licence conditions as the Parole Board considered necessary for management of their level of risk. Breach of any of these licence conditions could result in their recall to custody, whether or not they had been convicted of any further offence. In a further break with the previous traditions of secrecy surrounding staff reports and internal documentation, prisoners were now allowed access to their full parole dossier, and could make written representations to the board in determinate sentence cases and oral representations to Life Prisoner Tribunals. Section 2 of the 1993 Act introduced Life Prisoner Tribunals into our legal system for the first time. Initially applying only to discretionary life prisoners, and to those who had received their mandatory life sentence prior to the age of 18, these tribunals were introduced in recognition of the growing European jurisprudence on the precise meaning of a life sentence, and its conformity or otherwise with Art.5(4) of the Convention. This provides that:

"Everyone who is deprived of his liberty by arrest or detention shall be entitled to take proceedings by which the lawfulness of his detention shall be decided speedily by a court and his release ordered if the detention is not lawful".

In *Thynne, Wilson and Gunnell v United Kingdom* (Series A, No. 190-A E.C.H.R.), decided in October 1990, three discretionary life sentence prisoners serving their sentences in England had sought to challenge, in terms of Art.5.4, the absence of any legal mechanism whereby they could challenge the lawfulness of their continued detention after the expiry of the "tariff" period fixed by the sentencing court. The Court held that "the factors of mental instability and dangerousness are susceptible to change over the passage of time and new issues of lawfulness may thus arise in the course of their detention". In terms of Art.5.4, the applicants were entitled to take proceedings to have the lawfulness of their detention decoded by a court. The determination of their continued detention after the expiry of the tariff period should be determined by a judicial process, and not by a politician's decision. Recognising the crucial importance of this decision, appropriate legislation was passed in both Scotland and England (Criminal Justice Act 1991).

Legislation on crime and imprisonment continued apace, and the 1993 Act had already been amended by both the Crime and Punishment (Scotland) Act 1997 and the Crime and Disorder Act 1998, before the Scotland Act 1998 set up a Scottish Parliament, to which was devolved the administration of crime and criminal justice. In terms of s.57(2) of the Scotland Act, it became unlawful for any member of the Scottish executive to act in any manner contrary to the terms of the Convention, and thus, in October 2001, the Act was further substantially amended by the Convention Rights (Compliance) (Scotland) Act 2001.

The Convention Rights (Compliance) (Scotland) Act 2001

1–15   In terms of this Act, every prisoner sentenced to life imprisonment has a "punishment part" specified in his sentence. This is defined as the part of the sentence that is considered by the sentencing judge as "appropriate to satisfy the requirements for retribution and deterrence" relevant to the offence, having regard to the circumstances of the offence and of the offender. Every person sentenced to life imprisonment after February 2002 had a punishment part fixed at the time of sentencing, and every person already serving life imprisonment as at October 15, 2001 was entitled to have their case called before a single judge of the High Court (with a right of appeal against sentence), in order to have an appropriate punishment part fixed. Virtually all life prisoners in Scotland, apart from those whose release was imminent, therefore appeared in court and had punishment parts fixed. The average punishment part, which had been estimated in consultation before the Act came into force to be of the order of 10 years, in fact turned out to be 12.4 years (perhaps contrary to the expectations of those members of the tabloid press who consider all judges to be "soft on crime").

At the conclusion of the punishment part, the decision on whether to release the prisoner on life licence falls to be considered by a tribunal comprising three members of the Parole Board, with a legally qualified chair. Once the punishment part of the sentence has been served in full, the prisoner is entitled to have his case considered speedily by a tribunal. In practice, the first such hearing will take place within three working days of the expiry of the punishment part. The decision of the tribunal on whether or not to direct release of the prisoner is binding on Ministers (1993 Act, s.2(4)). In terms of s.2(5)(b) of the Act as amended, the Parole Board shall *not* direct release unless "the Board is satisfied that it is no longer necessary for the protection of the public that the prisoner should be confined". If release is directed, this is intimated to the prisoner, his legal representative if appropriate, to Ministers and to the prison within fourteen days of the hearing. Release must follow as soon as possible thereafter — usually on the next working day. It is thus at this stage that the interests of public protection take precedence over any question of revulsion at the nature of the offence itself. The question the tribunal must ask is "Is the level of risk to the public that this prisoner *currently* poses manageable by way of supervision in the community?" The operation of the tribunal system will be discussed in detail in Chapter 9, but at this stage it may be instructive to note that at present fewer than 20 per cent of life prisoners are released immediately after the expiry of their punishment part. In this regard, it should of course be noted that, at the time of writing, every life prisoner whose case has been considered for the first time since February 2002 was already serving his sentence prior to the coming into force of the Convention Rights Act, and thus had no expectation of his case being considered by a tribunal at the date of his conviction.

The Scotland Act 1998 had already made it unlawful for any member of the Scottish Executive to act in a manner contrary to the ECHR, and the Human Rights Act 1998 finally came into force for the entire country in October 2001. By then, the old familiar practice of a prison governor awarding loss of remission (in effect extending the time a prisoner spent in custody) after a private hearing within the prison at which he was customarily required to adjudicate on the credibility of a member of his own staff against that of a sentenced prisoner, had been dropped, quietly and without publicity. There can be little doubt that, viewed objectively, the conduct of these hearings was not in conformity with Art.6.1, which provides that in determination of civil rights and obligations or any criminal charge, "everyone is entitled to fair and public hearing ... by an independent and impartial tribunal established by law". Following *Campbell and Fell v United Kingdom*, this had been virtually inevitable.

Prisoners (and sometimes prison staff) have shown a far greater **1–16** willingness to resort to the courts over the past decade, in order to seek redress in respect of perceived injustices. In particular, the growth in the number of specialist practitioners in the field of Human Rights law and the swift procedures available for determination of matters by Petition for Judicial Review have proved attractive to prisoner litigants, and Scottish Ministers and the Parole Board regularly find themselves in the Court of Session seeking to justify their decisions. Undoubtedly the most significant and wide-ranging case yet decided by the Scottish courts was *Napier v The Scottish Ministers*, 2005 S.C. 229. In that case, evidence was heard over several days in respect of numerous aspects of prison conditions, and it will be analysed in full elsewhere in this book.

The prison population continues to increase, from a daily average of 5993 in 1996–97 to 6779 in 2004–05. Perhaps, more disturbingly, after the daily average dropped for two consecutive years in 1999–2000 and 2000–01, to a recent low of 5883, the population increase in the past four years has exceeded 15 per cent, at a time when the number of recorded offences in Scotland shows a decline.

Legislation continues apace. The courts are given more and more varied sentencing powers. Since September 30, 1998, the higher courts have been given the power to impose extended sentences on sex offenders and violent offenders sentenced to four years or more, where the court considers "that the period (if any) for which the offender would, apart from this section, be subject to licence would not be adequate for the purpose of protecting the public from serious harm from the offender" (1995 Act, s.210A(1)(b)). In January 2006, the Management of Offenders (Scotland) Act 2005 amended the 1993 Act yet again, by providing that all offenders convicted of a sexual offence and given a determinate sentence of between six months and four years imprisonment will no longer be released unconditionally, but will instead be released subject to licence conditions imposed by Scottish Ministers, and thus subject to the possibility of recall to custody. With effect from July 6, 2006, the provisions of the Management of Offenders (Scotland) Act 2005 s.15, which inserted a new Section 1AA into the 1993 Act, provide that certain low risk long-term and short term prisoners may further qualify for early release subject to the requirement to comply with the conditions of a Home Detention Curfew. It is estimated that this will affect over 2000 prisoners a year, and the provisions will be considered in detail in a later chapter.

1–17   Following publication of a consultation document on "Release and Post Custody Management of Offenders" in June 2006, the Scottish Executive introduced the Custodial Sentences and Weapons (Scotland) Bill in October 2006, the provisions of which are designed to end automatic and unconditional early release of offenders, and to achieve greater clarity in sentencing. At the time of writing, the Bill is still in progress through the parliamentary process, and it is not clear when, and in precisely what form, it will eventually be enacted. The salient proposals within the Bill will be addressed in later chapters. Ministers are considering the construction of new prisons, and a capacity of at least 8000 places, with all of these expected to be filled within the decade, has been openly discussed. At present Scotland's detention rate per 100,000 head of population stands at 135 — lower than England, and not increasing as rapidly, but still one of the highest in Europe, and continuing to rise substantially, as will be seen from the table below. It is clear that our politicians expect the prison population to rise yet higher, and have budgeted accordingly.

Country	Average Prison population per 100,000 in 1990	Average Prison Population per 100,000 in 2004	Percentage increase/decrease
England & Wales	93	143	53%
Scotland	95	135	42%
Northern Ireland	112	102	–9%
France	81	88	9%
Germany	84	97	15%
Portugal	85	123	45%
Italy	55	97	76%
Belgium	71	88	24%
Netherlands	44	127	189%
Sweden	60	78	30%
Finland	72	66	–8%
Austria	83	108	30%

CHAPTER 2

ADMISSION INTO PRISON

2–01 In most cases, a person admitted to prison in Scotland has either been remanded in custody awaiting trial for a criminal offence punishable by imprisonment, or has been convicted of an offence punishable by imprisonment, and is therefore either in custody awaiting sentence, or serving some form of custodial sentence imposed following upon conviction. There are a number of rarer circumstances in which a person may be admitted to prison; these are discussed at the end of this chapter.

REMANDS IN CUSTODY AWAITING TRIAL

2–02 There are two forms of criminal procedure in Scotland: Solemn Procedure, where the prosecution proceeds on indictment either in the High Court of Justiciary or before a sheriff where the case is considered to be serious enough to justify trial on indictment before a jury, and Summary Procedure.

Summary Procedure

2–03 Summary Procedure takes place either in the sheriff court, where the sheriff sits alone, or in the district court, where the case calls before a stipendiary magistrate, or a justice or justices of the peace. The law governing the periods of remand in custody is to be found in the Criminal Procedure (Scotland) Act 1995 (hereinafter "the 1995 Act"). Where an accused person first appears in court on a Summary Complaint, is called upon the plead, and tenders a plea of not guilty he may be ordained (ordered) to appear, released on bail pending the determination of his trial, or remanded in custody. In terms of s.147(1), a person charged with an offence in summary proceedings who tenders a plea of not guilty "shall not be detained in that respect for a total of more than forty days after the bringing of the complaint in Court unless his trial is commenced within that period, failing which he shall be liberated forthwith and thereafter he shall be forever free from all question or process for that offence". This period may be extended only where the sheriff is satisfied that delay in the commencement of the trial is due to the illness of the accused or of a judge, the absence or illness of a necessary witness, or any other sufficient cause which is not attributable to any fault on the part of the prosecutor. In the event of the sheriff granting such an extension, the accused has, in terms of s.147(3), the right to appeal that decision to the High Court, which may affirm, reverse or amend the determination made by the sheriff. In practice, in most modern Scottish courts, where the accused is remanded in custody, his trial will normally commence within three to five weeks of the date of his remand.

It should of course be noted that at present, with a few statutory exceptions, the most common ones being offences under s.41 of the Police (Scotland) Act 1967 (nine months), the Misuse of Drugs Act 1971 (twelve months), and where an offence is aggravated by being committed whilst on bail (where the court has the power under s.27(5) of the 1995 Act to increase the sentence by up to six months), the sheriff's maximum power of sentence on a summary complaint is one of six months imprisonment (of which the accused must, in terms of the Prisoners and Criminal Proceedings (Scotland) Act 1993 serve one half, although he remains liable to further imprisonment if he commits another imprisonable offence before his sentence end date).

Mentally disordered offenders

Occasionally a person will appear from custody on summary **2–04** complaint, and it will appear to the prosecutor that that person is suffering from a mental disorder. In that situation, the accused is customarily not called upon to plead, and may, in terms of s.52 of the 1995 Act, be committed to hospital. However, s.52(5) provides that "No person shall be committed to a hospital under this section except on the written or oral evidence of a registered medical practitioner". In practice such evidence is not always available where the accused has been in custody for less than 24 hours, and thus the courts occasionally find themselves compelled to detain an accused in custody pending receipt of the appropriate evidence, and pending the court being satisfied, as required by s.52(2) that a hospital is available for his admission and suitable for his detention. Should the matter proceed by way of a plea of insanity in bar of trial, it should be noted that s.54 requires this to be certified by the written or oral evidence of two medical practitioners. Again, it is competent in terms of the statute to remand the accused in custody if no appropriate hospital has been identified, pending the making of a "temporary hospital order".

Since October 5, 2005, the court's' powers to deal with persons
who may be suffering from a mental disorder have been significantly widened by the coming into force of s.52B–J of the 1995
Act, as inserted by the Mental Health (Care and Treatment)
(Scotland) Act 2003. In terms of these sections, prosecutors and
ministers have the power to apply to the courts for "assessment
orders", in terms of which offenders may be admitted to hospital.
The nature of these orders, and the circumstances in which they
may be granted, fall outwith the scope of this book. It is, however,
to be hoped that the number and length of remands in custody of
apparently mentally disordered offenders, which have long proved
unpopular with lawyers, medical practitioners and the courts, will
diminish considerably in future.

Solemn Procedure

2–05   Solemn Proceedings are almost inevitably commenced by the
service of a petition on the accused, after which he appears in private before the sheriff within whose jurisdiction the offence (or at
least one of the offences if the petition contains more than one
charge) was allegedly committed. While the procedures have
changed radically over the centuries, the terminology used is
effectively that which our eighteenth century forebears would
recognise. At the first appearance of an accused on petition, he is
customarily committed for further examination, although in modern practice the court no longer takes any part in the examination
of the accused. He is not called upon to plead, as the charges on the
initial petition may be very different to those upon which he ultimately stands trial, and while the accused retains his age-old right
to emit a Judicial Declaration, in terms of s.34(3) of the 1995, such
declarations remain rare in modern practice. Bail may now competently be granted for all offences, although the position of the
Crown in murder cases stated below should be noted.

Bail

2–06   Prior to 2000, bail was competent for all offences except murder
and treason, but that distinction, which had become somewhat
academic since the abolition of the death penalty, has now been
withdrawn. Since the coming into force of the Bail, Judicial
Appointments, Etc. (Scotland) Act 2000 it is now specifically provided by s.24(1) of the 1995 Act that all crimes and offences are
bailable. While it remains competent for the court to grant bail to
an accused facing a murder charge, following some well-publicised
cases where persons facing murder charges were released on bail,
the Lord Advocate issued new guidelines on July 28, 2006, to the

effect that bail will always be opposed by the Crown at the first calling of a petition alleging murder, and any grant of bail will be appealed to the High Court. With effect from that date, bail can only be unopposed at any stage in the case upon the specific instructions of Crown Counsel.

Since the coming into force of the Human Rights Act, it is now the invariable practice of the Crown, where bail is to be opposed and the accused is facing a remand in custody, to insert onto the service copy of the petition (and onto the principal seen by the sheriff) a "custody statement", setting out in broad outline the evidence the Crown have in their possession that is sufficient to indicate the involvement of the accused in the commission of the alleged offence. The practice was expressly approved in *Brown v Selfridge*, 1999 S.C.C.R. 809 and *Hynd v Ritchie*, 2002 S.C.C.R 755. There is no prescribed form for such a statement, although it must at least give notice, in broad terms, of the sources of evidence upon which the Crown will rely in attempting to prove the charge — thus bald statements such as "Two civilian witness identify the accused as being at the locus and he made relevant admissions to the police" or "Fingerprints identified as belonging to the accused were found inside the locus" are commonly appended to petitions. In theory, the sheriff may refuse to commit the accused if the custody statement does not disclose at least a *prima facie* case against him.

Where bail is opposed, the decision of whether to grant or refuse bail is one for the presiding sheriff. Guidelines as to when bail is and is not appropriate were set out by Lord Justice-Clerk Wheatley in *Smith v McC*, 1982 S.C.C.R. 115. In that case it was held that there were certain general considerations, which should regulate the granting of bail. There should be a presumption in favour of bail, unless it were shown that there were good grounds for opposing it, and that these would tend to fall into two categories, namely: (a) protection of the public and (b) the administration of justice. Bail should normally be refused where the accused was already in a position of trust (e.g. already on bail, on probation, on community service, on deferred sentence or being supervised in the community on parole licence). Other circumstances that might persuade a court against a grant of bail would include: the accused's record, any previous breaches of bail or supervision, the absence of a fixed address, previous failures to attend court, allegations of threats to intimidate witnesses or otherwise interfere with the course of justice, or (rarely) the serious nature of the charge itself.

While these do not have the force of law, and are not uncom- **2–07** monly departed from in practice, it is fair to say that the more the factors that are regarded as militating against bail are found in a particular case, the more likely it is that bail will not be granted. It is now settled law that where the Crown do not oppose bail, the sheriff is not entitled to look behind the Crown's decision and refuse to admit the accused to bail (*M.A.R. v Dyer*, 2005 S.C.C.R 818). Effectively, there are three situations in which it is both lawful and appropriate to commit someone into prison before their guilt has been judicially ascertained, in both solemn and summary proceedings, namely: (1) Where there is objectively considered to be a risk that the accused, if liberated on bail, will interfere with the course of justice by either failing to attend when required or interfering with the course of justice by interfering with witnesses, destroying or falsifying evidence, and thus thwarting a fair trial, (2) Where the accused has a history of proven or alleged non-compliance with court orders, by purportedly breaching bail conditions or allegedly offending whilst under the supervision of the court by way of probation, community service or deferment of sentence for good behaviour, or, (3) Where the accused declines to accept the bail conditions proposed by the court (this last situation being not unknown where the alleged offence is of a "political" nature).

The granting or refusing of bail has long been a politically controversial issue, with two powerful forces ranged against each other, holding opposite views. On the one hand, there are many who observe that all persons refused bail before trial are presumed innocent, that many are in fact acquitted, and many others do not receive a custodial sentence. They observe that the average length of a remand in custody is less than 28 days, and question whether locking someone up — who denies the offence and therefore presumably entertains a hope of acquittal — at public expense, and with the attendant disruption to his home and family life, is necessary in so many cases. They also note that a significant number of suicides in custody are those of remand prisoners.

2–08   Ranged against them are those who point to the large number of persons convicted of offending whilst subject to bail, sometimes breaching four or five bail orders before finally being detained in custody — the so-called "bail bandits". They also draw attention to the occasional high-profile case where an offender has been perceived as a "good risk" in terms of bail, and yet has offended in a serious manner whilst subject to bail. To this group, the grant of bail by the courts increases the risk to the public and there should effectively be a presumption in law against the grant of bail, unless the accused can put forward a wholly persuasive argument.

Any decision in respect of bail inherently involves a risk assessment. In deciding whether or not to oppose bail, the Crown have the advantage of a police report, to which they can add their experience of similar offenders in similar cases. Where bail is not opposed, the court must presume that that decision is made for good and proper reasons, now specifically including grounds of public protection. Where bail is opposed, the matter then becomes one for the court, and for the exercise of judicial discretion, weighing up the interests of the public against the interests of the accused, and deciding where the proper balance lies. Such decisions are often difficult and anxious ones that frankly do not lend themselves easily to the world of the tabloid headline. Within any legal system there will always be some in prison who could safely be in the community, and some in the community whose level of risk indicates objectively a preference for them being in custody. It might perhaps be considered unfortunate, so far as this debate is concerned to note that the options available remain a stark choice between liberation to the accused's home address (albeit sometimes subject to curfew conditions enforceable by electronic tagging for twelve hours a day), and incarceration in prison, where a first time remand prisoner can find himself surrounded by drug abusers, inmates with vastly greater experience of prison, career criminals and the like. It should be noted that, despite a tentative step towards them in the Criminal Justice (Scotland) Act 1980, there are still no "halfway houses" in Scotland, suitable to house those who may not need the strictures of prison, yet cannot be trusted within the confines of their own locality.

In the situation where bail is not granted at first appearance, the accused will be taken immediately to the nearest prison that accepts remand prisoners of appropriate age and sex. At that stage, he is treated as "committed for further examination", and the Crown have a maximum period of eight days (*Herron v A, B, C and D*, 1977 S.L.T. (Sh Ct) 24) before he must be brought back before the sheriff, during which time they are obliged to complete their initial enquiries into the case. The 1995 Act makes provision for the prosecutor to seek to have the accused judicially examined before the sheriff in accordance with the provisions of ss.35–39 of the Act. This procedure was introduced by the Criminal Justice (Scotland) Act 1980, and authorises the prosecutor to question the accused insofar as such questioning "is directed towards eliciting any admission, denial, explanation, justification or comment which the accused may have". Defence solicitors swiftly realised that, at a time when they had no information at all as to the strengths or weaknesses of the Crown case, there was seldom a tactical advantage in advising their clients to offer the court an explanation at this stage, and accused persons therefore routinely declined to answer Crown questioning upon legal advice. After a brief flurry when every accused on petition was brought before a sheriff for judicial examination, its popularity rapidly dwindled, and it is now rarely used other than in murder charges.

2–09   Prior to the coming into force of the Human Rights Act, the Crown would routinely hold the accused in custody for seven or eight days before bringing them back to court for "full committal" — strictly speaking "committal until liberated in due course of law". It is now accepted that, where the Crown have completed their initial enquiries at an earlier stage, before the date upon which he would normally be brought back to court, he should be brought back earlier, in order that the sheriff may consider whether it is now appropriate to grant bail (*Burn, Petitioner*, 2000 J.C. 43). Again, these proceedings, which are of a fairly formal nature, should take place in the presence of the accused and his solicitor, although recently it has become competent for them to take place by way of live video link when the accused is remanded to HM Prison Barlinnie. In these cases, the sheriff, the procurator fiscal and perhaps the accused's solicitor will be within the precincts of the court. The accused will participate from a dedicated area within the prison operated by the Scottish Court Service, and will both see and hear the proceedings taking place within the courtroom. It is of the essence of these committal proceedings that a signed petition containing a relevant charge against the accused is placed before the sheriff. This may or may not be the same petition upon which he appeared the previous week. Even if refused previously, bail may be applied for on this appearance. While the Crown may oppose bail at first appearance on, inter alia, the grounds that their enquiries into the offence might be jeopardised if the accused were granted his liberty, the fact that they now seek a warrant for full committal indicates that their initial investigations are complete, and opposition to bail should therefore be on the grounds stated above.

Where bail is refused, the sheriff will issue a warrant committing the accused to custody until liberated in due course of law, and this warrant will accompany him into prison when he is escorted there.

Prevention of delay in trials

2–10   For centuries, Scots lawyers and judges took great pride in the speed with which cases proceeded to trial in Scotland. The "80-day Rule", requiring service of an indictment on the accused in custody within 80 days of his full committal, and the "110-day Rule", which until 1980 required the accused's trial to conclude within 110 days of full committal, and latterly required his trial to commence within the same period, were regarded as cornerstones of our legal system. Motions to adjourn custody trials in the High Court were, until relatively recently, rarely made, and even more rarely granted.

However, the growing burden of work in the High Court, the growing complexity of many trials, the difficulty in obtaining sanction for, and reports from, expert witnesses, last-minute non-availability of instructed counsel, the occasional tendency of witnesses not to attend for trial, and sheer pressure on court time, saw the position shift dramatically between around 1990 and 2004, to the extent that trials commencing on the first calling of an indictment became something of a rarity, and motions to adjourn, and to extend the statutory time limits, became commonplace. Between 1991 and 2005 there were no fewer than eighty cases reported in the Scottish Criminal Case reports dealing specifically with the question of time bar. It was obvious to all court users that the procedures set out in the 1995 Act were no longer adequate to ensure the smooth and efficient running of the court, so, following the recommendations contained in the Bonomy Report (*Improving Practice,* 2002), the Criminal Procedure Amendment (Scotland) Act 2004 substantially amended the 1995 Act, setting out new procedures for all cases indicted after April 1, 2005.

In terms of s.65 of the 1995 Act as amended, an accused may not be detained for more than 80 days by virtue of a warrant committing him for trial for any offence without being served with an indictment. It is important to note that he must *only* be in custody "by virtue of" the warrant, for the 80-day rule to apply. If, during his period on remand, he receives another custodial sentence, elects to serve the alternative of imprisonment in respect of an unpaid fine, is recalled by the parole board in respect of non-compliance with licence conditions, or abandons an ongoing appeal and serves a sentence previously imposed having been granted bail in the interim, these periods are *not* treated as forming part of the 80 days. If an indictment is not served within the statutory period, and it has not been extended by application to the court, then he is entitled to bail. This does not prevent the subsequent lawful service of an indictment on the accused — unlike the position in summary procedure, he is not forever free from all question or process for his alleged offence. A single judge of the High Court may grant an extension of the 80 day period if no indictment has yet been served. If an indictment has been served, the court in which the indictment is to call (which may of course be the sheriff court) may grant an extension on cause shown. Either Crown or defence may appeal to the High Court against such decision.

Under the new provisions introduced by the 2004 Act, it is no longer necessary for the trial of an accused person in custody to commence within 110 days of his full committal. Instead, where an indictment has been served to call in the High Court, the accused is entitled to bail if he has been detained by virtue of that warrant for a total period of 110 days without a preliminary hearing in terms of s.65 of the Act having taken place (unless the hearing has been **2–11** dispensed with in terms of s.72B(8), in which case time limits are determined by reference to the date on which the hearing would have taken place) In the event of the 110th day passing without the case calling in terms of the statute, and where the Lord Advocate has not authorised the grant of bail in terms of s.24(2), the accused is to be brought before the court at which he is required to appear, or before a single judge of the High Court to apply for bail. The prosecutor has a right to be heard, and to apply for an extension of the statutory time limits, but if he declines to make such application, or the court refuses it, then it is mandatory for the court to grant bail (although the prosecutor may be invited to address the court on the proposed conditions of bail). Curiously, in terms of s.25A of the 1995 Act as amended, where the accused declines to accept the proposed bail conditions, he continues to be detained in terms of the initial committal warrant, even where this means that his detention continues beyond the 110 day time limit specified in s.65(4).

The new provisions in respect of preliminary hearings in the High Court and First Diets in the sheriff court represent a radical and unprecedented change in Scottish criminal procedure. For the first time, the trial diet does not occupy the central point of a criminal prosecution. In terms of s.79, the prosecution and defence are required to be fully prepared and ready to address the court at the preliminary diet. Both sides must have cooperated in preparing a written list of all agreed matters in terms of the Lord Justice-General's Practice Note of 2005 in advance of the hearing. The court will regard failure to carry out necessary preparatory work without reasonable excuse as unacceptable, and the court will investigate any such failures and record the reasons for them. Given that both preliminary pleas (matters of competency and relevancy, validity of service, and pleas in bar of trial) and preliminary issues (separation of trials, challenges to special capacity, objections to admissibility, agreement of uncontroversial evidence or the existence of matters capable of resolution before trial) must now be addressed in full at the preliminary hearing, before a trial diet will be assigned, it will be seen that in the majority of cases the importance of this hearing will be central to the entire preparation and presentation of the case by both Crown and defence.

Trials of accused persons in custody must now commence within 140 days of full committal — again, should the trial not commence within that time, the accused is not free from prosecution for the offence, but merely has the same entitlement to bail as specified above.

REMANDS IN CUSTODY PENDING SENTENCE

There are a number of situations in which an accused person who **2–12** has either pled guilty to, or been found guilty of, an offence punishable by imprisonment, may be held in a prison or young offenders institution for a period of up to 28 days prior to being sentenced.

Where a court is considering imposing a custodial sentence on an offender aged under 21, it is mandatory in terms of s.20(3) and (4) of the 1995 Act for it to obtain a report from an officer of the appropriate local authority (commonly known as a Social Enquiry Report), together with any other information it considers relevant (for example up-to-date medical or psychiatric reports) in assessing the appropriate sentence for the offence. In current practice, it is standard for such reports to incorporate an assessment of the offender's suitability to perform Community Service, and where the court is in an area where Restriction of Liberty Orders ("tagging") are available, for the offender's suitability for such an order also to be addressed. The court shall not impose a sentence of detention on the offender unless it is satisfied that no other method of dealing with him is appropriate.

Section 204(2) provides that:

"a court shall not pass a sentence of imprisonment on a person of or over twenty-one years of age who has not previously been sentenced to imprisonment or detention by a court in any part of the United Kingdom unless the court considers that no other method of dealing with him is appropriate".

Again, in order to reach such a conclusion the court must be furnished by a report from an officer of the local authority, together with such other information about the offender as is considered relevant.

Similarly, where a person subject to a probation order commits **2–13** an offence and is prosecuted in the sheriff court or the High Court, the obtaining of pre-sentence reports is mandatory in terms of s.203(1). In addition to the three cases where the ordering of background reports from the local authority is mandatory, there are many other situations where the court may exercise its discretion and call for reports in order to consider whether a non-custodial disposal would be appropriate, even where an offender is over 21 and has previously served a prison sentence.

The maximum period for which a person could be remanded in custody for preparation of reports was formerly 21 days, but since June 27, 2003, s.201 of the 1995 Act provides for a remand of up to four weeks or, on cause shown, for eight weeks. An accused person remanded under these provisions has the right of appeal to the High Court against such remand (s.201(4)), but such note of appeal must be presented to the High Court within 24 hours of his remand. Where it is mandatory for the court to call for reports prior to passing a custodial sentence, it should not normally detain the person in custody unless there are good reasons for doing so (*McGoldrick and Monaghan v Normand*, 1988 S.C.C.R. 83). Such reasons commonly include previous non-cooperation with preparation of reports when at liberty, previous failures to attend for sentencing diets, or the offence forming part of a continuing course of criminal conduct, particularly when that course involves one or more recent breaches of bail conditions. The matter of sentence being for the court and not the prosecutor, the Crown has no right to oppose bail following a finding of guilt, although it has a locus to address the court to clarify any matters within its knowledge that are germane to the issues before the court.

Backdating sentences

2–14   A significant percentage of those ultimately receiving custodial sentences will have been remanded in custody, either awaiting trial or sentence or both, for a period of several weeks or months, before their fate is determined. Often the periods spent on remand are the equivalent, in practical terms, of a short-term sentence of some months duration, when statutory remission is taken into account, and the question of whether to backdate the ultimate custodial sentence to the commencement of the remand period can be a fraught one.

The Criminal Procedure (Scotland) Act 1975 ss.218 and 432 merely obliged the court to "have regard to" the period spent in custody prior to sentencing. This of course made it entirely competent either to backdate as a matter of routine, or to decline to backdate the commencement date of a sentence. For many years, practice varied from court to court and from sentencer to sentencer, with significant variations in the level of use of backdating. In 1975 the Thomson Committee (*Criminal Procedure in Scotland*, Cmnd 6218) recommended that sentences should always be backdated to the date when an intimation to plead guilty was made. Fourteen years later, the majority of the Kincraig Committee (*Parole and Related Issues in Scotland*, Cm 598) recommended that all sentences should be backdated to the date of the initial remand in custody, unless there were special reasons to order otherwise. Amendments were made to the 1975 Act by s.41 of the Prisoners and Criminal Proceedings (Scotland) Act 1993, and the law can now be found in s.210 of the 1995 Act (as further amended by the Crime and Punishment (Scotland) Act 1997. This now provides that a court, in passing a sentence of imprisonment, shall, in determining the period of imprisonment or detention:

"(a) ... have regard to any period of time spent in custody ... on remand awaiting trial or sentence, or spent in custody awaiting extradition to the United Kingdom, or spent in hospital awaiting trial or sentence by virtue of an order made under Section 52,53 or 200 of this Act;

(b) specify the date of commencement of the sentence; and

(c) if the person—

   (i) has spent a period of time in custody on remand awaiting trial or sentence

   (ii) is an extradited prisoner ...

   (iii) Has spent a period of time in hospital awaiting trial or sentence by virtue of an order under Section 52,53 or 200 of this Act,

and the date specified under paragraph (b) above is not earlier than the date on which sentence is passed, state its reasons for not specifying an earlier date."

While the decision on whether or not to backdate remains one for **2–15** the discretion of the sentencing judge, the practical effect of this provision has been to ensure that virtually every custodial sentence passed in Scotland is now backdated. This includes the backdating of all mandatory life sentences, following *Elliott v HM Advocate* 1997 S.C.C.R. 111. If the court elects not to backdate, the reason for this should be minuted (*Hutcheson v HM Advocate* 2001 S.C.C.R. 43). The only situations in modern practice where sentence tends not to be backdated are the relatively rare ones — for example where the offender has been convicted of an offence committed whilst on licence, has been recalled to custody by the parole board (thus stopping the remand period specified in s.65 of the 1995 Act), and the trial judge elects not to make an order under s.16 of the 1993 Act returning the offender to prison for the unexpired portion of the previous sentence, or where the sentence is imposed in respect of a breach of probation, where the time between the original remand and the imposition of the sentence will characteristically be of the order of several months at least.

CUSTODIAL SENTENCES

2–16 In present Scottish sentencing practice, as governed by the 1993 Act, there are effectively now five distinct classifications into which prisoners who have received custodial sentences may be grouped. These are:

1. Short-term prisoners
2. Short-term prisoners serving determinate sentences of over six months for sexual offences
3. Extended sentence prisoners
4. Long-term prisoners, and
5. Life sentence prisoners

It should be noted that the Custodial Sentences and Weapons (Scotland) Bill proposes to abolish the distinction between short-term and long-term prisoners detailed below. Instead, it is proposed that all sentences of imprisonment of more than fifteen days duration shall be "custody and community sentences", a specified part of which shall be served in full in custody, and the remainder shall be a community part, during which the offender will be subject to a degree of supervision by way of licence.

1. Short-term prisoners

2–17   In terms of s.27(1) of the Prisoners and Criminal Proceedings (Scotland) Act 1993 ("the 1993 Act"), which governs the determination of sentence for all prisoners sentenced on or after October 1, 1993, "short-term prisoner" means a person serving a sentence of imprisonment for a term of not less than four years. It is, however, crucial to note that the term "sentence" does not in fact refer only to a single sentence. Section 27(5) of the Act specifies that, for the purposes of any reference in the Act to the term of imprisonment to which a person has been sentenced, consecutive terms and terms which are wholly or partly concurrent fall to be treated as forming a single term if the sentences were passed at the same time; or, where the sentences were passed at different times (the term "times" presumably being preferred to "dates" to allow for the situation where the accused appears before two different sheriffs on the same date and receives consecutive sentences) and the person has not been released from the earlier sentence in terms of the Act at any time between the passing of the first and subsequent sentences. This practice is known as "single-terming".

In terms of s.1(1) of the 1993 Act, and subject to the exceptions in respect of sex offenders and offenders serving extended sentences discussed below, "as soon as a short-term prisoner has served one-half of his sentence, the Secretary of State (now the Justice Minister) shall, without prejudice to any supervised release order to which the prisoner is subject, release him unconditionally". Since July 6, 2006, in terms of s.3AA of the Act, it has also been open to Ministers to direct the release of certain low risk prisoners serving sentences of three months and over, for a period of no less than fourteen days and no more than four and a half months on Home Detention Curfew, in terms of which they will be required to reside at a specified address for at least nine hours per day, subject to the condition that their whereabouts are electronically monitored.

The overwhelming majority of prisoners within the Scottish prison system are short-term prisoners. This group encompasses all those sentenced to total periods *in cumulo* of four years or less, including fine defaulters sentenced to imprisonment in respect of non-payment of fines under s.219 of the 1995 Act (with the exception of those imprisoned for non-payment of fines exceeding £250,000 — group so rare as to be effectively unknown in practice). Of the average daily prison population, almost 90 per cent will fall into this category, and well over 95 per cent of all admissions to prison in any year will be in respect of short-term sentences.

Over the past decades there has been much debate over the **2–18** practical effect of Scotland sending so many fine defaulters to prison. In most years, at least a third of new admissions to prison are in respect of unpaid fines, and some spend only one night in custody. It is widely known amongst offenders that, where the alternative imposed by the courts is seven days, s.1(1) of the 1993 Act directs unconditional release after three days. As prisons do not have sufficient staff to organise release at weekends, prisoners are only released between Monday and Friday. Thus, if a prisoner arranges to be arrested on a Thursday to "serve" his seven day alternative, he must by law be released from prison the following day (as by Monday he would have served more than half of his seven days). In 2005–06 there were 6,213 receptions into prison for non-payment of fines (itself showing a continuing decline in the number of such admissions from the high of 10,134 in 1996–97), having been sentenced to an average period of 11 days (of which 5 or less are served in custody). In each case, the net effect was two-fold. Firstly, the sums levied by way of fines were irrevocably lost to the Exchequer, and secondly, the offenders were maintained at the expense of the state for the few days they spent in custody. This anomaly is addressed by cl.5 of the Custodial Sentences and Weapons (Scotland) Bill, which proposes that any sentence of under 15 days imposed by the courts shall be a "custody-only sentence", which requires to be served in full in prison.

In addition to this, there are clear social costs in respect of the disruption that can be caused to families by the short-term imprisonment of the person who may be the chief or only wage earner or income generator within the family, or the person listed as the sole recipient of benefits within the family unit.

It should be noted that The Sentencing Commission for Scotland published a consultation paper in June 2006, in which they called for the abolition of fines for offenders on benefits or with low disposable incomes, proposing that they be replaced with supervision orders or community service. In addition, they proposed the abolition of the current alternatives of imprisonment for all fines of less than £5000. At the time of writing, it is not known whether Ministers will accept all or any of these proposals.

2–19   The alternative sentences of imprisonment for non-payment of fines are specified in s.219 of the 1995 Act. Currently they are:

Amount of Fine or Caution	Maximum Period of Imprisonment
Not exceeding £200	7 days
Exceeding £200 but not exceeding £500	14 days
Exceeding £500 but not exceeding £1,000	28 days
Exceeding £1,000 but not exceeding £2,500	45 days
Exceeding £2,500 but not exceeding £5,000	3 months
Exceeding £5,000 but not exceeding £10,000	6 months
Exceeding £10,000 but not exceeding £20,000	12 months
Exceeding £20,000 but not exceeding £50,000	18 months
Exceeding £50,000 but not exceeding £100,000	2 years
Exceeding £100,000 but not exceeding £250,000	3 years
Exceeding £250,000 but not exceeding £1 Million	5 years
Exceeding £1 Million	10 years

Where the court imposes a fine on an offender, and the offender requests that he be given time to pay the fine, the court may order payment by such instalments as it considers appropriate (s.214(8)). Where the offender is given the opportunity to pay by instalments, the court shall not, on the occasion of its imposition of the fine, impose the alternative of imprisonment in the event of future default unless (a) the offender is personally present and (b) the court determines that, having regard to the gravity of the offence or the character of the offender or other special reason, it is expedient that he should be imprisoned without further enquiry in the event of default of payment (s.214(4)). If the court so orders, it shall state the special reason for its decision. While the Act does not expressly provide that the reason be minuted, good practice surely dictates that it should be.

Where an offender has been fined, and has not paid the fine in **2–20** whole or in part, in accordance with the instalment rate ordered by the court, and the alternative has not already been imposed, then it is mandatory in terms of s.216 for the court to make enquiry in his presence as to the reason for non-payment of the fine, before the alternative of imprisonment can be imposed, unless the offender is in prison at the time. Failure to attend for a means enquiry in terms of the section may result in a warrant of apprehension being issued. On the offender's attendance before the court, whether voluntary or not, the court may impose the alternative in respect of non-payment. Where the fine has been paid in part, the alternative must be reduced proportionately to the percentage of the total fine paid to date.

In an attempt to reduce the number of persons sent to prison for fine defaults, the court now has power under s.217 to place the offender under the supervision of an officer of the local authority pending payment of the fine in full. Where the offender is under 21, s.217(4) provides that the court shall not fix the alternative of imprisonment unless the offender has been placed under supervision, or the court is satisfied that it is impracticable to place him under supervision.

A further option open to the courts instead of sending a fine defaulter to prison is the imposition of a supervised attendance order, in terms of ss.235–237 of the 1995 Act. Such an order may be made where the offender is of or over 16 years of age, has had a fine imposed on him that has failed to pay in full and the court would have imposed the alternative of imprisonment, but the court considers that the imposition of a supervised attendance order is more appropriate than the serving or imposition of the alternative.

A supervised attendance order requires the offender to attend a **2–21** place of supervision and carry out such instructions as may be given to him by his supervising officer for a minimum period of ten hours and a maximum period of 50 hours where the fine is Level One (£200 or less), and one hundred hours in respect of any higher fine. The coming into force of the supervised release order has the effect of discharging the fine in terms of s.235(6). An order for a supervised release order may be made at a hearing where the court is considering allowing further time to pay a fine, as an alternative to the court fixing an alternative of imprisonment. In the event of breach of a supervised attendance order being admitted or proven, Sch.7, para.5 of the 1995 Act provides that the period for completion may be extended, the number of hours may be varied, or the order may be revoked. On revocation, the district court may sentence the offender to up to 20 days imprisonment, and the sheriff court to 30 days, regardless of the alternative hat may have been specified in terms of s.219.

There are special provisions authorising the court to proceed straight to the imposition of a supervised attendance order where the offender is aged 16 or 17 and the court considers that the offender would be unlikely to pay the fine it intended imposing within 28 days (s.236).

2–22   Where the court is considering imposing the custodial alternative upon an offender who has not previously received a custodial sentence from a court in any part of the U.K., the offender has a statutory right to legal representation. Section 204 provides that it a court shall not "impose imprisonment, or detention, under Section 214 (2) ... in respect of failure to pay a fine, on an accused who is not legally represented in that court and has not been previously sentenced to imprisonment or detention ... unless the accused either—

(a) applied for legal aid and the application was refused on the ground that he was not financially eligible; or
(b) having been informed of the right to apply for legal aid, and having had the opportunity, failed to do so".

A great many offenders are sent to prison by the summary courts — the district court and the sheriff court, where the sheriff sits alone without a jury and the cases proceed by summary complaint. The maximum custodial sentence competent in the district court is restricted by s.7(6) of the 1995 Act to one of 60 days imprisonment. In terms of s.5(2)(d) of the Act, the sheriff has the power on convicting any person of a common law offence to sentence them to a maximum of three months imprisonment, unless the offence is a second or subsequent offence inferring dishonest appropriation of property, or attempt thereat, or is a second or subsequent offence inferring personal violence, in which case the maximum sentence becomes six months in terms of s.5(3)(b).

However, where the accused pleads guilty, particularly at the pleading diet or intermediate diet stage, and the matter does not proceed to a trial diet, these powers are circumscribed by the operation of s.196 of the Act, which introduces a statutory duty to take into account, when passing sentence, the stage in proceedings at which the offender indicated his intention to plead guilty and the circumstances in which that indication was given.

"Discounts" in respect of pleas of guilty

The concept of offering discounts in respect of pleas of guilty was **2–23** controversial for many years. Lord Justice-Clerk Ross expressly disapproved of the practice in *Strawhorn v McLeod*, 1987 S.C.C.R. 413, observing that it was the right of every person charged with a criminal offence to put the Crown to the proof of their case. The fact that trials were considerably more burdensome on the public purse than pleas, and the fact that witnesses did not enjoy the experience of being repeatedly cited to court before a case finally resolved did not go unnoticed, and gradually more economic (some might say pragmatic) considerations began to prevail. An informal practice began to develop amongst some judges of recognising the utilitarian value of the guilty plea in respect of its savings to the public purse, by way of the imposition of a lesser sentence, and the practice was expressly approved by the High Court in the four conjoined appeals reported as *Du Plooy v HM Advocate*, 2005 J.C.1. The sentencing judge retains an element of discretion in selecting the level of discount (if any) to be applied, although the general view of the High Court was that the discount should not normally exceed one-third of the sentence that would otherwise be imposed. *Low v HM Advocate*, 2004 S.C.C.R appears to be authority for the proposition that the sentencing judge must give some discount in respect of a plea of guilty, even where the evidence was overwhelming and the accused's record of analogous offending was horrendous.

The practice was given statutory approval by the amendments to s.196 introduced by the 2004 Act. The court is now obliged, in addition to taking into account the stage at which the plea was offered and its circumstances, to state whether, having taken account of these matters, the sentence imposed is different from that which would otherwise have been imposed and if not, why not.

It might of course seem anomalous, not to say unfair, that the accused who elects to proceed to trial upon responsible legal advice to the effect that a crucial element of the Crown case may be defective (for example, a search alleged to be unlawful or a police interview in which admissions were unfairly obtained), and who is then found guilty after trial, should be punished more severely than the accused who elects not to argue such points. However, it must be borne in mind that, in solemn proceedings, such crucial objections to the admissibility of evidence must now be intimated at the preliminary hearing in the High Court, and at the first diet in the sheriff court, and that the court has power to hear debate or evidence on these points prior to the commencement of the trial, and must rule upon them in advance. In fact, s.79 expressly provides that an objection to the admissibility of evidence must now be raised by way of preliminary issue. In the sheriff court this must be intimated in writing two clear days before the first diet, and in the High Court intimation must be made seven clear days before the preliminary hearing. The court cannot grant leave for an objection of this type to be raised at the trial diet unless it considers that it could not reasonably have been raised before the jury was sworn.

2–24 In practical terms, the effect of *Du Plooy* and s.196 in a summary prosecution where the accused pleads guilty at an early stage, is to reduce the statutory maxima in the sheriff court to aproximately two months and four months imprisonment or detention, of which the accused serves one-half by virtue of s.1(1) of the 1993 Act.

A pragmatic issue appears to raise its head at this point. A person should not be imprisoned (and must not be imprisoned for the first time) unless the court considers that no other method of dealing with him is appropriate. In order to deprive a citizen of his liberty, it seems logical to conclude that that citizen's removal from the community is necessary for the greater good. This seems to indicate that that individual's continuing freedom is in some way detrimental to the well-being of society. If that be so, and if he accepts his guilt, will he be less of a threat to the social order on his release thirty or sixty days later? Within that period, he will not have learned any new skills, nor will he have been able to undertake relevant offence-focussed coursework. He will, of course, have been removed from circulation, and deprived of the temptation to behave in his previous manner, but can it be stated objectively, with any certainty, either (a) that his incarceration has made him a better citizen, (b) that his incarceration has been effective in deterring others from behaving in a like manner, or (c) that his incarceration has fulfilled some public desire to see him suffer for his misdeeds? Given the notion that custody should be a positive experience for those sentenced to imprisonment or detention, is there any evidence of positive benefits accruing from his short sentence?

Of course, sentencers are regularly faced with the dilemma of how to deal with those members of society who are, for whatever reason, resistant to external offers of assistance — those whose schedule of previous convictions disclose deferred sentences during which they have not been of good behaviour, who have not been deterred by fines, who have failed to comply with probation, or declined to attend for community service. In many cases, the court simply feels that it has run out of options — every feasible non-custodial option has been tried, yet the offender is back once more.

In that situation, the term "positive custody" is a misnomer, as the court is, in practical terms, imposing "negative custody".

Debate over the practical use of imprisonment has carried on for 2–25 many decades now, with many academic thinkers questioning the rationale by which society chooses to imprison certain members of its citizenry. There are simply no easy answers to the question of whether short prison sentences really do have a utilitarian value, nor is it easy to say whether the "right" offenders are sent to prison for the "right" reasons. In terms of penal policy, Scottish policy-makers have tended often to agree with policies formed in England, and sometimes in the USA. As both these countries imprison a higher proportion of its citizenry than Scotland, with little empirical evidence yet of a marked decline in offending rates, some might say that these are not necessarily the only models to be studied. Certain other European countries with crime rates not markedly different to ours seem able to imprison fewer of their offenders without any appreciable tearing of the social fabric, and it may be that our future legislators might be minded to look further afield in seeking solutions to the problems of crime within our society.

Automatic Early Release

The operation of automatic early release of short-term prisoners 2–26 remains controversial. It seems illogical that, when a judge has decided that the protection of the public dictates that an offender be imprisoned for three years, that precisely eighteen months after his admission to prison, that offender is released unconditionally, subject to no form of statutory supervision, regardless of his behaviour in custody or his perceived level of risk to the public. The offender has no automatic right to access drug or alcohol counselling should he so wish, no right to employment advice, or to the assistance of any body experienced in the care and resettlement of offenders. Should his behaviour deteriorate and his level of risk of reoffending increase, he is not subject to recall to custody by either the parole board or Scottish Ministers. The only sanction over his behaviour is that provided in terms of s.16 of the 1993 Act, which provides that, where he commits an offence punishable by imprisonment before the date on which he would (but for his release) have served his sentence in full, the court may, in addition to any penalty it imposes for the new offence, order that he be returned to custody for part or all of the unexpired portion of the previous sentence.

This provision remains unpopular with sentencers, politicians, the press and the public. It should be noted that prior to October 1, 1993, all prisoners serving less than 18 months were not eligible for release until they had served two-thirds of their sentence. Those serving longer were eligible for parole at the halfway stage, and eligible for release after serving two-thirds. When the governor's power to award loss of remission is added in, it was not unknown for a disruptive prisoner serving a three year sentence to spend at most a few months of that period at liberty in the community (although it should perhaps be noted that there was no equivalent to s.16 then — once he was out, he was out).

In January 2006, the Sentencing Commission for Scotland issued its response to a Scottish Executive consultation paper on parole and early release, in which it was not supportive of the continuation of automatic early release of prisoners serving up to four years. Following a period of consultation, the Executive published the Custodial Sentences and Weapons (Scotland) Bill 2007, the main terms of which are discussed at paras 2–39 and 2–40.

2. Short-term offenders serving determinate sentences for sexual offences

2–27   With effect from January 12, 2006, a new s.1A has been added into the 1993 Act by the Management of Offenders (Scotland) Act 2005. Anyone sentenced to a period of between six months and four years imprisonment for a sexual offence, as defined in the Sex Offenders Act 1997, is no longer released unconditionally. Instead, they are released subject to such licence conditions as Scottish Ministers consider necessary for the protection of the public, and are therefore liable to be recalled to custody in respect of non-compliance with licence conditions. These conditions are not negotiable, and remain valid whether the offender elects to "accept" them or not. It is not necessary for the offender to reoffend for his licence to be revoked.

It is not objectively clear why Ministers regarded this provision as necessary. The majority of sexual offenders commit their offences within the broad confines of a family unit, and reconviction rates for intra-familial sexual offenders are amongst the lowest for all offences. If the sentencing judge considers the offender to require compulsory measures of supervision after release, s.210A of the 1995 Act empowers him to impose an extended sentence, whatever the length of the custodial term may be. The Sentencing Commission expressly did not support the insertion of this provision, observing the absence of evidence that sexual offenders presented a greater risk of reoffending than any other group. It is not clear how many offenders will be affected by this change.

3. Extended sentence prisoners

With effect from September 30, 1998, the Crime and Disorder **2–28**
Act 1998 has introduced a new s.210A into the 1995 Act. This
provides that, where a person is convicted on indictment of a sexual
or violent offence, and the court intends to pass a determinate
sentence of imprisonment in relation to a sexual offence, or a sentence of four years imprisonment or more for a violent offence, and
the court considers that the period (if any) for which the offender
would be subject to licence would not be adequate for the purpose
of protecting the public from serious harm from the offender, the
court may pass an extended sentence on the offender.

It is mandatory in terms of s.210(4) that the court has before it a
written report by a relevant officer of the local authority, and the
court may elect to hear oral evidence from the officer.

If, after consideration of the risk assessment report and such
other evidence as the court considers appropriate, the sentencing
judge considers that protection of the public from serious harm
makes such a sentence necessary, he must then impose a sentence
consisting of two parts — the "custodial term" which the court
would otherwise have passed, and the "extension period" for which
the offender is to be subject to a licence, of such length as the court
considers necessary. The maximum extension period competent in
the High Court is 10 years for both sexual and violent offences. In
the sheriff court, the maximum extended sentence is the aggregate
of a custodial term not exceeding the maximum term he may
impose (currently five years) and an extension period not exceeding
three years.

The practical operation of extended sentences is complex. Where **2–29**
the aggregate of the custodial term and the extension period is less
than four years (for example, where the index sexual offence is not
regarded as of the utmost seriousness and attracts a custodial term
of twelve to eighteen months, but the risk assessment indicates a
high risk of reoffending), then licence conditions are selected and
imposed by Scottish Ministers. Where the total sentence is four
years or more, then the parole board selects and imposes the licence
conditions. Again, these are not negotiable in advance by the
offender, but the supervising officer may request clarification,
amendment, addition or deletion of any licence condition after
supervision has commenced.

Where the custodial term is less than four years, the prisoner is
released at the halfway point of the custodial part. Unlike a
determinate sentence prisoner though, he is released on licence. At
that point, the extension period comes into force in terms of s.26A
of the 1993 Act. He remains liable to revocation of his licence in

terms of s.17 (effectively, if Ministers or the parole board consider that he is in breach of his licence conditions to such an extent that he presents an unacceptable risk to the public), and the licence remains in force until the end of the extension period. If his licence is revoked, he is entitled to have his case considered by a tribunal of the parole board, and that tribunal shall direct his re-release if it is satisfied that it is no longer necessary for the protection of the public from serious harm that the prisoner should be confined (s.3A(4)). Such hearings are usually convened approximately seven weeks after the prisoner's return to custody. If the tribunal directs release, the prisoner must be re-released, subject to such licence conditions as the tribunal considers appropriate, as soon as possible thereafter. If re-release is not directed, the prisoner may require the Ministers to refer his case to the parole board not less than one year following the disposal of that referral, in terms of s.3A(2)(a) of the 1993 Act. At the end of the extension period, he is no longer subject to licence conditions, and if he is in custody on that date he must be released. He remains, of course, at risk of a return to custody in terms of s.16 as described above, should he commit a further offence punishable by imprisonment between the date of his release and his sentence end date.

2–30   Where the custodial term is four years or more, release at the halfway point is discretionary, and release on licence at the two-thirds point if not released prior to that date is mandatory. These provisions will be discussed in detail later in this chapter. At this point, the offender becomes subject to licence conditions for the full period from the commencement date of the extension period until his sentence end date. Again, the offender remains subject to recall on the same grounds as above, and retains his entitlement to a hearing by a tribunal in terms of s.17, with the difference being that, where he is considered to present an ongoing risk of serious harm to the public, he may be ordered to remain in prison until his sentence end date, subject, of course, to the decisions of any further tribunals convened in terms of s.3A.

In practice, revocation of the licences of extended sentence prisoners is far from rare. Given that it is necessary that they be assessed as a higher than average risk of reoffending before such a sentence is passed (indeed, were they not such a risk they would likely not receive an extended sentence), this is not surprising. While some are recalled because they are facing fresh charges, the supervisory nature of the extended sentence means that a great many are recalled because their whereabouts are unknown, they are not cooperating with supervision, they have failed to engage in offence-focussed coursework in the community designed to reduce their level of risk, or it is felt that their behaviour in the community is deteriorating to such an extent that they are no longer felt to present a manageable risk.

When a prisoner receives an extended sentence, the custodial part of which is less than four years, he is released at the halfway part of the custodial term, by virtue of s.1(1) of the 1993 Act. This is, however, subject to the provisions of s.26A, which provides that, where a prisoner subject to an extended sentence licence would otherwise be released unconditionally, he shall be released on a licence, which remains in force throughout the whole of the extension period, unless it is revoked in terms of s.17.

In terms of s.26A(5), the extension period begins on the date on which, apart from that subsection he would have been released unconditionally. Thus, where an offender receives an extended sentence of six years, comprising a three year custodial part and a three year extension, they will spend the first eighteen months in custody, then are released on extended sentence licence for three years, during which period they are subject to recall under s.17, then, for the final eighteen months of the sentence they are not on licence, but are at risk of recall in terms of s.16 in the event of their reoffending.

4. Long-term prisoners

Any prisoner serving a sentence, or combination of sentences, **2–31** amounting in total to a calendar period of four years or more, is defined by s.27(5) of the 1993 Act as a "long-term prisoner". In terms of s.1:

> "(2) As soon as a long-term prisoner has served two-thirds of his sentence, the Secretary of State shall release him on licence unless he has before that time been so released, in relation to that sentence, under any provision of this Act
>
> (3) After a long-term prisoner has served one-half of his sentence, the Secretary of State shall, if recommended to do so by the Parole Board under this section, release him on licence."

The above provision is now subject further to the parole board's discretion, since July 6, 2006, in terms of s.3AA of the 1993 Act to recommend to Ministers the release of certain low risk long term prisoners up to four and a half months before their Parole Qualifying Date, subject to the requirements of a Home Detention Curfew. It is currently anticipated that around 40 prisoners per year will be released on such a curfew. The operation of the scheme will be discussed in detail in a later chapter.

Release on parole is therefore discretionary at any point between the halfway and two-thirds point of the offender's sentence, and all release, whether on parole or not, is subject to the imposition of licence conditions, breach of which can result in recall to custody at any point up to the offender's sentence end date. The position in England and Wales is not the same, as recall cannot be ordered there during the final one-sixth of the offender's sentence, when the obligations of the licence have ceased.

2–32　　The practical operation of parole, including the operation of recall of long-term prisoners subject to parole and non-parole licenses, and the various options available to the parole board at each stage of the parole process, will be examined in detail in a later chapter. At this point it should be noted that every prisoner retains the option to "self-reject" from consideration for parole at the halfway stage. At present, around 8–10 per cent of long-term prisoners each year decline the opportunity to be considered for parole. It should also perhaps be noted here that, unlike short-term prisoners, long-term prisoners on licence are entitled, if so directed by the board, to receive assistance in the fields of employment advice, accommodation, drugs and alcohol counselling and offence-focussed coursework. Failure to cooperate with specific licence conditions in these regards may result in the revocation of the offender's licence.

It may be relevant to observe, in passing, that while offenders on non-parole licence have been returned to the community at the two-thirds point of their sentences, and thus have in theory been released "early", firstly their release is in accordance with a statutory provision, and secondly their release is specifically made conditional upon their compliance with certain conditions imposed upon them. The regular use by Ministers and the parole board of their powers to order recall to custody indicate the seriousness with which breaches of licence are considered.

It should be noted that the terms "parole licence", "non-parole licence" and "extended sentence licence" used throughout this book are not terms found in statute. There is no practical or legal distinction between the three, as they are not separate and distinct "types" of licence. The terms have grown into common use as a simple "shorthand" way of prison professionals and the parole board distinguishing those released on licence before the two-thirds point of their sentence, and those released on licence in terms of s.1(2) above, whether serving a determinate sentence with or without an extension period. Where a prisoner is released on licence, under whatever circumstances, that offender immediately becomes subject to licence conditions.

2–33　　For the avoidance of doubt, where a long-term extended sentence prisoner is released on licence, s.26A(5) provides that the extension period shall be taken to begin on the day following the date on which, had there been no extension period, the prisoner would have ceased to be on licence in respect of the custodial term. Recall under s.17 therefore remains competent throughout the entire duration of the extended sentence. Thus, where an offender receives a nine year extended sentence, comprising a six year custodial term and a three year extension, they must be released on licence in terms of s.1(2) after four years. They are then on licence for two years as a long-term prisoner on licence, then on licence for a further three years by virtue of their extended sentence. However, in practical terms their status does not change at the end of six years. The licence conditions remain in force throughout, and there is no need to issue a new licence at the end of the six year period. The distinction is purely theoretical, and there is one single licence operating throughout the whole five year period (presuming, of course, that it is not revoked, as, in that situation, a fresh licence will require to be issued upon the prisoner's re-release).

Long term prisoners transferred from foreign jurisdictions

Under the Repatriation of Prisoners Act 1984 (which gave effect **2–34** to the Council of Europe Convention on the Transfer of Sentenced Persons), a citizen of one state who has received a sentence in a country other than their own, may apply to serve the balance of their sentence in their home state. Where the receiving state agrees to accept the transfer of the prisoner, that state must continue to enforce the sentence passed within the sentencing state. In terms of Art.6(1)(b) of the Convention, the state proposing to receive the prisoner must, if so requested by the sentencing state, provide evidence of the relevant law confirming that the offence is a crime against the laws of the receiving state, before any transfer can be effected.

Sentences must be administered in accordance with the principle of continued enforcement; thus, a prisoner cannot be transferred from another jurisdiction to Scotland, then given automatic release in terms of the 1993 Act. Thus, where a long term prisoner's transfer takes places after the halfway point of the total sentence, he becomes eligible to be considered for parole. However, should parole not be granted, his sentence calculation operates in terms of the Sch.1, para.2 of the 1984 Act, as amended by the Crime (Sentences) Act 1997 and the Criminal Justice (Scotland) Act 2003. This provides that the prisoner's statutory entitlement to release on licence is on completion of two-thirds of the *balance* of the sentence outstanding at the date of transfer.

For example, an offender sentenced to six years imprisonment with effect from June 1, 2002 applies for transfer to Scotland, and arrives in a Scottish Prison on December 1, 2005, having served three years six months. The balance to be served on transfer is thus two years six months. The prisoner is already eligible for parole. Parole will usually be considered after four to six months, to allow for completion of a full dossier. If parole is not granted, the prisoner may be required to serve one year eight months in custody, this being two-thirds of the balance. Release is not therefore guaranteed by statute until August 1, 2007, 10 months before the sentence end date.

Given that this is, on the face of it, anomalous, this sentence calculation must be explained to the prisoner in full before he makes formal application for transfer under the 1984 Act and the Convention. The prisoner may, therefore, elect to remain in a foreign jurisdiction and be released in terms of their provisions.

5. Life Prisoners

2–35   Any person sentenced to life imprisonment, whether under a mandatory sentence for murder under s.205 of the 1995 Act, or a discretionary life sentence, remains subject to that sentence from the date of its imposition until death. However, only a tiny percentage of life prisoners in fact spend every day between conviction and death in prison.

Prior to 2001, the majority of life sentences were "straight" life sentences. The accused was convicted of murder, the court passed the mandatory sentence of life imprisonment, or he was convicted of an offence considered to merit a discretionary life sentence, and the prisoner simply disappeared into the parole system, with no idea when he was likely to be considered for release. Some years later, the Preliminary Review Committee, a body consisting of a part of the membership of the parole board, including the chairman and the judicial member, would give an indication of the period they would expect the prisoner to serve before he would be considered for release, and then a lengthy and secretive review process would commence, at various stages of which the parole board would indicate its views as to likely progression, which either would or would not be accepted by Ministers. The prisoner would have no access to the reports on which the recommendations were made. The ultimate decision on whether to release the prisoner and when, rested with the Secretary of State alone.

In a small minority of cases, barely over five per cent of all life sentences, due to the perceived heinousness of the offence, or due to the offender's previous history of serious violent and/or sexual offending, the trial judge would make a recommendation in open court at the time of passing sentence as to the number of years he felt the offender should serve before the Secretary of State could consider his release on licence, and effectively the offender knew from the outset that there was no realistic prospect of his being considered for release until he had served the recommended period in custody. It was possible for the length of such a recommendation to be appealed to the High Court (*Casey v HM Advocate*, 1993 S.C.C.R. 453). Of course, at the end of this period there was no guarantee that the Secretary of State would be minded to direct release, nor was there any legal mechanism whereby the prisoner could present his case for release to the Minister — both the deliberations of the parole board and the Secretary of State's decision as to whether to accept these recommendations took place in private.

All this began to change, largely as result of a number of Eur- **2–36** opean Court decisions unfavourable both to the concept of secrecy in decisions affecting individual liberty, and to the notion that the ultimate arbiter on release of life prisoners was a Minister rather than a judge. Following *Thynne, Wilson and Gunnell v United Kingdom* in 1990, the 1993 Act introduced Life Prisoner Tribunals for discretionary life prisoners and later, this was extended by the Crime and Punishment (Scotland) Act 1997 those sentenced for murder when under eighteen years old, in respect of whom the Lord Justice General, whom failing the Lord Justice Clerk, after consultation with the trial judge (if possible), had certified his opinion as to the minimum period to be served in custody. The prisoner would be entitled to legal representation, would be provided with a full dossier detailing his progress from date of sentence to the present, and parole board had the power to direct release, whether Ministers (who were of course also represented at tribunals) opposed release or not. The number of prisoners eligible for consideration by the tribunal system was small. Between 1995 and 1997, there were only 23 such tribunals. After the 1997 Act, the number of tribunals increased to an average of 40 per year.

The system of fixing punishment parts for all life sentence prisoners, long felt to be inevitable, came into force on October 8, 2001, when the 1993 Act was substantially amended by the Convention Rights (Compliance) (Scotland) Act 2001. Section 2 of the Act was amended so that the word "designated" was removed, and courts were directed henceforth to specify "the punishment part" applicable in each case. This required to be specified by the court in years and months (s.2(3A)), and was defined as:

"such part as the court considers appropriate to satisfy the requirements for retribution and deterrence (ignoring the period of confinement, if any, which may be necessary for the protection of the public, taking into account:

(a) the seriousness of the offence, or of the offence combined with other offences of which the life prisoner is convicted on the same indictment as that offence."

On the expiry of the punishment part, the Scottish Executive is obliged to refer the prisoner's case to the parole board, and a tribunal is convened, usually within the prison in which the prisoner then resides, where three members of the board, with a legally qualified chair, hear evidence and representations then issue a decision binding upon parties. It is customary for Ministers to be represented by an official of the Justice Department and a senior prison officer with personal knowledge of the prisoner, and virtually all prisoners are legally represented. The tribunal may direct release on licence only when it is "satisfied that it is no longer necessary for the protection of the public that the prisoner should be confined".

2–37   Where the board declines to direct release, s.2(5A) directs that they must give the prisoner reasons in writing for the decision not to direct his release on licence, and must fix the date when it will next consider the prisoner's case, being a date not later than two years after the date of its decision to decline to direct release. On that date, a further tribunal takes place, usually (but not necessarily) heard by a differently constituted quorum of the board. The procedure at these hearings will be discussed in a later chapter.

In terms of the schedule to the 2001 Act, all prisoners who had not expressly declined in writing to have a punishment part fixed (in practice, only those whose future liberation in terms of a prior board recommendation was imminent declined) were referred back to the High Court for a public hearing in terms of para.12, at the conclusion of which a single judge determined the appropriate punishment part for the offence. Ten such hearings took place on average each week, and between February 2002 and 2004 every prisoner serving life had a punishment part fixed.

These hearings were defined as criminal proceedings, with the punishment part forming effectively the minimum period the offender was required to serve, and therefore both the Crown and the defence had a right to appeal against any sentence felt to be inappropriate, either as excessive or unduly lenient. There is no record of any Crown appeal against an ongoing sentence, but there were, unsurprisingly numerous defence appeals, in the course of two of which, *McCreaddie v HM Advocate*, 2002 S.C.C.R. 912 and *Stewart v HM Advocate*, 2002 S.C.C.R. 915, the Lord Justice-General issued guidance as to the considerations that he considered the courts should take into account.

These guidelines immediately proved controversial, as they paid **2–38** no direct heed to either the question of progress in custody or the related issue of "legitimate expectation of release". Following the guidance in *Stewart*, a life prisoner who had progressed through his sentence in an exemplary manner and was already in open conditions enjoying fortnightly home leaves, based upon prior assessments by prison staff and the parole board, might find, following the imposition of the punishment part, that it would be some years before his case could be considered by a tribunal. This inevitably resulted in "model" prisoners considered to require the minimum level of supervision requiring to be re-graded, and often returned to closed conditions. The matter of whether the relevant provisions of the 2001 Act as affecting such prisoners were ECHR compliant was referred to the Privy Council in respect of alleged breaches of Arts 5, 7 and 14 of the Convention, and in the four conjoined appeals reported as *Flynn v HM Advocate (PC)*, 2004 S.C.C.R. 281, the views of the High Court were expressly disapproved, the Privy Council holding that it was contrary to ordinary notions of fairness to deny to a serving prisoner the benefit of such officially recognised progress as he had made towards his release, and ultimately overruled in *Flynn v HM Advocate (No. 2)*, 2004 S.C.C.R 702, in which the court recognised the need to have regard to progress during sentence. Behaviour in custody, being situated in open conditions, and having a legitimate expectation of release all became relevant factors in the fixing of punishment parts for those already serving life sentences as at October 8, 2001.

Once a prisoner is released on life licence, he is subject to monitoring in terms of a number of supervisory conditions imposed by the tribunal at the time of his release, usually designed to aid his transition back into the community. These will also be discussed in detail in a future chapter. Generally, if the licensee's response to supervision has been satisfactory and his licence has not been revoked at any time, the supervisory conditions are withdrawn after ten years, and from then on he remains only under an obligation to be of good behaviour and keep the peace. He can, of course, be recalled to custody at any time should Ministers or the parole board consider his risk to be unacceptable.

Proposals to alter the sentencing system

2–39   Just as this book was going to press, the Custodial Sentences and
Weapons (Scotland) Bill was approved by the Scottish Parliament,
although no date has yet been identified for any of its provisions to
come into force. The Bill, once enacted, will change utterly the way
in which sentences are pronounced, and the way in which liberation
dates are calculated. Clause 6 of the Bill proposes that, when
imposing a custodial sentence of fifteen days or more, the court
must make an order specifying the "custody part" of the sentence,
which represents an appropriate part to satisfy "the requirements
for retribution and deterrence". In specifying the custody part the
court must ignore any period of confinement that may be necessary
for the protection of the public. The custody part must be a minimum of one half, and a maximum of three-quarters, of the total
sentence, although where the period chosen is to exceed one-half,
the court must consider a greater proportion "appropriate", having
regard to the seriousness of the offence or offences, and previous
convictions of the offender, and, where appropriate, the circumstances in which a plea of guilty may have been tendered.

It is further proposed that, before the expiry of the "custody
part", Ministers must determine whether the prisoner would, if not
confined, be likely to cause serious harm to the public. If the
Ministers determine that the prisoner does represent a risk of serious harm, they may recommend that the prisoner continue to be
confined until the three-quarter point of his sentence, in which case
they must refer the matter to the parole board for Scotland, who
may direct the prisoner's release on community licence at the expiry
of the custody part, or may decline to direct release, in which case
they must give written reasons for their decision and (unless the
prisoner has less than four months to serve) direct the date on
which his case will next be considered.

Where very short sentences of around three and four months are
concerned, these proposals present as somewhat impractical. For
example, within two months of a prisoner receiving a four month
total sentence (divided into two equal halves), it is proposed that
Ministers will have determined his apparent level of risk of serious
harm, reached an informed decision, then forwarded the relevant
papers to the parole board, which will have been able to determine
the issues of risk (presumably at an oral hearing, as the prisoner
faces continued confinement), and issued its decision in writing to
the prisoner. This does seem somewhat of an ambitious timetable.

2–40   It further appears from the terms of cl.14 of the Bill, that every
prisoner who serves the "full" three-quarters of his sentence in
custody, is expected to be released on community licence, the

conditions of which are to be specified by the parole board. However, cl.27 provides that "supervision conditions", under which an offender must be under the supervision of a relevant officer of the local authority, and must comply with the requirements imposed by the officer, applies only to custody and community prisoners serving six months or more. Thus, for prisoners serving less than six months, there is no sanction specified for breaching such a licence, as it is proposed that the present s.16 of the 1993 Act is repealed in full, and not replaced. This may of course alter during the Bill's progress.

So far as extended sentences are concerned, it is proposed that the court specify a "confinement term" and the "extended sentence" itself. While it is not expressly so stated in the Bill as it stands, it is proposed that the phrase "confinement term" replace the phrase "custodial term" in s.210A(2). However, at present prisoners are entitled to release at the halfway point of a short custodial term, at which point the extended sentence licence comes into force, and to parole at the halfway point, and non-parole licence at the two-thirds point of a long-term sentence. It is, at present, not unknown for the courts to impose relatively short periods in custody followed by far longer periods on supervision in the community. Clause 6 of the current Bill does not explain in terms how this will operate in future, although doubtless this will be addressed during its passage through the Scottish Parliament.

YOUNG PRISONERS

In general, those remanded in custody or convicted and sent to a **2–41** Young Offenders' Institution will be between the ages of sixteen and twenty, although this is not necessarily the case. It is not always fully appreciated that the age of criminal responsibility in Scotland remains eight years, in terms of s.41 of the Criminal Procedure (Scotland) Act 1995. It is sadly not uncommon for children aged fourteen and fifteen to be prosecuted on indictment for serious offences, and to be sentenced to detention before they have attained the age of sixteen.

Section 208 of the 1995 Act provides that:

"Where a child is convicted on indictment and the court is of the opinion that no other method of dealing with him is appropriate, it may sentence him to be detained for a period which it shall specify in the sentence; and the child shall during that period be liable to be detained in such place and on such conditions as the [Scottish Ministers] may direct".

The definition of "child" is, however, not straightforward, and is not based solely on age. Section 307 of the 1995 Act provides that "child" has the meaning assigned to it for the purposes of Chapters 2 and 3 of Part II of the Children (Scotland) Act 1995. That definition is found in Section 93 of the Children Scotland Act, and provides that a child is—

"(i)   a child who has not attained the age of sixteen years;
(ii)   a child over the age of sixteen years who has not attained the age of eighteen years and in respect of whom a supervision requirement is in force; or
(iii) a child whose case has been referred to a children's hearing by virtue of Section 33 of this Act".

The third of these covers the situation of a child in respect of whom a referral has been made by a court in England, Wales or Northern Ireland.

2–42   It will therefore be seen that, where a young person is convicted on indictment, and he or she is subject to the supervision requirements of the children's hearing system, and the court nevertheless considers, after obtaining the reports required by statute, that a period of detention is necessary, that period need not be served within a Young Offenders' Institution or prison, as it remains entirely a matter for Ministerial discretion whether the sentence is to be served there or within a secure educational establishment.

Commonly, young offenders convicted as above will be admitted to one of the five small secure educational establishments in Scotland, namely Kerelaw in Ayrshire, Rossie near Montrose, St Mary's Kenmure in Bishopbriggs, Howdenhall and St Katharine's, both in Edinburgh. Remands to these establishments remain rare (in the first six months of 2004 there were 31 admissions, involving 27 different children). Once a child is admitted to secure school accommodation, they will customarily remain there until the end of their sentence or they attain the age of eighteen, whichever is the earlier. If, however, their behaviour is of such a nature that they cannot safely be managed within the school environment, the Scottish Ministers have discretion to direct a transfer into a Young Offender's Institution, even when the offender is still under sixteen. In practice, this power is very rarely used.

The particular problems arising from the need to deal appropriately with the needs of young offenders in prison, whilst also having regard to public safety, has exercised the minds of prison administrators and staff for generations. Around 40 per cent of all recorded crime is committed by young offenders. Since the era of William Brebner in the early nineteenth century, it has been accepted as sensible policy to keep young and immature prisoners separate from older, often more experienced offenders. Young offenders clearly lack the maturity and life experiences of older offenders (although any dividing line based purely upon age is inherently arbitrary), and much time, thought and effort has been put into finding ways to reduce the risk of teenagers entering custody for the first time becoming hardened career criminals in years to come. Borstal training was introduced, following the enactment of the Prevention of Crime Act 1908, in Polmont in December 1911, with the express intention of subjecting the offender "to detention for such term and under such supervision and discipline as appears the most conducive to his reformation and the repression of crime". Education, physical training and the learning of practical skills in the fields of plumbing, painting, joinery, labouring and the like were all provided, and the sentence of Borstal training soon became a popular one. It was finally abolished by the Criminal Justice (Scotland) Act 1980.

By that time, two further forms of sentence for young offenders **2–43** had come into being — the Criminal Justice (Scotland) Act 1949, perhaps influenced by the growth in support for military discipline in the years immediately after the Second World War, had provided for the introduction of detention centres, where young offenders were to receive a "short, sharp, shock", designed to make offenders realise that they had done wrong. The first detention centre in Scotland was opened in Perth in 1960, to be followed by one in Friarton in 1963, then in Glenochil in 1967. The ethos behind detention centre training was avowedly militaristic, and was very much based upon the provision of strict discipline.

In 1963, the Criminal Justice (Scotland) Act authorised the establishment of a Young Offenders' Institution, for those who were not felt to require either the military discipline of the detention centre, nor the educational focus of Borstal. By 1966, there were Young Offenders' Institutions in Edinburgh, Barlinnie and Dumfries.

In reality, the differences between the three forms of sentence were not significant, the distinctions in respect of offenders arbitrary, and the cost of operating three separate systems utterly disproportionate to the apparent benefits. Borstal training was abandoned in 1980, when Castle Huntly, Noranside and Polmont were re-designated as Young Offenders' Institutions, but detention centres remained in existence at Glenochil until the Law Reform (Miscellaneous Provisions) (Scotland) Act 1985 provided that there was to be one generic sentence for young adults under twenty-one. It should perhaps be noted that, in the five previous years, no fewer than seven inmates in Glenochil had committed suicide. The report into these deaths paved the way for the introduction of a balance between the need to maintain discipline in prison, and the duty of staff to develop an interest in the welfare of inmates. After 1985, the notion that officers should be specially trained to work with young offenders gained acceptance, as did the concept of every young offender having a personal officer, with staffing being organised on a group basis, to ensure that officers would know particular inmates well, and would be receptive to any concerns that may arise.

2–44   At present, almost all convicted young offenders in Scotland, regardless of where they lived at the time of conviction, are situated in HMYOI Polmont, although since December 2005 Friarton Hall, formerly a prison in its own right but now an annexe of HM Prison Perth, houses around fifty low supervision convicted offenders. Polmont has a capacity of 650, and is generally filled to between 90 per cent and 95 per cent of capacity. Its current approach is to work in partnership with a wide range of agencies to offer as wide as possible a range of interventions designed to reduce the risk of reoffending. Personal change and development is central to the present approach. Educational classes and vocational training programmes are offered. It is an unfortunate fact that the bulk of prisoners, especially young offenders, have been educated to an extremely basic level. Most have poor literacy skills, and many have effectively truanted their way through their secondary education. A recent study conducted by Her Majesty's Chief Inspector of Prisons for Scotland revealed that almost 50 per cent of all inmates in Young Offenders Institutions were dyslexic, as against a national average of between five and ten per cent. Rule 86(2) obliges the Governor to arrange a programme of educational classes which meets the needs of young offenders and can assist them to develop their potential. Educational staff working within prisons are employed by the local authority of the area where the establishment is situated, and require to possess appropriate qualifications and have undertaken relevant training in teaching before their appointment. The same applies in adult prisons, where again the provision of education is regarded as a vital part of the process of training prisoners for a return to the community.

In recent times the Scottish Prison Service has come under some criticism as a result of the policy of housing all young offenders from Stranraer to Wick in the same establishment. Many family members from areas outwith the Central Belt find it difficult to maintain regular face to face contact due to the distances involved in visiting. At present there are no plans to build new Young Offenders Institutions, or to spread young offenders more widely throughout the country.

The establishment admits prisoners of all supervision levels, and has its own "open" hall, from where young offenders serving longer sentences and holding low supervision status may access the community by way of placements and home leaves. It may be instructive to note that the number of suicides in young offenders' institutions has declined markedly in recent years.

It should perhaps also be noted that it is not obligatory for prisoners to be sent to adult prisons immediately they attain the age of twenty-one. The Governor of a Young Offenders Institution may, and in practice does, retain those prisoners who have less than three months of their sentence to serve as at their twenty-first birthday.

FEMALE PRISONERS

The rate of female imprisonment in Scotland has probably been the **2–45** part of the penal system most susceptible to changes in social attitudes. In the seventeenth and eighteenth centuries, there was no real notion of segregation within Scottish jails; once again it was the pioneering work of William Brebner that introduced separation of male and female prisoners.

In the mid-nineteenth century, when the bulk of persons sent to prison were serving short sentences for drunkenness, public order offences and immorality, around one in three prison inmates was female. This does not seem to have been the subject of any particular political or public concern. A great many women acquired numerous convictions for public drunkenness, and spent several short spells in custody as a result. As notions of crime and criminal justice developed throughout the nineteenth century, the focus of punishment moved more towards the perpetrators of violence and dishonesty, who tended to be male, rather than on those who were effectively public nuisances, and thus fewer and fewer women found themselves being sent to prison. By the start of World War II, the proportion of the prison population that was female had dropped below ten per cent, and by 1966 it was below three per cent. As recently as 1970, the Government was able to consider the possibility that imprisonment of women might cease altogether within the foreseeable future. Experience has clearly demonstrated that this is no longer likely. While the prison population in general has increased by 80 per cent in the last forty years, the female prison population has risen by 180 per cent, meaning that female prisoners now represent close to five per cent of all inmates. However, it may be instructive to note that recent Home Office statistics reveal that around 15 per cent of all arrests in England and Wales are of women, and 12 per cent of those on probation in England and

Wales are women. The female proportion of the English prison population also presently sits just below five per cent. Assuming that the pattern in Scotland is similar, it would appear that in fact a female offender may well be significantly less likely to receive a prison sentence, particularly for a summary offence, and more likely to be placed on probation, than a male offender.

Until November 2002, with the exception of a very small number of prisoners held for geographical reasons in designated units in Aberdeen, Inverness and Dumfries, all female prisoners were situated in HM Prison Cornton Vale, Stirling. The increase in the number of females in custody then necessitated the transformation of Darroch Hall, Greenock, into a female-only wing, to reduce overcrowding, pending the building of more accommodation at Cornton Vale. This hall held up to 55 female prisoners until August 2005, when they returned to Cornton Vale.

2–46   Patterns of offences committed by female offenders are markedly different from those of male offenders. A significantly lower proportion of female offenders are in custody for offences of serious violence, homicide or attempted murder, while admissions of women to prison for crimes of indecency, contraventions of the Road Traffic Act, possession of offensive weapons, theft by housebreaking and opening lockfast places, all of which are represented to a significant extent in male establishments, tend to be extremely rare. Generally, the bulk of female offenders are in custody for theft, drugs offences, breaches of the peace and minor assaults. Around 6 per cent of female prisoners are in custody for fine defaults. While the social stigma that might previously have been attached to a woman going to prison seems to have receded in the recent past, there is little doubt that the laddish culture that does not frown upon offending, and may even see going to prison as in some way "glamorous" does not have a female counterpart. To an even greater extent than is found in admissions to male establishments, the overwhelming majority of women admitted to prison have ongoing drug misuse issues. While figures for stated drug use amongst male prisoners on admission tend to be around the 60-75 per cent mark, the most recent study by Dr Andrew McClellan, HM Chief Inspector of Prisons for Scotland found that 98 per cent of inmates had drug problems. Victims of physical and sexual abuse form a depressingly high percentage of prison inmates. The same study by HMCIP revealed that 80 per cent were mentally ill and 75 per cent had a history of abuse and poor health. As with male establishments, most prisoners have received only a rudimentary level of education, and many are barely literate. Some may have, or have had mental health or other psychiatric difficulties, although again these are clearly not problems unique to the female prison system. There is a clear emphasis within the Scottish justice system on encouraging the use of non-custodial alternatives, and, when imprisonment becomes the only feasible option, on prisoners and staff using the time productively to achieve rehabilitation. The Ministerial Group on Women's Offending set up in 2000 to tackle the problem of the growing number of women being imprisoned had a remit to implement a package of measures designed to reduce the number of women held in custody. Action had been promised following the suicides at Cornton Vale in the 1990s. While there is evidence that courts will tend to used deferred sentences and probation as alternatives to custody, those whose drug misuse has spiralled out of control are often ill-suited to the regular appointment systems required by probation (or often the discipline involved in being in court for a specified time), when such orders are breached sentencers often find themselves feeling that they have no alternative to the imposition of a period of imprisonment, due to the absence of any further viable community-based resource.

Imprisonment of women, particularly remands in custody, short sentences for fine defaults and the large number of women incarcerated for minor offences against property remains controversial, particularly in England, where the female prison population is around 4,500, and where the suicide rate remains around ten per annum. In summer 2006, the Howard League for Penal Reform, noting the preponderance of offenders under thirty in women's prisons, noting the proportions who suffer mental health problems, drug and alcohol abuse, and who were the victims of domestic abuse, called for the closure of all fifteen English female prison establishments by 2011, arguing that barely a hundred of the offenders currently in custody were sufficiently violent and dangerous as to require continued detention, and arguing that over 95 per cent of women currently in prison should receive community disposals. It remains to be seen whether such pressures will even reduce the rate of increase in the courts' use of imprisonment for women, and it seems unlikely that there will be a marked decline in the use of imprisonment for women in the immediate future.

Only those born female can serve their sentences in a female prison. In the recent past a small number of male to female transsexuals have received custodial sentences, which have required to be served in male prisons.

In addition to r.133, which specifically provides that female **2–47** prisoners shall be kept entirely separate from male prisoners, there are only two rules that specifically affect only female prisoners.

Rule 134 imposes a duty on the medical officer to notify the governor if of the opinion that the prisoner is pregnant or is likely to give birth while still in custody. The governor shall not inform any friend or relative of the prisoner's pregnancy without her consent, except where the offender is under 18 years old and the governor considers it appropriate to do so, or where the prisoner is unable to give consent by reason of illness and the governor has no reason to think that consent would be refused.

Unsurprisingly, a pregnant prisoner cannot be required to undertake any strenuous work that could potentially endanger her health or that of the unborn child (r.134(3)(a)), and the prisoner has the right to be provided with food and drink that takes into account her dietary requirements during pregnancy. The governor retains a discretion in respect of the appropriate level of supervision required, and may require the pregnant prisoner to share her accommodation or cell with a suitable prisoner (r.134(3)(c)).

2–48   Rule 134(4) provides that a medical officer "shall arrange for the transfer of any prisoner who is pregnant to a hospital outwith the prison for the purposes of giving birth".

In terms of r.135, the governor may permit a prisoner to have her baby with her in prison, subject to any direction by Scottish Ministers and subject to such conditions as the governor thinks fit. Everything necessary for the baby's maintenance and care, including a suitable cot, shall be provided by the governor. A prisoner may, at her own expense, or at the expense of someone outside prison, provide other articles or food for her baby, subject of course to the governor's consent.

OTHER REASONS FOR ADMISSION INTO PRISON

Persons sentenced by courts-martial

2–49   It is still possible, although generally rare in peacetime, for a member of the armed forces to be sentenced to imprisonment by a court-martial carried out under the procedures set out in the Army Act 1955, The Royal Air Force Act 1955 or the Naval Discipline Act 1957, depending upon the offender being subject to the appropriate military discipline at the time of the offence. For some years there was a considerable degree of adverse criticism of the lack of ECHR compliance within the military justice systems, and the court-martial system was substantially reformed by the Armed Forces Act 1996, which introduced elements of independence previously lacking.

Prosecutions before courts-martial are conducted by military lawyers, who, while members of the Army Prosecuting Authority, are not part of the military chain of command. They retain unfettered discretion as to whether to prosecute and for what offences, after conducting a review of the evidence submitted to them. The defence may (and usually is) conducted by a civilian lawyer.

A District Court-Martial, heard by a Judge-Advocate and three members, who can be commissioned officers and/or warrant officers and who are subject to the legal guidance of the Judge-Advocate, hears routine cases and can impose punishments of imprisonment or detention of up to two years. In Scotland, s.84B of the Army Act 1955 as inserted by Sch.1 of the 1996 Act provides that a Judge-Advocate must be either an advocate or solicitor with extended rights of audience (a solicitor-advocate) in either the High Court of Justiciary or the Court of Session of at least five years standing. The new provisions of the Air Force Act 1955 and the Naval Discipline Act 1957 in respect of the qualifications for a Judge-Advocate in Naval and Air Force Courts-Martial are in identical terms. The Armed Forces Bill presently before Parliament proposes to raise that qualification period to seven years.

A General Court-Martial is heard by a Judge-Advocate and five **2–50** members, who can again be commissioned officers and/or warrant officers, and hears more serious cases. It has the power to award any sentence permitted by law for the offence in question.

Sentences imposed by courts-martial are all now served in civilian prisons. If the sentence is served in a Scottish prison, the Scottish rules of remission contained in the 1993 Act apply to any sentence calculation. This does create an anomaly, in that sentences imposed are based upon sentence guidelines applicable to England and Wales (where the effect of remission is taken into account in selecting the length of sentence), yet when the sentence is served in Scotland the Scottish rules apply. As sentencing practices between the two systems are never uniform, this can mean that at certain times it is more advantageous to a prisoner to be in one or other jurisdiction, dependent upon the remission regime in force at the material time. It is proposed that these anomalies will be removed by the present Armed Forces Bill.

It should perhaps be noted that the average daily population of those sentenced by a court martial in the last ten years has been between zero and two.

Persons awaiting deportation

There are currently two categories of prisoners held in custody **2–51** awaiting deportation. In terms of s.3(6) of the Immigration Act 1971, a person who is not a British citizen shall be liable to deportation if, after the age of seventeen he is convicted of an offence punishable by imprisonment, and on his conviction he is recommended for deportation by a court empowered to do so.

Where the prisoner is a "long-term prisoner" as defined in the 1993 Act, the provisions of s.9 come into play. This means that the decision on whether to release him on licence (which should inevitably trigger the deportation process) remains one for the Minister, not for the parole board. In practice, the board can still recommend early release on licence for such a prisoner, but the decision as to when the prisoner is released is for the Minister. In all such situations, the dossier supplied to the parole board should include a copy of the relevant order for deportation, so that all parties, including the prisoner, are in no doubt as to his status. Once deportation has been arranged, the prisoner should be taken by the prison authorities (in present practice, this means an organisation authorised to transport prisoners) to the appropriate airport, where the prisoner is placed on an aircraft bound for the receiving state. Once he is aboard, he ceases to be the responsibility of the Minister or the Prison Service.

In practice, release of a long-term prisoner does not take place until arrangements for the prisoner's deportation are in place. In the case of a short-term prisoner, as his liberation date has been fixed by statute, and as a recommendation for deportation is made on conviction, arrangements for his deportation should be in place as at the date of his release in terms of the 1993 Act.

Section 3(5) of the 1971 Act provides that "a person who is not a British citizen shall be liable to deportation:

(a) if, having only a limited leave to enter or remain, he does not observe a condition attached to the leave or remains beyond the time limited by the leave; or

(aa) if he has obtained leave to remain by deception; or

(b) if the Secretary of State deems his deportation to be conducive to the public good; or

(c) if another person to whose family belongs is or has been ordered to be deported."

2–52   It is competent for bail to be granted pending the determination of any deportation issue, and there are procedures for appeals against the decision to remand someone in custody. The rules governing the detention of persons liable to deportation can be found in Schs 2 and 3 of the 1971 Act. The procedures of the Immigration Tribunals and their decision-making powers fall outwith the scope of this book.

Quite clearly, any person taken into custody pending deportation for any of the reasons specified in s.3(5), and who is detained in terms of Schs 2 and 3 of the 1971 Act, has not been convicted or charged with any criminal offence, and accordingly r.3(1) of the

1994 Rules defines such person as an "untried prisoner". Their status is thus the same as that of a person remanded in custody in terms of the Extradition Act (see paragraph above), and they are afforded the same rights and privileges, while remaining subject to the same obligations.

Again, the number of persons held in custody in Scotland under these provisions remains low, seldom exceeding one per day.

The Scottish Prison Service issues weekly statistics on its website *www.sps.gov.uk*, and these specify the numbers of untried and convicted prisoners, the number of male and female prisoners, and the reason for their incarceration.

Civil prisoners

Unlike the situation in England, where imprisonment for certain **2–53** forms of civil debts, in particular unpaid Council Tax, remains both competent and commonly used, civil imprisonment in Scotland is virtually unknown. At common law it remains competent for a creditor to seek a warrant for the civil imprisonment of a debtor who has wilfully refused to pay aliment, although the ultimate sanction of imprisonment is extremely rarely imposed. In addition to this, there are number of quasi-criminal matters, where breach of an order of the civil courts can result in imprisonment. Contempt of court in civil proceedings, such as a wilful refusal to obtemper an order to disclose assets, or to disclose the whereabouts of a child in contested family proceedings, may be punished by the imposition of a fine, non-payment of which can be punished by the imposition of a custodial sentence as an alternative, or by the direct imposition of a sentence of imprisonment. Breach of an interdict granted in civil proceedings, where the procurator fiscal concurs in proceedings but does not intend to raise criminal proceedings, is again quasi-criminal in nature and can result in fines or imprisonment. Non-compliance with an order under s.45 of the Court of Session Act 1988 (where the court orders specific performance of a statutory duty and a person refuses to comply), and the issuing of a warrant granted under s.1(1) of the Law Reform (Miscellaneous Provisions) (Scotland) Act 1940 (wilful refusal to comply with a decree *ad factum praestandum,* a procedure whereby the civil courts can order someone under a legal duty to perform an obligation due to another person), can also result in committal to prison, although both are extremely rare in modern practice.

Violation of a power of arrest granted in terms of a matrimonial interdict (which is of course now open to cohabiting couples or same sex partners) in terms of s.15 of the Matrimonial Homes (Family Protection) (Scotland) Act 1981 can result in "detention" for up to 48 hours, if such request is made to the court, in a situation where the Crown again have expressly waived their right to prosecute the alleged offender. The decision whether to order such detention is at the discretion of the sheriff. Given the maximum length of the detention provided, and the fact that it is only competent when criminal proceedings are not to be commenced, such detentions are virtually unknown in practice. In view of the time periods involved and the fact that the court can only authorise that the person breaching the power of arrest be "detained", such persons would be held in police, rather than prison custody.

For most of the past ten years, the average daily population of penal establishments of those servicing civil imprisonment has varied between one and two.

Civil prisoners retain the same rights to request a visit from a medical or dental practitioner (subject to payment of their expenses), and to visits by any person with whom the prisoner wishes to communicate as do untried prisoners (1994 Rules, rr.34 and 56).

Breaches of immigration legislation

2–54   There are also a very small number of persons held in custody for breaches of immigration legislation, who are awaiting deportation, and some whose detention in a Scottish prison is pending the determination by the Scottish courts of an application for extradition. These will be dealt with in more detail later in this chapter.

Asylum seekers

2–55   There are of course a far larger number of persons of all ages currently detained pending the determination of their applications to remain in the United Kingdom for political asylum. While it is manifest that these people are not free to come and go as they please, and while they remain in conditions of compulsory detention, the centres in which they are held are not in fact defined as "prisons", nor are they under the management or control of the Justice Department. The questions surrounding the treatment and detention of asylum-seekers, and the conditions in which they are held, therefore falls outwith the subject matter of this book.

Prisoners awaiting extradition

2–56   This is now governed by the terms of the Extradition Act 2003. Where an arrest warrant is issued by a judicial authority of a Category 1 territory, specifying the name of the alleged offender, the details of the alleged offence, including the time and place of its commission, the breach of the law of the state seeking extradition, and the foreign court's power of sentence, and that the warrant is issued with a view to securing the extradition of that person to the state in question, or alternatively where the warrant specifies that an identified offender has been convicted in a foreign court, sentenced, and is now unlawfully at large, the offender may be arrested by a constable or customs officer within the UK and brought forthwith before a judge. The relevant information contained in the warrant must also be placed before the court.

Extradition proceedings in Scotland must be conducted by the Lord Advocate (or his deputes or procurators-fiscal) unless he is requested by the authority seeking the warrant not to do so (s.191), and he is under a duty to give advice to any such persons as he considers appropriate on any matters relating to extradition proceedings.

The subject of extradition, and the procedures under the Act in respect of search, arrest and identification, are beyond the scope of this book. However, the judge at the first hearing of a request for extradition may either remand the suspect in custody or grant bail (s.8), and the hearing must commence within 21 days starting with the date of arrest, in terms of s.8(4). Adjournment is competent, and bail may be granted if the case is adjourned. In terms of s.21, the judge is obliged to consider whether extradition would be compatible with the Convention. Where a person facing extradition is facing charges in the UK, extradition proceedings must be adjourned until that case is disposed of (s.22), but where the person is serving a prison sentence adjournment of the extradition proceedings is discretionary (s.23). Unusually, where it is decided that there is insufficient evidence to convict, and the prosecution is withdrawn, this renders extradition on the same charges incompetent, but where it is decided that there is insufficient evidence to prosecute, the suspect may be extradited.

Where the judge grants an order for extradition, and it is not **2–57** appealed, then in terms of s.36, the person must be extradited within ten days of the court's decision unless the court and the relevant authority seeking the warrant agree a later date, in which case the ten day period runs from that date. There is an exception under s.37 where the person is serving a sentence of imprisonment, in which case the judge may seek an undertaking (in terms specified by him) on behalf of the Category 1 territory.

Appeal against an order for extradition is competent, and not unusual. The procedures for appeal are set out in detail in the Act, and at this stage it is sufficient only to observe that extradition cannot take place until all appellate proceedings before the domestic courts have been terminated. In addition to this, it remains competent to petition the *nobile officium* of the High Court of Justiciary (see *Wright and Brown, Petrs*, 2005 J.C. 11) and to petition the Court of Session for Judicial Review (see *Brown, Petr* 2004 S.C. and *Wright, Petr*, 2005 S.C. 453). In either case the existence of proceedings before the domestic courts operates to prevent extradition pending their final determination, from which it can be seen that those not granted bail in proceedings commenced under the 2003 Act may find themselves in custody for periods amounting to several years in complex cases where the sentences available to the courts in the authority seeking warrants so merit them.

In these situations, where the persons in custody have not been convicted or sentenced for any offence within the UK, they remain treated as untried prisoners in terms of r.3(1), with all the different rights and privileges associated with that status, in respect of an entitlement to a greater number of family visits, medical and dental visits, not being obliged to work or undertake education within prison, and the right to wear non-prison issue clothing. They must, so far as practicable, be kept apart from other categories of prisoner (r.14). They are, however, obliged to comply with the same standards of order and discipline as convicted prisoners, and may be subject to report and punishment for breach of rules. In this regard, their situation may be contrasted with those serving sentences but who have appealed against conviction and/or sentence. As the presumption of innocence manifestly does not apply to those convicted, they are required to comply with the standard regime for sentenced prisoners pending determination of their appeal. It should be noted that the number of prisoners in custody pending extradition proceedings remains low, on average fewer than five per day.

CHAPTER 3

BASIC STRUCTURES AND PERSONNEL OF THE SCOTTISH PRISON SERVICE

The Prison Service within Scotland (which now includes the private **3–01** sector) has the responsibility for administering the incarceration of an enormous diversity of individuals. At any one time, the Scottish Prison System is likely to have responsibility for the management of several thousand individuals of vastly differing ages, races, genders and personal circumstances. Around five per cent of prison inmates are female, and a similar percentage are non-British citizens. Within the general body of the prison population, there are those of considerable intellectual achievement and academic qualifications, and those with no academic qualifications whatsoever. There are those who freely and wholeheartedly accept their guilt, and those who do deny their guilt entirely. The Scottish Prison Service is responsible for the management of a small number of offenders over the age of sixteen, and a small number of offenders over that age of eighty.

The smooth running of the prison system requires not merely the employment of a full complement of staff within all establishments and in its administration, but also the input of a considerable number of outside agencies. The provision of medical, educational and religious services will be discussed in a later chapter. The operation of prison-based and throughcare social workers, in particular in respect of preparation for release and supervision on licence, and the visiting functions of the Parole Board for Scotland, will likewise be covered elsewhere.

The administration of all these people is governed at present by the Prisons (Scotland) Act 1989, which provides that all powers and jurisdiction in relation to prisons and prisoners continue to be exercisable by the Secretary of State. Since the passing of the Criminal Justice & Public Order Act 1994, it has been competent to for the private sector to be involved in the running of Scottish Prisons, and since 1999, there has been one private prison initially operated and run by Premier Prison Services, but since 2003 operated under the auspices of Serco Group plc and run, within the Scottish Prison System at HM Prison Bowhouse, Kilmarnock.

Since the coming into force of the Scotland Act 1998, the administration of prisons in Scotland has fallen within the remit of the Justice Minister.

GENERAL SUPERINTENDENCE OF PRISONS

3–02 In terms of s.3 of the 1989 Act, it is the responsibility of the Justice Minister to appoint the governors and other officers of prisons including medical officers, the medical practitioner duly registered under the Medical Act, together with the appointment of Prison Chaplains who are required, in terms of s.3(2) to be a Minister or a Licentiate of The Church of Scotland.

Inspection of prisons is governed by s.4 of the 1989 Act, which provides that officers duly authorised by the Justice Minister shall visit and inspect all prisons and determine the state of the buildings, the conduct of officers, the treatment and conduct of the prisoners and all manners concerning the management of Prisons. It remains the duty of the Minister to report to parliament as to the condition of prisons, as to the punishments inflicted within prisons, and the offences for which they were inflicted.

The place of confinement of prisoners is not a matter for the courts, but is a matter for Ministerial discretion, in terms of s.10 of the 1989 Act. In practice, the decisions as to transfer of prisoners are made, not by the Minister directly, but by appropriately qualified civil servants, based upon recommendations by staff within the particular establishment. The movement of prisoners is generally governed, to a greater or lesser extent, by their supervision status and by their behaviour in custody. It is therefore not uncommon for prisoners serving longer sentences to progress from closed conditions to conditions of lesser security within National "Top End" facilities, which are specific halls within closed establishments but in which prisoners have a greater degree of freedom of movement and association, and from thence on to open conditions, from which they can take home leaves to their proposed release addresses, in the period immediately before they are due for release.

3–03 Obviously, the process can work in reverse. If a prisoner fails to comply with the requirements of open conditions, for example by involvement with drugs, involvement with subversive activities, threatening or aggressive behaviour towards staff or absconding, then they can be downgraded and returned to closed conditions. The supervision classifications will be discussed later in this chapter. It should be noted that it is currently proposed that, with effect from 2007, staff will be involved in a continuous process of risk assessment for all prisoners serving sentences of over fourteen days.

In the case of a life sentence prisoner in top end conditions holding a low supervision category and being considered for an outside work or college placement, the decision on whether to approve the first grant of temporary release or not requires to be made at Ministerial level. Temporary release, and the rules governing it, will be discussed in detail in Chapter Five.

THE STRUCTURE OF THE SCOTTISH PRISON SERVICE

Prison Board

At present, the Scottish Prison Service is run by a Prisons Board, **3–04** consisting of the Chief Executive, six Directors, with responsibility for Human Resources, Prisons, Health and Care, Corporate Services, Finance and Business services and Prison Services, and three non-executive Directors. All members of the board are appointed by the Justice Minister. The Scottish Prison Services has held devolved agency status since April 5, 1993. It has an annual budget of £320 million, and employs around 4500 people at fifteen prisons and a training college outside Falkirk, and operates a central storage facility in Fauldhouse, West Lothian. Its headquarters are presently situated at Calton House, Redheughs Rigg, Edinburgh.

Governors

Each institution within the Scottish Prison Service is run by a **3–05** governor, whose duties are specified in s.33 of the 1989 Act. In order that the governor may carry out his statutory obligations in terms of s.33, in practice a number of governor grades, deputies and assistants need to be appointed. With exception of the open estate — which currently has one governor, plus one deputy governor for each of HM Prison Noranside and HM Prison Castle Huntly — each directly managed establishment in Scotland has its own governor, assisted in all the larger establishments by a deputy governor, and a number of hall governors, responsible for the maintenance and administration of specific halls within establishments.

Prison Officers

The training and development of Prison Officers has undergone **3–06** some radical changes in the course of the past twenty years. Prior to 1986, there was a specific distinction between those who entered the prison service at governor grades, and those who entered as prison officers. Since 1986 that distinction has been withdrawn. Following the coming into force of the 1994 Rules, a much greater emphasis has been placed on training and development of prison officers. Now, after an induction week within a prison establishment, newly recruited officers spend six weeks in the Officer Foundation Training Course at the SPS College in Polmont. Within the first two years of service, all new recruits are required to attain a Level S3 SVQ in Custodial Care. The functions and duties of prison officers have changed radically over the past two decades. The former public image of prison "Warders" as dour, humourless and robotic has taken some time to shift from the public imagination, but since 1989, the Scottish Prison Service have issued mission statements, setting out their specific policies. In 1989, the mission statement read: "The Mission of the Scottish Prison Services is to keep in custody those committed by the Courts, to maintain good order in each Prison, to look after inmates with humanity, and to provide them with all possible opportunities to help them lead law abiding and useful lives after release". Currently, the Scottish Prison Service Mission Statement sets out that the key aims for the prison service remain "custody, order, care and opportunities".

As a result, prison officers spend a great deal more time now engaged on the delivery of course work and offender programmes. A great many prison officers are qualified facilitators, who engage in delivering programmes such as the Sex Offenders Treatment Programme ("STOP", which is itself divided into a number of different modules), the Violence Protection Programme, Basic and Advanced Drug Awareness, Alcohol Awareness, Domestic Violence, and others, which are discussed later in this chapter. Long term prisoners are afforded a "personal officer" on their admission to each establishment, and every prison in Scotland in which long-term prisoners are incarcerated employs officers holding the rank of Lifer Liaison Officer and Early Release Liaison Officer to deal particularly with the specific needs and demands of long term and life sentence prisoners.

The private prison system

3–07   There is, as stated previously, at present only one private prison in Scotland, namely HM Prison Kilmarnock, Bowhouse. This is operated by Premier Prison Services Ltd on behalf of the Scottish Prison Service, and has a contractual maximum capacity of 692 prisoners. It is a closed mainstream high security establishment, operating a similar regime to that available elsewhere within the Scottish Prison System, and is thus broadly analogous to the security conditions that would be found in Shotts, Glenochil and

Perth. It accommodates male adult prisoners, including remands, short term and long-term prisoners. It does not have a National Top End facility, but prisoners are able to apply from Kilmarnock to be transferred to a National Top End establishment operated by the Scottish Prison Service.

The 2006 Rules apply in HM Prison Kilmarnock in exactly the same way as they do in other Prisons, by virtue of the provisions of r.3. However, it should perhaps be noted that Kilmarnock does not have a Governor, but is administered by a "Director", who is a senior member of prison staff, responsible to a controller, who is a crown servant appointed by the Justice Minister. The director carries out the majority of the functions of the governor of an SPS establishment, except where such functions have been conferred upon the controller in terms of s.107(4) of the 1994 Act. References to an "officer" in the 2006 Rules also apply to "prisoner custody officers", as certified in terms of the Criminal Justice and Public Order Act 1994 s.107. Every officer performing custodial duties shall be a prisoner custody officer, and there are specific provisions in r.4 of the 2006 Rules regulating the suspension of the certificate of a prisoner custody officer, where the officer has been charged with a criminal offence, disciplinary action is being taken against him, he is alleged to have acted improperly in the course of his duties, or he appears to be unfit by reason of illness.

Staff to prisoner ratios in Kilmarnock are significantly lower than those in other mainstream high security establishments, although it should be noted that there is a considerably greater use of surveillance technology within Kilmarnock, and consequently a higher average number of misconduct reports, although the most recent report by HM Chief Inspector of Prisons for Scotland observes that this number fell markedly between the inspections in 2003 and 2005. Recent reports indicate that systems within HM Prison Kilmarnock are becoming more closely aligned with those within the public sector. Uniformed staff in Kilmarnock wear Premier Prison Service uniforms, not those worn elsewhere within the prison system.

In June 2006, a contract was awarded to Addiewell Prison Ltd to design, construct, finance and manage a second private prison, expected to house 700 inmates, at Addiewell, West Lothian. This prison is currently expected to be open and fully operational in 2009, and will be the second private prison in Scotland.

DUTIES OF OFFICERS

3–08　These are specified in detail in rr.148–153. It is the duty of every officer and employee to conform to the 2006 Rules, to obey any lawful instructions of the governor or of the Scottish Ministers, and to inform the governor promptly of any breach of these rules or any abuse or impropriety which comes to their knowledge.

Business or pecuniary transactions

3–09　Business or pecuniary transactions by staff members with prisoners or in connection with the prison are specifically prohibited by r.149, except with the express permission of Ministers. Except with the authority of the governor, no officer or prison employee is permitted to bring in or take out, attempt to bring in or take out, or knowingly allow to be brought in or taken out, or deposit in any place any article whatsoever, with the intent that it shall come into the possession of any prisoner.

Rule 150 provides that "No officer or employee shall:

   (a)　receive any unauthorised fee, gratuity or other consideration in connection with his or her duties as an officer or employee;

   (b)　directly or indirectly, have any interest in any contract in connection with the prison or any other prison; or

   (c)　receive any fee, gratuity or other consideration from or on behalf of any contractor at, or any person tendering for a contract in connection with, the prison or any other prison."

Power of search

3–10　In terms of r.151, the governor may order the carrying out of a search of any officer or employee, and of any article of property belonging to any officer or employee which is in his or her possession whilst in the prison, or which is kept by them in his or her locker or any other place within the prison. A search of an officer or employee in terms of this rule shall be carried out within the prison, by at least two officers of the same sex as the officer or employee being searched, outwith the sight of any other person, and as expeditiously and decently as possible (r.151(4)). A search under this rule of any clothing or other article of property belonging to an officer or employee which is being worn or, as the case may be, otherwise in their possession whilst in the prison, or which is kept by them in their locker or any other place within the prison, may, in addition to being carried out by hand, be carried out by the use of equipment involving the application of a suction device or a swab on or to such possessions in order to collect particles from their surface, and analysis of any such particles as may be found, for the purpose of ascertaining whether any consists of a controlled drug or an explosive substance, or by the use of metal detecting equipment, and in accordance with any such procedures and conditions as may be specified in a direction by the Scottish Ministers.

The power of search conferred above shall include power to use reasonable force where necessary.

Communications to the press and other media

Communications to the press and other media are governed by 3–11 r.152, which specifies that no officer or employee shall make, directly or indirectly, any unauthorised communication to a press representative or any other person concerning matters which have become known to them in the course of his or her duties, nor shall they, without the authority of the governor or, in such circumstances as Ministers may specify by direction, publish any matter or make any public pronouncement relating to the administration of any institution to which the Act applies or to any person who may be lawfully confined therein.

Code of conduct

The Scottish Ministers have power, in terms of r.153, to approve 3–12 a code regulating the conduct and discipline of officers and employees, and any such code may include provision regulating the procedures which may be invoked where it is suspected that the acts or omissions of an officer or employee may constitute misconduct, the disciplinary action which may follow in the event that an officer or employee is found to have misconducted himself and the rights of appeal granted to any such officer or employee.

HER MAJESTY'S CHIEF INSPECTOR OF PRISONS FOR SCOTLAND

While the role of Prison Inspector dates back to 1835, when the 3–13 government first appointed five prison inspectors for the United Kingdom, the post as an independent one fell into desuetude in 1903 when, after the death of the incumbent Major W.G.B. Willis, the Prison Commissioners and the treasury agreed that the post did not require to be filled. Thereafter, the function of inspection of prisons became part of the remit of the prison commissioners, and separate annual reports into prison conditions were not issued.

Inspection proceeded in a rather ad hoc manner throughout the twentieth century, which became increasingly inappropriate as complaints about prison conditions grew, prisoners became more adept at publicising their complaints, and large parts of the prison estate were substantially damaged in riots. A non-statutory form of Inspectorate was set up in January 1981, following the Report of the May committee in 1979 and eventually, s.7(1) of the Prisons (Scotland) Act 1989 provided that the monarch may appoint a person to be Chief Inspector of Prisons for Scotland, and the Inspectorate was placed on a statutory footing. All holders of the office of Chief Inspector since 1981 have been lay persons appointed from outwith the Prison Service. The Inspector is appointed for a term of five years at a time.

The statutory duties of HM Chief Inspector of Prisons for Scotland are specified in s.7(2)–(5). It is his duty to inspect or arrange for the inspection of prisons, and to report to the First Minister on them, and in particular to report to the Minister on the treatment of prisoners and the conditions in prisons. At present, the Inspectorate has a staff of four, not including the Inspector himself.

The Inspectorate also retains the responsibility for inspecting and reporting on conditions within the nine Legalised Police Cells (LPCs), where prisoners may, by reason of their geographical remoteness from mainstream prisons, be held briefly waiting trial or transfer to prison. The nine locations of LPCs are Campbeltown, Dunoon, Oban, Hawick, Thurso, Lochmaddy, Kirkwall, Lerwick, and Stornoway

3–14   The Minister may refer specific matters connected with prisons in Scotland and prisoners in them to the Inspector, and direct that he report on them, and the Inspector is obliged to provide a yearly report to the Scottish Parliament in such form as the Minister shall direct. In addition, the Inspectorate aims to carry out a full inspection of each prison within Scotland once every three years, and therefore the Inspectorate will publish on average five reports on specific establishments each year. The Inspectorate determines its own timetable for the carrying out of inspections. Each full inspection normally lasts between one and two weeks, depending on the size and complexity of the establishment. Following each inspection a report is prepared, which is submitted to Scottish Ministers and published. Such reports are now also available on the Scottish Executive website. In addition to the programme of full inspections, follow up inspections — which normally last one or two days — are undertaken on each establishment not subject to a full inspection. All reports are submitted to Scottish Ministers. All inspection reports are published in full, save occasionally parts of reports that the Inspectorate has indicated should not be published as they touch on confidential matters involving security. It is for the Inspector to decide whether or not to hold a press conference on the publication of the annual report. The Inspectorate's main statutory responsibility is the regular inspection of individual establishments. In carrying out this function, the specific matters that are inspected and reported on include physical conditions within establishments, quality of prisoner regimes, morale of staff and prisoners, facilities and amenities available to staff and prisoners, questions of safety and decency, and the establishment's contribution to preventing re-offending. It is not the function of the Inspectorate to investigate or adjudicate upon the complaints of individual prisoners (that falls within the remit of the Scottish Prisons Complaints Commissioner), although clearly members of the Inspectorate will meet and discuss matters with prisoners and staff. The Inspectorate has no direct input to the policy or management of the Scottish Prison Service, although recommendations contained in its reports may have implications for either or both.

THE SCOTTISH PRISONS COMPLAINTS COMMISSIONER

Since the 1994 Rules came into effect, it has been recognised that, **3–15** for prisoners' rights to be meaningful, there must be a form of internal complaints procedure to the governor. Most inmates are familiar with the "CP" forms issued when they wish to raise complaints about matters directly affecting their day-to-day life in custody, whether in respect of complaints about food standards, refusal of privileges, conditions in worksheds, minor disagreements with officers, problems of access to educational, religious or other external bodies, downgrades or any other matter that properly forms part of the everyday life of a custodial institution. This ensures that, where a matter has not been satisfactorily resolved at hall level, there is a direct avenue whereby prisoners may raise their concerns with the governor and receive a written reply within a reasonable time.

In order to establish a uniform system for responding to complaints throughout the system, and further to provide some form of independent scrutiny of the governors' decision-making processes, the office of Scottish Prisons Complaints Commissioner (which remains on a non-statutory basis, although a recommendation to place the post on a statutory footing was made in 2005) was set up in December 1994, following a recommendation within the Justice Charter for Scotland. It was recognised that the holder of the post had to be seen as entirely independent of Ministers. It is the

Commissioner's function to act as Ombudsman in respect of complaints by individual prisoners, and thus this post does not in any way impinge upon the role of the Inspector. The commissioner has jurisdiction to adjudicate upon any matter within the competence of SPS, including any adjudication by the governor, but he has no locus to raise matters relating to sentencing or parole with the appropriate bodies. He currently employs a staff of three, and deals on average with around 400 complaints annually, although the number of complaints filed in 2005 reached an all-time high of 460, 37 per cent of them emanating from one establishment, HM Prison Dumfries. It should perhaps be noted that of the 172 complaints filed in Dumfries, the overwhelming majority emanated from a total of five prisoners. Most of these are dealt with by correspondence, although the Commissioner and his staff will regularly visit prisons and interview prisoners. Conciliation is now actively encouraged, and the number of cases resolved by this method increased from 58 in 2004 to 127 in 2005. In any case in which he is not satisfied with the manner in which a complaint was dealt with internally, the Commissioner may make recommendations to the Chief Executive of the Scottish Prison Service. Interestingly, the bulk of complaints in 2005 emanated from the two prisons housing virtually all Scotland's convicted sex offenders, namely Peterhead and Dumfries. The Commissioner provides an annual report to Scottish Ministers, which is published by the Commission.

VISITING COMMITTEES

3–16 These bodies were set up in modern times by s.7 of the Prisons (Scotland) Act 1952, and re-constituted by ss.8 and 19(3) of the 1989 Act, and the rules made thereunder, which provided that the Secretary of State appointed members of Visiting Committees for establishments holding prisoners under 21 (two members of such committee were required to be justices of the peace, and it was obligatory to appoint women members), while local authorities retained their involvement in the prison system, as first granted in 1877 when prisons passed into state control, by appointing the members to Visiting Committees for adult establishments. Over the last fifty years in particular, their power and influence has waxed and waned considerably. In the period when there was little prison unrest, little debate about the uses of imprisonment, and no real move towards the concept of prisoners' rights, they would carry out their duties in respect of frequent visiting and hearing prisoners' complaints, but would not necessarily take a proactive role in the addressing of prisoners' grievances, or report particularly often to the Secretary of State on matters within their remit.

Prior to 1985, the Visiting Committees would sometimes be called upon to adjudicate on allegations of serious disciplinary breaches by prisoners, and they had the power to award punishments, including loss of remission, effectively adding days onto a prisoner's sentence. It was the exercise of this power by the broadly analogous Boards of Visitors in England that was criticised by the European Court in *Campbell and Fell v United Kingdom*, (1984) E.H.R.R. 165, and, following the decision in *R v Secretary of State for the Home Department, Ex p Tarrant*, [1985] Q.B. 251, in which it was held that, in view of the seriousness of the penalties available to the Board of Visitors, legal representation should be allowed, the practice of allowing visiting committees to ward unlimited loss of remission was suspended. The power was absent from the 1994 Rules, and the visiting committee no longer exercises a disciplinary function. In practice, this has assisted them in carrying out their remaining supervisory functions, as prisoners are more likely to air their grievances freely to those whom they do not perceive as part of the disciplinary system.

As concerns began to grow about prison conditions, and as the concept of prisoners rights grew, the Visiting Committees' role as "watchdog" over prisons and as a quick and cheap method for the addressing of complaints meant that their use and influence increased. In terms of s.8(2) of the 1989 Act, any member of the committee was empowered to visit the prison at any time, to have free access to any part of the prison, and to any prisoner. Their functions were reconstituted in terms of the 1994 Rules, which provided in r.135 that:

> "A visiting committee shall cooperate with the Secretary of State and the Governor in promoting the efficiency of the prison and shall enquire into and report to the Secretary of State upon any matter in which he may ask it to enquire".

An association of Scottish Visiting Committees has been set up, for **3–17** the purposes of arranging training for members, and to ensure cooperation in respect of representations made to Ministers.

The rules governing the present constitution and functions of the Visiting Committees are now to be found in rr.154–164 of the 2006 Rules. The councils having responsibility for the appointment of members of the Visiting Committees for each adult establishment, and the number of members to be appointed by each authority, are specified in detail in Sch.2 of the 2006 Rules. The rules of appointment by councils are specified in r.155(2).

In terms of r.155(4), "Any person with a direct financial interest in any contract for the supply of goods or services to any prison shall not be eligible for appointment to a visiting committee in terms of this Rule". Rule 155(7) provides that:

"A member of a visiting committee shall cease to hold office if—

(a) he or she resigns;
(b) either the council who appointed the member or the Scottish Ministers terminate the member's appointment if either is satisfied that—

   (i)   the member has failed satisfactorily to perform his or her duties;
   (ii) the member is for any other reason incapable of carrying out his or her duties;
   (iii) subsequent to his or her appointment, the member has been convicted of such a criminal offence, or their conduct has been such, that it is not fitting that he or she should remain a member; or
   (iv) the member has a direct financial interest contrary to the terms of rule 163; or

(c) having been appointed a member whilst also a member of the council, the council terminate his or her appointment by reason of having ceased to be a member of the council."

3–18 The Scottish Ministers retain the duty to appoint members of the committee for Polmont Young Offenders Institution in terms of s.19(3) of the 1989 Act and r.156. This provides that a minimum of one third of members, and not fewer than two members, shall be women.

Rule 157 provides that each committee shall appoint a chair, a deputy chair and a clerk, the chair and deputy holding office for four years, and obliges the chair to report the membership of the committee to the Ministers immediately after the first meeting. In terms of r.157(3) the visiting committee for a prison shall meet at the prison at least once in every period of three months. The committee has the power to delegate certain duties to subcommittees, and must retain minutes of its meetings.

The general duties of visiting committees are specified in r.158. A visiting committee shall co-operate with the Scottish Ministers and the governor in promoting the efficiency of the prison and it is under a duty to inquire into and report to the Scottish Ministers upon any matter into which they may ask it to inquire.

The committee must immediately bring to the notice of the **3–19** governor any circumstances relating to the administration of the prison or the condition of any prisoner which appear to it to be expedient to report for the governor's consideration, and in terms of r.158(2)(b) bring such circumstances to the notice of the Scottish Ministers "if it appears to the committee that the Governor has not remedied any matter which the Committee has notified to the Governor in terms of sub paragraph (a) within such period as appears to the committee to be reasonable".

The visiting committee shall from time to time inquire into the state of the prison premises and must inspect, in particular, the food and drink provided to prisoners and in relation to any such inquiry they are obliged to record particulars of every visit made, together with any deficiencies found during such visits, in the committee's minute book, and promptly send a copy of such particulars to the Scottish Ministers and to the governor.

The visiting committee shall also discharge such other (unspecified) duties as the Scottish Ministers may from time to time assign.

Matters considered by the committees are strictly confidential. **3–20** r.158(5) states "No person who is or has been a member of a visiting committee shall disclose any information mentioned in paragraph (6) which the person holds or has held as a member."

The information referred to above is any information obtained by any member of a visiting committee which relates to the prison, any officer of the prison or any prisoner, and on terms or in circumstances requiring it to be held in confidence. This, of course, does not apply in the context of the committee's own reports to Ministers or the governor.

SHERIFFS AND JUSTICES OF THE PEACE

Section 15(1) of the 1989 Act permits any sheriff or justice of the **3–21** peace to visit any prison within their jurisdiction, or in which a prisoner is confined for any offence committed within their jurisdiction. They may examine the condition of the prison and the prisoners, and may enter any observations on the condition of the prison or on any abuses found therein, into the visitors book kept by the governor. By virtue of s.15(2), for obvious reasons a sheriff or justice of the peace can only communicate with the prisoner on the subject of his treatment. Where an entry has been made in the visitors book in terms of this section, it is the duty of the governor to bring this to the attention of the visiting committee on their next visit. In practice, the use of this power by sheriffs and magistrates is relatively rarely used, although it is understandably not uncommon for newly appointed sheriffs in whose jurisdiction larger prisons may be found to visit the institution soon after their appointment.

TRANSPORTATION OF PRISONERS TO AND FROM PRISON

3–22 This task is no longer undertaken by the Scottish Prison Service. Since November 2003, the contract for all prisoner transportation to and from courts has been awarded to Reliance Custodial Services for a seven year period, and since October 2004 all transportation of prisoners from every prison to every court and *vice versa* has been by way of a Reliance prisoner escort vehicle. In addition, reliance are responsible for inter-prison transfers and certain external escorting services, including escorting prisoners on compassionate visits. The fact that prisoners are therefore often not known to the escorting services did, in the early stages, give rise to a number of well-publicised escapes, but as at the time of writing these have become considerably less common. The practice of employing outside contractors to transport prisoners for compassionate visits has come in for some criticism, as many feel that it would be preferable for a prisoner facing a potentially traumatic meeting with members of his family to be accompanied by staff with whom he has built up a rapport. However, it should perhaps be noted that there is as yet no evidence of any increase in the number of escapes, attempted escapes or other adverse incidents since the privatisation of prisoner transport.

OFFENCE-FOCUSSED COURSEWORK

3–23 One of the most obvious changes in the management of prisons has been the vast amount of time and money spent on arranging and delivering coursework in custody, designed to reduce the risks of re-offending. Until 1993 there were no official programmes in Scotland designed to assist offenders in learning more about the triggers to their offending, and to reduce the risk of re-offending.

Initially, the only coursework available was for sex offenders. The first Sex Offenders Treatment Programme (STOP) was delivered on twenty occasions between 1993 and 2000, before its replacement by the STOP 2000 programme. Since 2002, further programmes have been developed to address the areas of Cognitive Skills, Problem Solving, Anger Management, Drug and Alcohol Awareness, and relationship and parenting skills. By 2006, no fewer than 1,064 programmes and approved activities had been undertaken within the Scottish Prison System. There is some evidence recently ingathered by SPS that indicates that successful completion of relevant offence-focussed coursework may reduce the likelihood of re-offending within two years of release by 10-15 per cent (R.K. Hanson, "The first report of the Collaborative Outcome Data Project on the effectiveness of psychological treatment for sex offenders" in *Sexual Abuse: A Journal of Research and Treatment*, 2002, 14, 169–194).

At present, there are five Accredited Programmes (programmes that are delivered to a high quality and have achieved Accredited Status from an external panel of experts), namely:

(1) The Sex Offender Treatment Programme (STOP 2000)
(2) Adapted STOP
(3) Extended STOP
(4) Cognitive Skills
(5) Anger Management (Kilmarnock)

The first three of these are only available within HM Prison **3–24** Peterhead (although the adapted programme can be provided for offenders under 21 in HMYOI Polmont). The "core" STOP 2000 programme runs for 210 hours, taking place over a period of around nine months, and received full accreditation in 2001. It is designed to provide the opportunity for prisoners to address their sexual offending behaviour, and the treatment goals are to challenge thinking patterns, develop victim empathy and develop relapse prevention skills. The programme is run by way of group-work sessions, as there is at present no facility anywhere within the Scottish prison system for one-to-one work on offending behaviour. It is not necessary for the prisoner to have pled guilty to the offence to be accepted onto the programme, and the issue of its suitability to all those convicted of sexual offences remains controversial. Those who have ongoing appeals against conviction obviously cannot be requested to undertake coursework based upon a presumption of guilt, and those who deny their offences are often either assessed as unsuitable for the coursework, or do not complete the course. Clearly, once the appellate process is concluded, prison staff must proceed on the basis of the conviction and sentence, and it is not unknown for prisoners who have previously pled guilty to use delaying tactics to avoid having to address aspects of their behaviour, but there has been some criticism of the present policy that suggests that all prisoners convicted of a sexual offence or offences should be encouraged throughout their sentence to undertake groupwork, even when they continue to deny their offences. In the recent past, those who maintain their denial are often transferred to other establishments where no such offence-focussed work is available. At present, there are two to three core STOP programmes run each year in Peterhead.

The use of the STOP programme, with its emphasis on group-work, as opposed to person-to-person counselling, has long proved controversial in Scotland. Due to the small size of the convicted sex offender population in Scotland, there is to date no statistical analysis of its effectiveness, but a study of 43 similar programmes run in the United States of America, Canada, and England and Wales, completed in 2002, and reviewing the cases of around 9000 prisoners, discovered that while approximately 18 per cent of high risk offenders who had not undertaken a sex offender treatment programme reoffended within five years, the figure dropped to 19 per cent amongst those who had (R.K. Hanson, "The first report of the Collaborative Outcome Data Project on the effectiveness of psychological treatment for sex offenders" in *Sexual Abuse: A Journal of Research and Treatment*, 2002, 14, 169–194).

The Adapted STOP programme has broadly similar goals, but is designed to be used by adult prisoners or young offenders with learning disabilities or borderline learning disabilities to address their sexual offending behaviour. It runs for 160 hours, and was accredited in 2005. It is available in Polmont and Peterhead. It relies considerably less on written material, and more on pictorial representations, and the treatment goals encompass increasing sexual knowledge, modifying offence justification thinking, gaining an understanding of victim harm and developing an ability to recognise feelings in themselves and others. The "cut-off" point to be assessed as suitable for this programme is whether the prisoner's measured IQ is below 80.

3–25   The Extended STOP programme lasts for 150 hours, and is designed to help prisoners who have completed STOP 2000, but who require further work to understand their sexual offending and how to control it. It goes without saying that successful completion of the core programme is a prerequisite to acceptance onto this programme. Around one month after the completion of the core programme, the prisoner is psychometrically tested, and if the result of this reveals an ongoing unmet need, and there is sufficient time available before his liberation date, he will be invited to participate in this programme, which received its accreditation in 2005. Its treatment goals are to enable the prisoner to develop a deeper understanding of the patterns underlying sexual offending and how to control them.

Of the five accredited programmes, the most widely used is the 76 hour Cognitive Skills course, introduced in 1995, accredited in 1998, and currently available in Barlinnie, Cornton Vale,

Edinburgh, Glenochil, Greenock, Low Moss, Perth, Peterhead, Polmont and Shotts. In the past four years, 208 such courses have been run in Scotland. The course is designed to address the needs of any offender who has difficulties with thinking skills, which may affect their social functioning. Unsurprisingly, given that the entire pool from which candidates for this course are selected consists of those convicted and imprisoned for a criminal offence or offences, a vast number of inmates are assessed as suitable for this course. It comprises seven modules; problem solving, social skills, creative thinking, values enhancement, negotiation skills, management of emotions and critical reasoning. Each group undertaking the course usually starts with between ten and twelve members, two of whom on average do not complete the course, either by deselecting themselves or by being deselected.

The Anger Management course developed by Premier Prison Services and offered in HM Prison Kilmarnock received its accreditation in 2002. It runs for 30 hours. It should be noted that the Anger Management programmes still provided by the Scottish Prison Service in Barlinnie, Cornton Vale, Greenock, Perth, Peterhead, Polmont and Shotts, which were developed by SPS psychologists and accredited in 1999, have no longer been accredited following the lapse of accreditation in 2005. The Kilmarnock course is designed to address the needs of any prisoner who has problems in temper control, and is therefore only suitable for a percentage of violent offenders, as many such offences, being premeditated, are not born of anger. The programme addresses the issues of why and when to control anger, how to reduce anger and how to modify and improve behavioural coping skills. The programme in Kilmarnock is broadly the same as the non-accredited Anger Management programmes available elsewhere in the SPS.

In addition to the accredited programmes (and the Anger Management programmes discussed above), there are a number of other programmes delivered without accredited status. These are— **3–26**

(1) Problem Solving Skills Training
(2) Rolling STOP
(3) Violence Prevention Programme

The Problem Solving Skills Training programme runs for 60 hours. It was introduced in 1999, accredited the following year, but its accreditation has also lapsed in 2005. It is currently available in Glenochil and Kilmarnock, and its aims are to teach the offender problem-solving skills, and how to use these skills to address offending behaviour. This course places some emphasis on self-management and perspective taking, in order to place problem solving skills in a social context.

The Rolling STOP programme is available in Polmont, Barlinnie, Edinburgh and Peterhead. It runs for between 60 and 100 hours, depending on the prisoner's level of needs and his perceived speed of progress, and is designed to enable either adult prisoners sentenced to four years or more to address their sexual offending behaviour in full, or to help adult prisoners who have completed the core STOP 2000 programme, but who might not need to complete the full Extended STOP programme, to carry out further offence-focussed work prior to release.

3–27   The Violence Prevention Programme is designed specifically for those offenders at the highest risk of future violent re-offending. It is targeted at the adult male population, and is currently available only in Shotts and Glenochil. Only those with a history of violent convictions and a long pattern of violent offending are likely to be accepted onto this course. The programme lasts for 200 hours, lasting around six to nine months, and is divided into ten modules which, together, explore the offender's use of violence. The programme is designed to challenge the attitudes and motivation behind violent offending, and to teach skills to assist violent offenders to replace past violent offending patterns with more pro-social behaviours.

In addition to the coursework available above, the Scottish Prison Service runs a number of other approved activities.

A 22 hour long Alcohol Awareness course is currently available in Aberdeen, Edinburgh, Cornton Vale, Glenochil, Greenock, Inverness, Low Moss, the Open Estate, Perth, Peterhead, Polmont and Shotts.

3–28   There are several short courses in respect of drug use and drug awareness available. Since 2001, the Lifeline Course, developed by SPS psychologists and lasting 50 hours has been available. In addition to this, the Drug Action for Change course, lasting 25 hours, is on offer at Cornton Vale, Edinburgh, Greenock, Inverness, and Low Moss, while the 40 hour SMART recovery course is available within Inverness, Shotts and the Open Estate. The 36 hour First Step addictions course is offered in Aberdeen, Barlinnie, Dumfries, Glenochil, Perth and Polmont. It will thus be seen that every mainstream establishment in Scotland offers some form of addiction-based coursework. A new more intensive drug awareness course, lasting four weeks and consisting of groupwork five days per week, commenced in June 2006.

For its part, HM Prison Kilmarnock has developed and uses the 24 hour Over-Comers course and the 16 hour Advanced Drug Awareness course.

Inter-personal skills have often been an issue of concern in respect of their relevance to offending, and HM Prison Peterhead developed a 35 hour relationship skills course, now available in Aberdeen, Dumfries, Edinburgh, Perth and Peterhead. HM Prison Shotts developed a 25 hour course on coping skills for long term prisoners called "START", which is currently only available at Shotts. Kilmarnock has developed and uses a 16 hour Alternatives to Violence course.

For female offenders, HM Prison Cornton Vale has developed **3–29** and offers a course called "Connections for Women", which runs for 23.5 hours.

Positive Parenting classes for young offenders are provided at HM YOI Polmont, while Greenock and Low Moss offer parenting classes for adult short-term offenders, and Shotts runs a course entitled "Encouraging the Long-Term Father". An anxiety and sleep management course developed at Cornton Vale is now offered in Aberdeen, Cornton Vale, Dumfries, Greenock and Shotts.

EMPLOYMENT

All prisons that house convicted prisoners have links with job **3–30** search and advice agencies within the community, and most long-term and life prisoners approaching the end of their sentences, and who have not obtained a concrete offer of employment will be offered these services as a matter of course, as there is some evidence that those who access employment upon release are at a reduced risk of returning to custody, although it has also long been recognised that the existence of criminal convictions, especially those resulting in prison sentences, has a detrimental effect on a person's value in the labour market. In custody, much time is spent in offering skills-based courses designed to suit prisoners' particular needs, in order that they can put their newly-learned skills to use in the community. All long-term establishments provide both educational opportunities and vocational training, and a great many long-term prisoners access college and university courses from custody. As release approaches, prison staff will offer assistance in respect of putting prisoners in touch with relevant outside agencies experienced in the field of job search advice. The largest organisation in Scotland, currently offering services in thirteen towns and cities as far apart as Stranraer and Inverness, is APEX Scotland.

OVERCROWDING

3-31 In common with the rest of the United Kingdom, Scotland's prisons are permanently stretched to and beyond their official capacities, particularly in respect of adult male prisoners. While there are occasions when HM YOI Polmont, HMP Cornton Vale and HMP Peterhead (which houses only adult convicted sex offenders) operate at just under 100 per cent capacity, as at the end of financial year 2004-05 the national daily average population was 6,779, as against a design capacity of 6,396, meaning that Scotland's prisons are running at 106 per cent of their "ideal" capacity. By February 2007, the average daily prison population stood at around 7,153, or over 112 per cent of capacity, the overcrowding being found almost entirely in the prisons taking short-term convicted prisoners (Barlinnie, Aberdeen, Greenock, Edinburgh, and Inverness). HM Prison Craiginches, Aberdeen, not uncommonly finds itself housing 140 per cent of its recommended number of inmates.

The detrimental effects of this on prisoners and staff have been commented upon for many years. In his most recent report, published on November 1, 2006, HM Chief Inspector of Prisons for Scotland identified nine specific ways in which overcrowding causes harm, namely:

(1) It increases the number of prisoners managed by prison staff who, as a result, have less time to devote to screening prisoners for self-harm or suicide, prisoners with mental health problems and prisoners who are potentially violent. Risk assessments will inevitably suffer.

(2) It increases the availability of drugs since there are more people who want drugs and prison staff have less time to search.

(3) It increases the likelihood of cell-sharing: two people, often complete strangers, are required to live in very close proximity. This will involve another person who may have a history of violence and of whose medical and mental health history the prisoner will know nothing; and it will involve sharing a toilet within the cell.

(4) It increases noise and tension.

(5) It makes it likely that prisoners will have less access to staff; and that they will find that those staff to whom they do have access will have less time to deal with them.

(6) The resources in prison will be more stretched, so prisoners will have less access to programmes, education, training, work etc.

(7) Facilities will also be more stretched, so that laundry will be done less often and food quality will deteriorate.
(8) Prisoners will spend more time in cell.
(9) Family contact and visits will be restricted.

It is manifest that the Scottish courts imprison more people than the prison service can readily accommodate. This clearly has a detrimental effect on any attempts at proper rehabilitation, education and vocational training, and, in respect of short sentences, often means that no practical work is undertaken during the offender's spell in custody. While sentencers will inevitably feel that the decision to imprison someone was the only appropriate one to make in the circumstances of the case, and while availability of prison places cannot be a reason for not imprisoning someone who is felt to require to be removed from the community, it remains a concern that the limitations of the present range of non-custodial sentencing options, and the proposed increase in the length of sentence actually served in prison to three-quarters of the total sentence in some cases, can only serve to exacerbate the over-crowding problem in the near future. In England, the crisis has become so acute that it has been proposed that some offenders do not commence their sentences until a prison place is available. **3–32**

With a growing number of imprisonable offences on the statute book, with parliament regularly increasing the statutory maximum sentences for some offences, with the prospect of sentencing guidelines being issued in future, with press and parliamentary pressure encouraging sentencers not to be seen as "soft", and with a significant percentage of those given non-custodial "alternatives" (although that presupposes the imprisonment is the norm) failing to comply with these, resulting in the majority of cases in custodial sentences being imposed, it is clear that the problem of over-crowding will remain a vital issue for Ministers and the Prison Service for many years to come.

Bruce Short Solicitors
3 Rattray Street
Dundee
DD1 1NA
LP44 Dundee

CHAPTER 4

DAILY LIFE IN PRISON

4–01 As previously stated, prior to 1994 the rules governing daily life in prisons were limited, afforded no concept of prisoners possessing rights, and were often made by standing orders, the terms of which were not a matter of public knowledge. Since the Prisons and Young Offenders Institutions (Scotland) Rules 1994 ("the 1994 Rules") came into force, it has been considerably easier for staff and inmates to know how to approach particular situations within prison, not least because r.5 obliged the governor to ensure that a copy of the Rules and any directions made under them, as in force from time to time, shall be "readily available for inspection by officers and prisoners in each accommodation block and in the prison library. The rules have been replaced, with effect from March 26, 2006, by the Prisons and Young Offenders Institutions (Scotland) Rules 2006 ("the 2006 Rules"), which consolidated the various amendments since 1994. Rule 7 of the 2006 rules is in the same terms as the former r.5.

Central to the 1994 and 2006 Rules is the distinction between privileges, which may be awarded and withdrawn at the discretion of the governor of each prison, and rights. Rule 49(4) specifically provides that a system of privileges shall not make provision that would prejudice or derogate from any right specified in the 1994 Rules or any direction made thereunder, and that any right specified in the rules shall not be regarded as a privilege, and cannot be forfeited under r.119(1)(b). Discretionary privileges include the items of property a prisoner may keep in his cell, arrangements for purchase of items within or outwith the prison, additional recreation or library facilities, and use or possession of tobacco (prisons are specifically exempted from the terms of s.4 of the Smoking, Health and Social Care (Scotland) Act 2005). The regulations governing smoking tobacco in prison can be found in r.31 of the 2006 Rules.

The 2006 Rules are divided into seventeen separate parts. With the exception of supervision categories and female prisoners, dealt with in a previous chapter, and release from custody, dealt with in a subsequent chapter, the principal rules are dealt with here in the order in which they appear.

RECEPTION, RECORDS, CLASSIFICATION AND ALLOCATION.

These are governed by rr.8–15. No person can be admitted to **4–02** prison unless a valid warrant is produced at the time committing him into custody. On admission, every prisoner is to be searched as expeditiously and decently as possible by an officer of the same sex, in accordance with the provisions of r.106. Strip-searching is permissible, but must be carried out by two officers, outwith the presence of other prisoners. If any prohibited article (for example drugs, weapons or a mobile telephone) is found on admission, this may be passed to the police. Every prisoner must be interviewed by an officer on admission, in order to identify any problems that may require immediate attention, and a medical examination must take place within 24 hours of first admission into prison, and within 72 hours of transfer from another establishment, unless there is an apparent cause for concern, in which case the examination must take place within 24 hours.

On first admission, the prisoner is advised as to how he may inform up to two persons and his legal adviser. Where the prisoner is a foreign national, he is informed of his right to contact a diplomatic representative of his choice. A refugee or stateless person is informed of his right to contact a diplomatic representative of a state which he considers may look after his interests, and an organisation or authority whose principal purpose is to serve the interests or civil rights of refugees or stateless persons.

Fine defaulters must be advised of the facilities available to arrange for release upon payment of the balance of the fine (r.11(5)).

Where the prisoner is serving a determinate sentence, as soon as **4–03** reasonably practicable he must be advised of his liberation date. Where he is a long-term prisoner, he will be advised of both his Parole Qualifying Date and his Earliest Date of Liberation. Where he is a life prisoner, the warrant committing him to prison will specify the commencement date of the sentence and the length of the punishment part.

The rules of the prison, its routine and regime, its complaints procedure, the manner in which he may maintain contact with family and friends, and his rights of appeal must be intimated to him in writing on admission.

The prisoner is then registered. His height, weight and distinguishing marks are noted, and he is generally photographed. Fingerprints may be taken, but if the prisoner is untried and subsequently acquitted, these must be destroyed unless the procurator fiscal requests their retention in connection with other

proceedings. He is then assigned a supervision category, in terms of
rr.16 and 17, which on admission will be "high", although a
reduction in supervision category to "medium" may be directed
within 72 hours. Low supervision status is earned by behaviour in
custody.

Supervision Classifications

4–04   Prior to 1966, there were no specific security classifications for
prisoners. Security was regulated by standing orders, which were
not available to prisoners or the public, and thus not open to any
challenge. However, there were a number of well-publicised escapes
by high profile prisoners from English establishments in the early
part of the decade, culminating in the assisted escape in October
1966 of the Soviet spy George Blake, then serving 42 years for
espionage offences, from Wormwood Scrubs. Within days of his
escape an inquiry was set up, under the chairmanship of Lord
Mountbatten. Its report was published in December 1966, based
almost entirely on examination of the English system (the only
prison visited in Scotland was HM Prison Inverness, which at the
time housed many of the more dangerous prisoners in Scotland
within its "cages"), and it recommended that each prisoner be
allocated a specific "security category", based upon their perceived
level of risk to the public and likelihood of escape.

Initially, there were only four security categories, which remained
in force throughout the United Kingdom until 1998, namely:

Category A:

A prisoner who would place national security at risk, or be highly
dangerous to the public or to prison staff and their families or to the
police in the event of an escape and who must be kept in conditions
of maximum security.

Category B:

A prisoner who is considered likely to be a danger to the public
and who must be kept in secure conditions to prevent his escape.

Category C:

A prisoner who is considered unlikely to be a danger to the public
and who can be given the opportunity to serve his sentence with the
minimum of restrictions.

Category D:

A prisoner who is considered not to be a danger to the public and who can be given the opportunity to serve his sentence in open conditions.

After over thirty years in operation, these categories were **4-05** beginning to be perceived as less than entirely useful to the smooth running of the prison system, and in 1998 the Rules were substantially amended. A new category — "Limited D" was devised in respect of:

> "A life prisoner who may participate in activities approved by the Secretary of State for the purpose of testing his suitability to be assigned security category D".

This category enabled life prisoners who had served many years in custody, and who did not present as a management problem, to be allowed further exposure to the community by way of outside work or college placements, as part of the preparation for release, prior to being transferred to open conditions.

It was obligatory for every prisoner to be allocated a security category (untried prisoners could not be assigned a category lower than category B) in accordance with their level of risk of danger to the public, and a formal review of security categories had to take place at least every twelve months. The approval of the Secretary of State was necessary before either Limited D or full D categories could be awarded. Where the governor assigned any prisoner Category A status, it was his duty to inform the Secretary of State forthwith, and there were lengthy and complex review procedures set out within the 1994 Rules for review of this status.

By the end of the twentieth century, a system of security classi- **4-06** fications based upon the need to prevent prisoners escaping had become somewhat anomalous. The overwhelming majority of prisoners in closed conditions had neither the means nor the motivation to escape, and improved security made escape from closed establishments considerably harder than had been the case three decades before. While escapes were not unknown, they were more commonly from work placements, escorted leaves or open conditions, and the security categories recommended in 1966 were no longer relevant to the day-to-day administration of virtually all Scottish inmates. Challenges to security classifications through the internal complaints procedure became a regular feature of the governor's workload, and many such complaints reached the desk of the Scottish Prisons Complaints Commissioner, increasing the day-to-day workload of prisons in manners that could not have been foreseen thirty years previously. To base someone's prison status upon a theoretical risk of escape was unpopular with prisoners, staff and administrators. Thus, with effect from April 30, 2002, the former Security categories were replaced by Supervision levels, as specified by r.4 of the Prisons and Young Offenders Institutions (Scotland) Rules 2002, which deleted the whole of the previous security classifications and rules, and replaced them with the new supervision levels, now to be found in r.16 of the 2006 Rules, namely:

High Supervision:

A prisoner for whom all activities and movements require to be authorised, supervised and monitored by an officer.

Medium Supervision:

A prisoner for whom activities and movements are subject to limited supervision and restrictions.

Low Supervision:

A prisoner for whom activities and movements are subject to minimum supervision and restrictions, and who may be given the opportunity to participate in supervised or unsupervised activities in the community.

4–07 In order that an appropriate category is assigned for every prisoner under the new system, seven specific criteria are specified in r.17. These are:

> "(a) the seriousness of the offence for which the prisoner has been convicted;
> (b) the prisoner's previous convictions;
> (c) any outstanding charges;
> (d) the length of time that the prisoner has spent in custody;
> (e) the prisoner's conduct in custody;
> (f) the prisoner's trustworthiness and stability; and
> (g) any other criteria as may be specified in a direction made by the Scottish Ministers for the purposes of this rule."

The regulations governing the assignment of supervision levels are fairly complex, particularly now that classifications in Scotland are no longer analogous to those in England and Wales. Rule 17(3) allows Ministers to issue directions making provision for the relative importance of each of the above criteria in assigning a supervision level.

With the exception of prisoners whose admission is by way of **4–08** temporary transfer or a restricted transfer in terms of para.6(1) of Sch.1 to the Crime (Sentences) Act 1997, or a transfer under paras 2 or 3 of Sch.1 of the 1997 Act, who are assigned for their period of detention in Scotland a supervision level which is, in the governor's opinion, the nearest equivalent to their classification in the prison in which they were detained immediately before the transfer took place, every prisoner, on reception, shall be assigned high supervision level (r.17(4)).

Supervision levels are, of course, liable to change, especially during the currency of a long-term sentence. Rule 17(5) provides that, within 72 hours of reception, the supervision levels of all prisoners shall be reviewed in accordance with the provisions of the 2006 Rules. Following that review, the governor must keep supervision levels under review and shall formally review them within six months, and thereafter at least once every twelve months.

With the exception of the award of high supervision status, and subject to r.19, following the assignment of a supervision level, or the review of such level, r.18 obliges the governor to inform the prisoner in writing either, in the case of the assignment of a supervision level, why that level is appropriate, or in the case of a review that has resulted in no change in the prisoner's level, the reasons why a lower level is not appropriate. If the prisoner requests it, the governor may be required to provide the prisoner with a copy of any document to which he has had regard, and a summary of any other information of which he was aware and to which he had regard, unless the governor considers, in terms of r.18(3), that disclosure of the document or information would, if disclosed, be damaging to the prisoner on the grounds of being likely to adversely affect the health, welfare or safety of the prisoner or another person, that it would be likely to result in the commission of an offence, that it would be likely to facilitate an escape from legal custody or the doing of an act prejudicial to the safekeeping of persons in custody, that it would be likely to impede the prevention or detection of offences or the apprehension or prosecution of suspected offenders, or that it would otherwise be damaging to the public interest.

There are of course a great many situations in which a prisoner **4–09** faces the assignation of a higher supervision level, usually due to proven or suspected misconduct. Decisions to "downgrade" a prisoner, and apply a higher supervision level, are amongst the most controversial a governor can make, as they can often have far reaching consequences for the prisoner and their prospects of onward progression. Prisoners are therefore afforded the right to make representations before certain reviews can take place, and these are governed by r.19.

This rule applies in four specific situations, namely:

(1) Where a governor is minded to assign a higher supervision level than the existing level assigned;

(2) Where the governor is minded to assign a supervision level other than low supervision to a prisoner who is eligible to be considered for release on parole in terms of the provisions of Pt I of the 1993 Act;

(3) Where the governor is minded to assign a supervision level other than low supervision to a life prisoner who has served the "punishment part" of his sentence as defined in s.2(3) of the 1993 Act; or

(4) Where the governor is minded to assign a level other than low to a prisoner whose sentence does not fall within paras (2) and (3) above, but who has served such part of his sentence as may be specified in a direction made by the Scottish Ministers.

In these situations, as in terms of r.18 above, the governor shall provide the prisoner with a written notice informing him of the supervision level he is minded to assign, and his reasons therefore, and may once again provide the prisoner, on request, with copies of the documentation and information on which he proposes to make his assessment, subject to the exceptions specified in r.18(3) discussed above.

4–10 There are, however, two crucial distinctions provided by r.19. Firstly, r.19(2)(iii) specifically entitles the prisoner to make written representations to the governor in relation to the proposed assignment of a supervision level, and r.19(3) obliges the governor, if he declines to produce a document or other information on the grounds that its disclosure is likely to be damaging, to inform the prisoner in a written notice, of the gist of the information against him.

The award of a prisoner's supervision level is clearly crucial to his progression or otherwise, and decisions on whether to upgrade or downgrade prisoners require to be objectively justifiable. A prisoner holding a medium supervision level is precluded from progression to open conditions, from where home leaves may be taken to his proposed release address or area. In the case of a long-term prisoner approaching a parole qualifying date, the decision not to award a lower supervision level for a period of at least six months may substantially reduce the chances of their being granted parole, and in those circumstances the governor's decision may be scrutinised by the Internal Complaints Committee, and if their decision is not to the prisoner's liking he may refer the matter to the Scottish Prisons Complaints Commissioner, and ultimately, in some situations, he may seek to apply to the Court of Session for judicial review of the decision. The scope and use of judicial review will be discussed in a later chapter.

Of equal significance is the situation where the governor elects to downgrade a prisoner, resulting in many situations in their transfer back from open to closed conditions. In many situations the evidence of breach of discipline is clear and unequivocal (for example absconding, the provision of two positive drug tests on separate dates, violence towards prisoners or staff or other disruptive behaviour), but a considerable of downgrades within the modern system are based upon intelligence gathering, and its assessment.

Each establishment has its own intelligence gathering system, and **4–11** every prisoner has an intelligence file in which any matters of concern are noted and classified according to their level of reliability, which is assessed according to the source, its own history of reliability, and the extent to which the allegation is corroborated by other evidence or information. Particularly in the recent past, when there have been a great many allegations of prisoners in open conditions having easy access to drugs, and of certain prisoners being involved in the introduction of drugs into prison for onward supply, the ingathering of intelligence and its assessment has become a major part of prison work. As stated above, not all of the intelligence gathered can be revealed to the prisoner; disclosure of a considerable amount of such information might compromise its source and could lead to certain repercussions. However, where a prisoner is advised that intelligence reveals that his behaviour is not consistent with that expected of a low supervision prisoner in open conditions, to the extent that he is to be downgraded and returned to closed conditions (Most commonly in the present era for alleged involvement in supplying controlled drugs), he is advised of the gist of this information.

Where appropriate, redacted versions of the intelligence file, from which all matters that could identify sources or witnesses, may be seen by the Parole Board for Scotland and the Scottish Prisons Complaints Commissioner, and, where the prisoner is sufficiently aggrieved to seek judicial review of the decision to downgrade him based upon intelligence, this redacted information can be placed before the court. Obviously, the whole use of intelligence, which by its very nature cannot be tested fully either before a court or a tribunal, remains an area of some controversy. This matter will be considered in more detail in the context of parole decisions in Chapter 7.

Special security measures

4–12   In terms of r.20, the governor may impose additional security
measures, additional to the standard measures contained in Pt 10 of
the Rules, on any high supervision prisoner, where the governor
considers that these measures are necessary in the interests of the
health, safety and welfare of the prisoner or any other person, or to
prevent an escape from legal custody or the doing of any act prejudicial to the safe keeping of persons in legal custody.

PHYSICAL AND PERSONAL ENVIRONMENT

4–13 For as long as burghs and states have been locking up offenders,
this subject has been one of the most controversial. Argument over
the standard of prison conditions has raged for at least two centuries, and the debate between those who consider that standard
prison conditions should be as spartan as possible, to make prison
such an unpleasant place to reside that no-one in theory would ever
wish to return there, and those who consider that, when one is
deprived of liberty, one does not use human feelings and emotions,
and that a measure of comfort is consistent with encouraging
prisoners to engage more with those responsible for their care.

  Rule 22 of the 2006 Rules creates, for the first time, a presumption that all prisoners should be accommodated in a single cell or
room (subject to the provisos that the nature of the accommodation
or the circumstances in prison may not permit this, in which case
the governor or medical officer may authorise sharing of cells). Rule
23(1) provides that each cell or room used to accommodate prisoners shall be fitted with a means of communication with an officer.

  Rule 23(2) provides that:

> "Each cell or room used to accommodate prisoners, and any
> other part of the prison in which prisoners are otherwise kept,
> or to which they ordinarily have access, shall be of an adequate
> size and be lighted, heated and ventilated and furnished as is
> necessary for the health and safety of prisoners."

4–14 Rule 24 obliges Ministers to provide sufficient beds and bedding for
prisoners, r.21 obliges the governor to provide prisoners with sufficient wholesome and nutritious food and drink, having regard to
the prisoner's age, health and, so far as practicable, his religious or
dietary requirements, while r.30 obliges the governor to provide
access to washing, bathing and showering facilities at least twice a
week. In terms of r.21(3), the governor is under a duty to ensure, on

a daily basis, that he tastes some food and drink prepared for prisoners, for the purpose of checking its quality and condition, that he checks that the quantity of food and drink provided is adequate, and that the conditions under which such food and drink are prepared and served (or reheated prior to serving) are inspected by an officer. If the inspection reveals any deficiency, then the governor must remedy the deficiency as soon as possible

Sanitation — "slopping out"

It will be noted that the 1994 Rules made no specific provision in **4–15** respect of sanitation facilities within prisons. In cell sanitation was not a concept that had occurred to the prison builders of the nineteenth and early twentieth centuries, and for generations prisoners endured the daily routine of "slopping out" their chamber pots when their cells were opened in the morning. This practice became increasingly unpopular and anachronistic as the overwhelming majority of the populace lived in homes with separate indoor toilet facilities, and, as new prisons and prison halls began to emerge with integral sanitation, the continuing practice of slopping out in older establishments became less and less acceptable.

It should be noted, however, that criticisms of prison conditions were by no means exclusively related to the issue of slopping out, although that was the most obvious manifestation of concerns over prison conditions. In 1991 Lord Woolf (as he then was) and Judge Tumim recommended the elimination of slopping out in English prisons. As they put it in their report into the Prison Service in England and Wales, "to lock up prisoners for long periods at a time with no alternative but to use a bucket for their basic needs, which then has to remain in the cell, sometimes for many hours ... is not just". They described slopping out as " a blot on our prison system ... which undermines the justice of the sentence which prisoners are serving" It appears that, with a few particular exceptions, the practice had been eliminated in England by 1996.

The Committee For the Prevention of Torture visited Barlinnie in 1994, inspected C Hall, and issued a report on their findings. The CPT was established in terms of the European Convention for the Prevention of Torture, which was ratified by the UK on February 24, 1988 and entered into effect on February 1, 1989. Since 1989, the committee has had the power to authorize a delegation, comprising independent and impartial experts from member states, to visit any institution within a member state. No notification of the intention to visit is required, nor is it usually given, and the establishment is under a duty to admit the CPT delegation.

Following their visit, the published report observed that **4–16** conditions within Barlinnie's C Hall were quite unsatisfactory. They identified the triple vices of overcrowding, inadequate lavatory facilities and poor regime activities as all present. They regarded the chamber pots then in use as small and inconvenient to use. They recommended that the provision of integral sanitation be accorded a very high priority, and observed that the Scottish Prison Service had informed them that it should be *possible* (my italics) to introduce integral sanitation into all cells by 1999. The CPT had hoped that this could have been received by an earlier date.

Work on the provision of integral sanitation proceeded on a gradual basis until 1998, when refurbishment work was suspended. The rolling programme of refurbishment came to a halt shortly after the Scottish Ministers took office in July 1999.It is not clear whether, at that stage, the Scottish Prison Service had in mind its comments to the CPT or their observations thereon, but a revised timetable was prepared, in terms of which the target date for the elimination of slopping out was revised to 2004, and then to 2008.

In December 1999 Scottish Ministers decided to claw back the sum of £13m from the Prison Service Budget. This money was spent on what were described as "other priorities" within the Justice Department, such as a drug enforcement agency, tackling domestic violence, and establishing a witness support scheme for the sheriff court. The Justice Minister told the Scottish Parliament "Government is about making choices; these are the choices we have made".

4-17   The then Justice Minister Jim Wallace had stated to the Scottish Parliament on April 18, 2002, "We believe that slopping out is unacceptable ... how can we reasonably expect prisoners to reform and become valued members of society if we do not even provide them with a toilet?" Despite this the eradication of slopping out continued to be regarded as a low priority, until the case of *Napier v The Scottish Ministers*, 2004 S.L.T. 555 was decided.

This was the first case in which the court was required to determine whether present day conditions for remand prisoners in Scotland necessarily complied with minimum Convention rights, and the court heard evidence from a number of medical and other experts, and reviewed a number of judgments of the European Court of Human Rights in determining whether such conditions as were accepted to be the norm within Barlinnie in 2001 were compliant with Article 3. In particular, reference was made to the judgements of the European Court of Human rights in *Peers v Greece*, No.28524/95, 74, E.C.H.R. 2001-III, which held the conditions in a segregation unit to be degrading, even where there was no evidence of a positive intention to humiliate or debase the applicant, and *Yankov v Bulgaria*, issued on December 11, 2003, in which the court observed that "ill-treatment must attain a minimum level of severity if it is to fall within the scope of Article 3", but that the assessment of such minimum level was relative and dependent on all the circumstances of the case.

The Basis of the Decision in Napier

Article 3 of the Convention is in very brief and stark terms. Headed "*Prevention of Torture*", it reads in full:

"No one shall be subjected to torture or to inhuman or degrading treatment or punishment".

The petitioner, who had a history of atopic eczema dating back to infancy, was remanded in custody, and found himself in C Hall of HM Prison Barlinnie. Within approximately two days of his admission, his eczema flared up and evidence disclosed that he drew this to the attention of prison staff immediately. It was not in dispute that an eruption of eczema such as was suffered by the petitioner could be a result of stress. Two psychiatrists who gave evidence at the proof were agreed that the conditions in which he was detained on remand were bound to have had some impact on his mental state. **4–18**

Evidence was led from a number of experts in a whole range of different disciplines. A Professor from the University of Strathclyde and a Civil Engineer gave evidence on the adequacy of the cell for occupancy by two people, having particular regard to sanitation, living space, lighting and ventilation. This evidence concluded that a cell with a total floor area of 8.47 square metres was inadequate for occupation by two prisoners. The level of illumination by natural and artificial light was considered by two further experts. The lighting evidence demonstrated that there was inadequate natural light within the cell, and that the level of artificial illumination was less than that which would be desirable. The respondents did not challenge the petitioner's evidence that the ventilation within the cell was inadequate. An environmental psychologist, whose speciality is the study of how people interact with their surroundings, provided the court with a detailed opinion on the effect of the conditions on the petitioner.

There was a great deal of evidence led on the practice of "slopping out" and its consequences for the petitioner's health. Several prisoners and staff gave evidence of their personal experiences of the practice. A Professor from St George's Hospital Medical School, University of London, gave evidence of the risk of infection that was posed by detention conditions, in particular the slopping out process. In addition to this, the court heard evidence from a number of experienced examiners of prison conditions, including the former Chief Inspector of Prisons for Scotland, the Head of Secretariat of the Committee for the Prevention of Torture, the Director of the International Centre for Prison Studies at King's College, University of London, and the last two holders of the post of Scottish Prisons Complaints Commissioner.

The Court's Conclusions

4-19   Having considered the evidence, and a number of authorities in which the European Court of Human Rights had considered whether prison conditions in other countries complied with Art.3, Lord Bonomy concluded, that:

> "to detain a person along with another prisoner in a cramped, stuffy and gloomy cell which is inadequate for the occupation of two people, to confine them there together for at least 20 hours on average per day, to deny him overnight access to a toilet throughout the week and for extended periods at the weekend and to thus expose him to both elements of the slopping out process, to provide no structured activity other than daily walking exercise for one hour and one period of recreation lasting an hour and a half in a week, and to confine him in a "dog box" for two hours or so each time he entered or left the prison, was in Scotland in 2001, capable of attaining the minimum level of severity necessary to constitute degrading treatment and thus to infringe Article 3."

He then addressed the specific question of whether the petitioner had been subjected to "serious ill-treatment", applying the test set by Lord Hope of Craighead in *Pretty v United Kingdom* (European Court of Human Rights, April 29, 2002) (Application no 2346/02). He expressly rejected the submission that the standard of proof in an alleged violation of Art.3 was the criminal standard, and applied the general standard appropriate to civil litigation. He noted that the petitioner's solicitors had requested a transfer to better conditions as early as May 22, and that this had been refused on May 24. He observed that the water he could take to his cell was inadequate for the purpose of washing his eczematous skin, and that he had persistently sought transfer, being extremely anxious about the link between his skin complaint and prison conditions. Having considered expert medical, psychological, scientific and technical evidence, he was satisfied that the petitioner was exposed to conditions of detention which in their totality were such as "to diminish his human dignity and to arouse in him feelings of anxiety, anguish, inferiority and humiliation", and accordingly held that there had been a breach of Art.3, resulting in an award of damages in favour of the petitioner.

As at the date of publication, the practice of slopping out has, with the exception to date of HMP Peterhead, been virtually eradicated from Scotland's prisons. However, it may be instructive to observe the absence of any specific right to integral sanitation in terms of the 2006 Rules.

PRISONERS' CLOTHING

While every untried prisoner has the right in terms of r.25 to wear **4–20** his own clothing both in prison (unless that right has been forfeited after an escape or an attempted escape, by virtue of r.119(1)(e)), and on occasions when he is required or permitted to be outwith the establishment, this is subject to the provisions of rr.25(2) and (3), which provide a number of exceptions. Rule 25(2) creates exceptions where particular clothing may be required for legal proceedings, where the medical officer considers the prisoner's clothing prejudicial to his health or that special clothing is required on medical grounds (r.25(2)(a)), where the governor considers that the clothing is in poor condition, may be prejudicial to security, good order or discipline (for example, the wearing of a t-shirt bearing a sectarian or racist slogan), or is incompatible with the facilities at or management of the prison (r.25(2)(c)), or where special or protective clothing is required for the particular work or activities being undertaken by the prisoner (r.25(2)(d)). The regulations relating to convicted prisoners, in terms of r.26, are permissive only, and leave the right to wear one's own clothing at the discretion of the governor. The provisions of r.25(2) are incorporated into this rule as matters the governor may choose to take into consideration in exercising his discretion.

In addition, where the Minister considers, in relation to any prison, that it is not appropriate to permit prisoners, or particular categories of prisoner, to wear their own clothing in that prison, he may specify by a direction, that the prisoners' rights to wear their own clothing shall not apply in relation to any prisoner, or any category of prisoner, in that prison. In practice, in most mainstream closed establishments prisoners now wear uniform sweaters and shirts that identify both the prison and the hall, thus preventing unauthorised movement of prisoners during the working day.

The Minister is obliged in terms of r.27 to provide suitable clothing for every prisoner where the prisoner either has insufficient clothing, does not wish to wear his own clothing, or is not permitted in terms of r.25 or 26 to wear his own clothing. Such clothing must be of good condition, appearance and fit, and is suitable for the health and safety of the prisoner. It is issued to the prisoner on a personal basis, the obligation to maintain and repair it rests with the governor, and where prison-issue clothing requires to be worn by the prisoner on occasions when he is outwith the prison, it must not give any visible indication that the prisoner is such a person. Rule 28 specifies that the governor must ensure that every prisoner has sufficient clothing to enable him to change his socks and underwear daily, and have a clean change of other clothing as often as is necessary for the purposes of health and hygiene.

HEALTH AND WELFARE

4–21 This is governed by rr.32–42. Rule 32 obliges the Justice Minister to make arrangements at every prison for the provision of appropriate medical services and facilities. A medical officer has a general duty under r.33 to attend prisoners who complain of illness at such times and with such frequency as he judges necessary in the circumstances, and in terms of r.34 the governor must, without delay, bring to the attention of a medical officer any prisoner whose physical or mental condition appears to require his attention.

Where a medical officer considers it appropriate to call another medical practitioner or specialist into consultation, or to refer the prisoner to another practitioner, he must first inform the governor (r.35(1)(a)), and thereafter make such arrangements as are necessary. Where the medical officer considers that the condition of a prisoner's health requires treatment outwith the prison, the duty to make arrangements for transfer to the appropriate facility rests with the governor.

Where a prisoner is confined to his cell for breach of discipline in terms of r.119(1)(d), a medical officer shall visit him as soon as practicable and no later than 24 hours after that confinement. If the medical officer considers on medical grounds that cellular confinement is not appropriate, then he must notify the governor in terms of r.36(1)(d), and he shall give effect to the medical officer's opinion without delay.

4–22 Where the medical officer considers on medical grounds that a prisoner should either — (a) be confined in special conditions; (b) not participate in specified activities; (c) participate in specified activities only in such conditions as the medical officer considers necessary; or (e) not be placed under a restraint by a body belt in terms of r.97 (injuring or threatening to injure himself or others, damaging or threatening to damage property, or creating or threatening to create a disturbance), then again r.37(1) obliges him to notify the governor, who shall give effect to his opinion without delay.

The provision or otherwise of medical treatment has always attracted a considerable number of complaints. A significant percentage of internal complaints, and thereafter complaints to the Scottish Prisons Complaints Commissioner, relate to alleged or perceived deficiencies in medical care, whether by failure to attend the prisoner with sufficient urgency, or failure to prescribe appropriate medication or other treatment. Given human nature, and the fact that a large number of inmates within certain establishments are illicit drug users during their sentences, there can be little doubt that many such complaints are malicious, and that many reports to medical officers are designed to provide either an excuse to obtain drugs, or are intended to provide a valid reason for failure to attend work in prison. On the other hand, it must be recognised that each medical officer has a "patient list" of some hundreds of adult males, a disproportionate percentage of whom were already suffering from alcohol or drug related illnesses before their admission to prison.

RELIGION

This is governed by rr.43–47 of the 2006 Rules. Rule 43 provides **4–23** that every prisoner shall be allowed to observe the requirements of his religious and moral beliefs subject to and in accordance with the provisions of the 1989 Act, the 2006 Rules and any direction made for the purposes of the Rules, and the governor is under a duty to ensure that every prisoner is informed of the facilities which exist for religious practice.

Where a prisoner indicates that he is a member of a specific denomination, the relevant member of the Chaplaincy Team will visit the prison as soon as practicable after their reception into prison, and thereafter at such times as the prisoner and the member of the Chaplaincy Team may agree, conduct religious services or meetings at such times as a member (after consultation with the governor) considers appropriate, and make any other arrangement, subject to the approval of the governor, which are considered necessary for the preservation of such religious ministration to such prisoners. A member of the Chaplaincy Team may also make arrangements, subject to approval of the governor, for the purpose of enabling a prisoner to be visited by a minister of any religious denomination or any authorised representative.

In terms of r.45, where a visiting minister is allowed to visit prisoners, the governor shall make arrangement, so far as practicable, to enable him or her to conduct religious services or meetings for prisoners, and to make any other arrangements which the minister considers necessary for the provision of his ministration to such prisoners.

4–24 Except in a situation where the prisoner has been removed from association in terms of r.94, or where the governor considers that, due to exceptional circumstances, it is necessary to prevent him from attending a service in the interest of good order, every prisoner who belongs to a religion or a religious denomination may attend such services or meetings of their denomination as may, with consent of the governor, be arranged by the chaplain or minister concerned (r.46(1)).

In terms of r.46(4) any visit to a prisoner by a member of the Chaplaincy Team shall be held out with the sight and hearing of an officer except where the member concerned requests otherwise or where the governor considers that it would be prejudicial to the interests of security or the safety of the member for an officer not to be present.

In terms of r.47, the governor is under a duty to provide for such literature and other materials as the governor considers appropriate for prisoners' religious needs, and each prison shall, so far as reasonably practicable, be allowed to have in their possession and for their personal use religious books, items and materials appropriate to his or her religious denomination, and to engage in the practises of their denomination.

PRIVILEGES AND PRISONERS' PROPERTY

4–25 The operation of the system of privileges, and the distinction between rights and privileges, has been discussed before. The system of privileges as established by the governor of each establishment must be in terms of r.49 of the 2006 Rules. In terms of r.49(3), a system of privileges established under the Rule shall make provision at least in relation to any items of property which the governor may allow a prisoner to have in their room and cell, the arrangements whereby a prisoner may purchase items within or out with the prison, the use of recreational library facilities provided or the participation recreational activities organised by virtue of r.90 (the provision of reasonable facilities and opportunities for prisoners to participate in recreational activities out with normal working hours), the arrangements whereby a prisoner may have tobacco in his or her possession, the circumstances in which privileges may be withdrawn from a prisoner, and any other matter as may be specified in a direction made by Scottish Minister under and for the purposes of this Rule. In terms of r.49(5), the governor shall ensure that every prisoner is provided with information in a manner which enables him to understand it, in relation to the application of the system of privileges, and the circumstances in which privileges may be withdrawn. Where the governor withdraws any privileges enjoyed by a prisoner or refuses to grant a privilege to one prisoner which is enjoyed by other prisoners, he shall give reasons for that decision to the prisoner concerned.

PRISONERS' PERSONAL PROPERTY

The possession, reception and use of personal property is governed **4–26** by rr.50–52. The right of a prisoner to receive a possess personal property within prison is not unfettered. In terms of r.50(2) the governor may refuse to receive any item of property sent to the prisoner for a prisoner and where appropriate may return it to the sender. Any items belonging to a prisoner received into the prison other than property purchased by him within the prison, letters or written communications sent to the prison, or perishable or edible property, must be recorded by an officer in the prisoners record. Where a record is prepared, the prisoner concerned shall, in terms of r.50(4), be given the opportunity to check its accuracy and thereafter be required to sign it.

The governor shall make arrangements for the safe storage of all items of property belonging to a prisoner, except for items which a prisoner is allowed to keep in his or her room or cell or on his or her person. However, where the governor is of the opinion that any item of property belonging to or sent to the prisoner and which has been received into the prison is prejudicial to health, safety, security or good order, in terms of r.51(2) the governor shall notify the prisoner, and except where it is reasonably practicable for the prisoner to arrange for disposal, make arrangements for the disposal or (if the item if perishable) the destruction of any such item.

Every prisoner shall be entitled, in terms of r.52, to keep in their room or cell such items as property may be specified in a direction by Ministers. Without prejudice to that, the governor may allow any prisoner to have in his or her possession or to keep in their room or cell such items of property as are compatible with the size and furnishing of the room or cell, matters of health, safety, security and good order and any other matter which the governor considers relevant.

PRISONERS' MONEY

4–27 In terms of r.53, the governor may specify in relation to any prisoner or category of prisoners, whether such prisoner or category may have cash in their personal possession, or, if any prisoner is permitted to have cash in their possession, the maximum amount of cash which that prisoner may possess, or the denominations in which that cash may be held. Rule 53(2) provides that the governor shall hold on behalf of the prisoner any other money belonging to the prisoner which represents earnings paid for work carried out in terms of r.88, or has been received into the prison and does not exceed any restrictions as to the amount of money a prisoner may receive as may be prescribed in a direction made for the purposes in r.60(2). A prisoner may withdraw money held on his or her account by authorising the governor to deduct such sums as are required for the purpose of making specific payments to persons out with the prison or for the purpose of purchasing any article in prison or to be delivered into prison, subject to the proviso that the governor may specify in relation to any prisoner or any category of prisoner the maximum amount which may be so withdrawn during any specified period, and for the purposes of purchasing any article either in prison or to be delivered to prison. It is the governor's duty, in respect of each prisoner, to keep a record of all money deposited in an account held by the governor, in terms of r.53(5). While the prisoner may of course, during his time in custody, open or continue to maintain an account at a bank or building society, the use of any such account is subject to the other provisions of the 2006 Rules.

A prisoner who wishes to obtain books, newspapers, writing materials or other means of occupation during his time in custody shall be entitled to arrange, at their own expense or at the expense of someone out with the prison, the delivery to the prison of such books, newspapers, writing materials and other means of occupation as a prisoner may wish to use.

COMMUNICATIONS

4–28 Every prisoner, in terms of r.55, may be kept informed of current affairs by means of books, newspapers, periodicals or a radio or any other medium the governor may allow. In practice, the vast majority of prisoners now have access to have a television set in their own cell. The governor may, in terms of r.55(2) restrict or impose conditions as the exercise of any such entitlement where the governor considers it necessary to do so to protect the prisoner from self-injury or to protect the prisoner from injuring others.

PRISONERS' CORRESPONDENCE

This has long been a controversial issue within Scottish Prisons. **4–29** The original provisions of the 1952 Rules made all letters into and out of prison subject to censorship, limited the category of person to whom a person could write, and permitted the prison authorities to stop letters, or parts of them which were considered to be objectionable. This was one of the areas that was ripe for challenge in terms of its apparent breach of Art.8 of the European Convention of Human Rights, which reads which reads "Everyone has the right to respect for his private and family life, his home and his correspondence". A number of United Kingdom prisoners therefore took matters relating to correspondence to the European Court of Human Rights. The first case was *Golder v United Kingdom*, (1975) 1 E.H.R.R. 524, and this case was followed by a number of cases. In *Leech v Secretary of State for Scotland*, 1991 S.L.T. 210 the Court of Session held that the rules then in force permitting staff to read prisoners' correspondence were valid. However, the following year the European Court of Human Rights came to a different view in *Campbell v United Kingdom* (1992) 15 EHRR 137, in which the court observed, "The reading of a prisoner's mail to and from a lawyer ... should only be permitted in exceptional circumstances when the authorities have reasonable cause to believe that the privilege is being abused in that the contents of the letter endanger prison security or the safety of others or are otherwise of a criminal nature." That decision was then applied in England in *R v Secretary of State for the Home department, Ex p Leech*, [1994] Q.B. 198.

Gradually, the Rules on correspondence were progressively liberalised, until the 1994 Rules created a general right on behalf of prisoners, subject to certain limited restrictions, to send and receive letters and postal packages by means of the postal services or otherwise. These Rules have been substantially incorporated into the 2006 Rules.

Correspondence to and from court is governed by r.57. This applies only to letters and packages which are either addressed to a court, and which the prisoner gives to an officer for the purposes of posting to that court, or are sent to a prisoner at the prison by the court. A prisoner wishing to send a letter or package to a court shall mark prominently on the outer face of the envelope or packaging the words "Legal Correspondence" and their own name. Any letter or package marked in such a way shall not be opened by an officer unless (a) the offer has cause to believe it contains a prohibited article; (b) the officer has explained to the prisoner concerned the reason for that belief; and (c) the prisoner concerned is present (r.57(5)). Where the letter or package is found to contain any prohibited article, the governor shall seize and detain that article. For the purposes of this Rule, "court does not merely include the District Courts, Sheriff Courts, High Court, Court of Session, Privy Counsel and House of Lords, but also includes the European Court of Justice, the European Court of Human Rights, the European Commission of Human Rights, the Principal Reporter to the Children's' Panel, the Scottish Criminal Cases Review Commission and the Parole Board for Scotland."

Correspondence from and to legal advisers is governed by r.58. Again, this Rule applies to letters and packages address to a legal adviser and given to an officer for the purpose of posting to that legal adviser or are sent to the prisoner at the prison by a legal adviser. Once again the words "Legal Correspondence" must be marked prominently on the outer face of the envelope, and once again, the letter or package may only be opened by an officer in the same conditions as apply in r.57. It should be noted that, while a letter to a court shall not be read by an officer under any circumstances, a letter opened by an officer in terms of r.58(4) shall not be read by an officer except where para.6 applies. This applies in exceptional circumstances, where the governor has reasonable cause to believe that the contents of the letter endanger the security of the prison or the safety of any person or relate to a criminal activity. Where the governor is of such opinion, the prisoner shall be informed that letter of written material shall be read, and the reasons why, and the letter or written material shall be read by the governor or an officer specially authorised by the governor for that purpose.

OTHER CORRESPONDENCE

4–30 Any letter of package to which r.58 does not apply, and which a prisoner wishes to send or which is sent to the prisoner may be opened by an officer. In terms of r.29(2) the contents of any such letter or package may only be read by an officer where the officer considers that they be or may contain anything in contravention of the restrictions specified in any direction by the Scottish Ministers for the purposes of r.60. Where a letter or package is found to contain anything that contravenes these regulations or it contains something which the prisoner may not be permitted to receive and officer may prevent the letter or package or anything contained in it being sent of received by the prisoner, and may deal with the letter or package or anything contained in it in accordance with such arrangements as may be specified in a direction by Scottish Ministers. The restriction on prisoners' correspondence governed by r.60.

In terms of r.60(2) Ministers may specify by direction restrictions for the purposes of prescribing the circumstances which an offer may read a letter, and the offers may be authorised to do so, any restrictions as to the number of letters and packages which a prisoner may send, to prescribe restrictions as to the amount of money which a prisoner may send of receive in any form, the times and frequency at which prisoners may send or receive money, the persons, authorities and organisations to whom a prisoner is prohibited from sending any letters and packages, and any particular restrictions and conditions which shall apply where a prisoner wishes to send letters and packages to prescribed organisations and persons with whom the prisoner is not otherwise prohibited from corresponding, and the nature and description of letter, written materials and items of property which in general a prisoner may not send or receive.

Rule 61 provides that every prisoner shall be allowed to send one letter per week, the postage of which shall be paid for by Scottish Ministers, and the governor shall provide the prisoner with all necessary writing materials for this purpose, which comprise one ball point pen, one sheet or writing paper and a reasonable number of further sheets if the prisons so requires, and an envelope. Rule 61(3) provides that the governor may, for the purposes of r.61, allow the prisoner to send more than one letter per week at the expense of the Scottish Ministers if it appears to the governor that this is justified in the prisoner's circumstances.

TELEPHONES

A prisoner may have the use of a telephone in custody, subject to **4–31** the provisions of r.62(2), which provides his entitlement of a telephone will be subject to the provisions of any direct which Scottish Ministers may make in relation to the groups or categories of prisoners who may have the use of a telephone; The times of day and circumstances of which a telephone may be available for use; The conditions applicable to the use of such a telephone; And the logging and monitoring and recording by any means by an officer of telephone calls made by a prisoner. Where an officer informs a prisoner that he or she may not have the use of a telephone, the officer shall inform the prisoner of the reasons for that decision.

In practise, all prisoners within the Scottish Prison Service have at least some access to a telephone on a daily basis. Phone cards, allowing use of a pay phone, are regularly purchased from prisoner's personal cash, and calls are made from dedicated pay phones situated within the prison establishment. For reasons of security these calls are monitored and recorded. The level of monitoring of calls proved controversial. The Scottish Prison Service, for reasons of security, set up a system that restricted prisoners' access to the public telephone system by putting in place a number of restrictions. These were:

(i)   the prisoner can only make calls to a person whose number is on a list of pre-approved numbers ("PAN"), although it should be noted that calls to solicitors and the Scottish Prisons Complaints Commissioner are exempted;

(ii)   that list is limited to a maximum of 20 numbers;

(iii)   the numbers on the pre-arranged list have been submitted to and approved by the governor;

(iv)   the calls made are logged, allowing the prisoner making the call to be identified (by virtue of his PIN number), as well as the number called and the time and duration of the call;

(v)   the calls may at any time be recorded and/or monitored by prison service staff; and

(vi)   the calls are preceded by an automated message to any person answering the number called to the effect that the call originates from a Scottish prison, that it may be recorded and/or monitored and that if the individual does not wish to accept the call he or she should simply hang up.

Given the number of security measures in place in terms of heads (i)–(v), which might be thought to reduce the chances of abuse of the telephone system to arrange, for example, drug transactions or witness intimidation to virtually nil, it came as little surprise that restriction (vi), which could result in a person unconnected with the prisoner, but who happened to answer a phone at an approved number learning of the prisoner's situation, was challenged as not being in conformity with Art.8 of ECHR. The matter was considered by the court in March 2007 in *Potter, Petitioner*, [2007] CSOH 56, unreported. Perhaps unsurprisingly, the Executive conceded that the recorded message did constitute a *prima-facie* breach of Art.8, but sought (unsuccessfully) to argue that the interference was justified on one or more of the public interest grounds in Art.8(2). Lord Glennie, in granting the prayer of the petition, held that there was no statutory authority for the imposition of what was, in fact, a blanket policy, and ruled therefore that the actions of Ministers were both *ultra vires* and not in conformity with the "in accordance with the law" provisions of Art.8(2).

Only communication on prison authorised pay phones is permitted in terms of the Rules. The use or possession of mobile phones in custody is strictly prohibited, and constitutes a disciplinary offence under r.113 and Sch.1(I), which forbids any prisoner from having in their possession or concealed about their body or in any body orifice, any article which they are not authorised to have. The increasing popularity of mobile phone technology, and the attendant reduction in the price of mobile telephone communications has meant that a great many instances of prisoners being found with mobile telephones and being disciplined accordingly have occurred in recent years.

It has of course been recognised for a long time that one of the **4–32** greatest difficulties suffered by prisoners is the lack of communication with their families, and obviously family contact continues to be encouraged, and it is for this reason principally that telephone calls are now permitted. However, the prevalence of drug misuse within custody, and the evidence of a considerable number of family members being pressurised, either directly or indirectly, to introduce drugs into prison for prisoners has meant that, as the use of telephone technology increases, the issue of surveillance and monitoring of telephone calls has required to increase proportionately, subject of course to being in accordance with the law.

VISITS TO CONVICTED PRISONERS

Rule 63.1 governs visits to prisoners other than untried prisoners **4–33** and civil prisoners. Subject to the provisions of r.77, which authorises the governor to prohibit a prisoner from receiving a visit from any person in particular where the governor considers it is necessary to prohibit the visit in the interests of security, discipline or the prevention of disorder or crime, and to r.78, which allows the governor, for certain specified reasons, to hold visits in closed visiting facilities to prevent the obtaining of prohibited articles or for the preservation of security, a convicted prisoner shall be entitled to a minimum of one visit of thirty minutes in any period of seven consecutive days, or a minimum of two hours visits time in any period of twenty eight consecutive days for the purposes of receiving visits in terms of these Rules. In practise, some establishments allow standard visits of slightly longer duration than this.

Where the prisoner is a young offender and not untried, and where rr.77 and 78 do not apply, the governor may allow not fewer than two visits of not less than thirty minutes in any period of seven consecutive days in terms of r.63(3). The governor has a discretion as to the number of persons who shall be allowed to visit a prisoners at any one time, and where a prisoner receives a visit in terms of the Rule, the visit shall take place within the sight of an officer, but except for the governor otherwise authorises, no officer shall listen to any conversation between the prisoner and his or her visitor.

Occasionally a situation may arise where it is not practicable to allow prisons the minimum period for visits specified in terms of this Rule, due to the circumstances pertaining in the prison, or a lack of facilities at a particular time. In that situation, Scottish Ministers may, by direction, provide that para.2 shall apply subject to such reduced minimum periods as may be specified in the directions.

A prisoner is only entitled to receive a visit from a prisoner at another prison in exceptional circumstances, and with the express prior consent of the governors of both establishments. In the event that either or both governors refuse consent, the prisoners concerned shall each be given an explanation of the actions of such refusal (r.63(7)).

4–34 In terms of r.63.8, a governor shall only permit a visit by a friend or relative of a prisoner who is or has previously carried on the profession or vocation of journalist, author of media representative if the person is visiting of a personal basis and not for professional or vocational purposes, and before being admitted to prison that person gives a written undertaking to the effect that any material obtained during the visit will not be used for professional or vocational purposes and in particular for publication or broadcast or use on or transmission by any form of electronic medium and will note be disclosed to any other person for use by that person or anyone else for the purpose of journalism, broadcasting or publishing. This Rule does not apply if the former journalist is either now a member of a recognised religious body, or is a lawyer, procurator fiscal, police officer, representative of the diplomatic service or other person with specific rights to attend the prison in terms of the 2006 Rules.

The Rules in respect of untried and civil prisoners are somewhat different. They are to be found in r.64 of the 2006 Rules, and they provide that an untried prisoner or a civil prisoner shall be allowed to receive a visit of at least thirty minutes duration on any day of the week other than a Saturday or a Sunday, and other than on January 1, or December 25, in each year, and, where the prisoner has not received a visit on every day of the preceding Monday to

Friday, a visit of at least 30 minutes duration on a Saturday or a Sunday.

Rule 64(2)(b), affords the governor discretion to allow a visit of such duration as he or she thinks fit on a Saturday or a Sunday or on January 1, or December 25, in any year. Again, a visit may take place during such hours and subject to the other provisions of the Rule under such conditions the governor may specify and the number of persons who shall be allowed to visit a prisoner at any time shall be at the discretion of the governor. Rule 64(4) provides that the visit shall take place within sight of an officer, but that no officer shall listen to any conversation between the prisoner and the visitor except where the governor otherwise directs. Again, where Ministers consider that it sir not practicable to allow untried prisoners as civil prisoners the minimum period for visits specified in terms of the Rule, they by direction provide that this Rule shall apply in relation to untried prisoners subject to such reduced minimum period as may be specified in the direction. The same Rules are relative to visits by journalists provided in r.63(8) apply to untried prisoners in terms of r.64(6).

ACCUMULATED VISITS

In terms of r.65(1) a life prisoner or prisoner serving a sentence of **4–35** more than twelve months who has served at least six months of that sentence and who has moved from one prison to another, whether or not for the purpose of enabling him to use any accumulated unused allowance of visits, and who has accumulated unused allowance of visits in terms of r.63 shall be entitled to carry forward the accumulated period of unused allowance, and to use as accumulated allowance that the prison to which he or she is moved in addition to the allowance in terms of r.63 at that prison.

This entitlement is subject to any direction given by Scottish Ministers in relation to the circumstances in which a prisoner may not be allowed to carry forward his accumulated visits, or may by restricted from carrying forward any accumulated allowance of visits, and conditions which may be imposed by the governor, where a prisoner is entitled to carry forward such an allowance. This Rule applies equally to young offenders in respect of r.65(4).

VISITS BY LEGAL ADVISERS

4–36 This is governed by r.66. A prisoner shall be entitled to receive a visit from his or her legal adviser at any reasonable time for the purposes of consulting about any legal matter in which the prisoner is or may be directly interested. This visit may take place within sight of an officer but, in terms of r.66(2)(b) shall take place out with the hearing of any officer. A legal adviser may use sound recording equipment to record discussions with the prisoner in terms of this Rule, subject to such conditions as the governor may specify.

The entitlement of prisoners to regular confidential consultations with their legal advisers is one that has tended to be jealously guarded.

It should, however, be noted that, in terms of the Legal Aid (Scotland) (Fixed Payments) Regulations 1999, when the prisoner is awaiting trial on a Summary Complaint (whether on remand in respect of that matter or not) agents are no longer paid by the board for the time spent in visiting the prisoner, merely paid for the mileage incurred in travelling to and from the Prison. In respect of Solemn Proceedings, while there is no specific restriction upon the number of visits to a prisoner that can be carried out in connection with the preparation of his defence, the Scottish Legal Aid Board retains a right not to pay the solicitor and/or counsel of the visit, if they consider that the visit was unnecessary, or that insufficient new matters were discussed to justify a separate attendance upon the prisoner. In addition to this, it should be noted that, following the conviction in March 2006 of a solicitor for supplying Class A drugs into a prisoner within HM Prison, Barlinnie, the question of increasing the level of surveillance upon solicitors during visits has been raised. It may be that an attempt is made in future to vary the terms of r.66, although any proposed alteration would require to comply with the duties of Ministers in terms of s.57(2) of the Scotland Act not to act in a manner which will be incompatible with the European Convention on Human Rights, and to the right enshrined in Art.6(3) of the Convention whereby every person charged with a criminal offence is entitled to adequate time *and facilities* for the preparation of his defence.

VISITS BY REPRESENTATIVES OR OFFICIALS OF THE CROWN

4–37 In terms of r.67, a procurator fiscal or any person acting under the authority of the procurator fiscal may, for the purpose of discharging their public duties, visit and examine a prisoner at any reasonable time. Such a visit may take place in such an area of the prison and under such conditions as the governor may specify except that such visits shall take place within the sight of an officer but out with the hearing of any officer, in terms of r.67(2).

A police constable may, on production of the written authority of either the procurator fiscal or the chief constable, visit any prisoner for the purposes of interviewing that prisoner, providing the prisoner is willing to be interviewed, see any prisoner for the purposes of identification, or see any prisoner for the purpose of charging that prisoner with any offence (r.68(1)). Such visit may take place in such area of the prison and under such conditions as the governor may specify, with the crucial distinction that the police visit shall take place both within the sight of an officer and within his hearing (r.68(2)).

VISITS BY REPRESENTATIVE OF DIPLOMATIC SERVICES AND NATIONAL OR INTERNATIONAL AUTHORITIES OR ORGANISATIONS

These are governed by r.69. Where a prisoner is a foreign national, **4–38** r.69(1) provides that he shall be entitled to communicate with and receive a visit at any reasonable time from a diplomatic representative of his or her choice. Where a prisoner is a refugee or a stateless person, he shall be entitled to communicate with and receive a visit at any reasonable time from a diplomatic representative of a state that he considers may look after his or her interests or, subject to such limit as to numbers of authorities or organisation as the governor may reasonably impose, an authorised representative of an national or international authority or organisation whose principal purpose is to serve the interests of refugees or stateless persons or to protect their civil rights. In this case, in terms if r.69(3) the visit take place within the sight of an officer, but no officer shall listen to any conversation between the prisoner and the visitor unless either the prisoner or the visitor otherwise requests.

SPECIAL VISITS

In terms of r.70, an untried prisoner, a civil prisoner, an appellant, a **4–39** prisoner remanded in custody awaiting sentence or further enquiry, or, who while serving a sentence of imprisonment is subject to a further charge under the 1995 Act, shall be allowed a visit at any reasonable time to consult a registered medical practitioner where

the governor considers that to be in the interests of justice, or any
other person for the purposes of the preparation of their case. In the
case of an untried prisoner, this includes complying with the condition of bail which requires to deposit of a sum of money in terms
of s.24(6) of the 1995 Act, while in the case of a civil prisoner, he or
she is entitled to receive a visit for the purpose of discussing the
proceedings in respect of which he or she has been committed to
prison. In the case of an appellant or a prisoner awaiting sentence
or awaiting prosecution in other matters, again any visit may be
granted at the governor's discretion. The number of persons
allowed to visit shall be at the discretion of the governor, and, while
the visit takes place within the sight of an officer, no officer shall
listen to any conversation between the prisoner and the medical
practitioner, or any other visitor, except where the governor
otherwise directs. Visits by Members of Parliament, etc. Rule 71
provides prisoners shall be entitled to receive a visit from a Member
of the United Kingdom Parliament, the Scottish Parliament, or a
representative of a European Parliament. Again such visit takes
place within the sight of the officer, but out with the hearing of the
officer unless the Member or representative or prisoner request
otherwise or the governor so requires for reasons of security. It is
permissible to use sound recording equipment for such visits in
terms of r.71(3).

OTHER VISITORS

4–40 In terms of r.72 the Scottish Public Services Ombudsman or any
person authorised by them may visit the prisoner at any time with
that prisoner's consent. Again such visits shall take place out with
the hearing of any officer and with the Ombudsman or representative request otherwise or the governor otherwise requires so
for the reasons of security, in terms of r.72(2)(b). Visits by journalists are governed by r.73(2), which states, "A Governor shall
permit visits to prisoners by persons to whom this Rule applies only
in exceptional circumstances and where satisfied it is appropriate to
permit such a visit". Such meeting shall take place within the sight
of an officer and within the hearing of an officer, and before the
journalist, author or media representative is admitted to prison,
they must give a written undertaking not to conduct an interview,
take photographs, filming or sound recording except with the
express prior consent of the prisoner and the governor, subject to
such conditions as the governor considers necessary, that the person
shall not make any payment or gratuity to the prisoner or any other
person in relation to the holding of the interview or any material

contained in it, and that any material obtained at the interview or photographs, films or recordings so taken will not be used for professional or vocational purposes or for publication or broadcast by any form of electronic medium by the person or anyone else except in accordance with the prior written consent of the governor, and subject to and in accordance with such conditions as the governor may impose. Rule 74 governs visits by Members of the Parole Board in terms of r.15(3) of the Parole Board (Scotland) Rules 2001. The purposes of these Rules will be discussed in a later Chapter. Such a visit may take place within the sight of an officer, but shall take place out with the hearing of any officer unless a Member of the Board or the prison otherwise requests. Rule 75 covers the position of visits by Members or employees of the Scottish Criminal Cases Review Commission. Such visits in terms of r.75(2) shall take place within the sight of an officer but out with the hearing of an officer unless the Member or Employee of the Commission or the prisoner otherwise requests. Where a prisoner is charged with a Breach of Discipline and the prisoner wishes to call a person as a witness at the enquiry into the charge and the governor considers that the prisoner should have the opportunity to discuss with that person whether they could give evidence which would be relevant to defence of the charge, the prisoner shall be allowed to receive a visit at any reasonable time from that person for the purpose of discussing whether that person could give relevant evidence at the hearing. Such visits shall take place within the sight of an officer in terms of r.76(4) but "No Officer shall listen to any conversation between the prisoner and the visitor except where the Governor otherwise directs".

It should be noted that all entitlements to receive visits in terms of the 2006 Rules are subject to the proviso that the governor may prohibit any prisoner from receiving a visit from any person where the governor considers that it is necessary to do so in the interests of security, discipline or the prevention of disorder or crime. Where the governor considers that any undertaking given by the visitor has been breached or that there has a contravention of any of the restrictions specified in the foregoing paragraphs, the governor may terminate the visit.

CLOSED VISITS

These are governed by r.78. This Rule and its predecessors have **4–41** been amongst the most controversial provisions within the Prison Rules. This Rule sets out the circumstances in which a visit requires to be held in closed visiting facilities. Where the governor is of the opinion that there are reasonable grounds for suspecting that the prisoner has previously obtained or is likely in the future to attempt to obtain from any visitor any prohibited article or property which the prisoner was not or would not be authorised to possess in the part of the prison, his behaviour make it necessary for the purpose of security and control for a visit to be received in closed visiting facilities, a previous visit to the prisoner has been terminated due to the conduct of the visitor, a person who wishes to visit the prisoner has previously been refused access to the prison or the governor is of the opinion that it is necessary to ensure that the visit is genuinely required for any of the purposes specified in r.70, then the governor may make an order, in terms of r.78(1) in relation to any particular visit or every visit that such visits take place within closed conditions. Unlike standard visits, which take place in visit rooms, and where physical contact between the prisoner and their visitors is permissible, closed visits take place in single rooms, where the prisoner and the visitor are separated by a glass screen. Therefore physical contact between the prisoner and visitor, or the passing of any items between the two is an impossibility. The imposition of closed visits may be revoked by the governor at any time, and any order made in relation to closed visits shall be reviews by the governor not less than once every three months.

The punishment of placing a prisoner on closed visits shall not, in terms of r.78(4) be made as a punishment in respect of a breach of discipline within the meaning of Pt 11 of the 2006 Rules.

Obviously, the whole issue of closed visits, with its intendment disruption upon family life, is a controversial one, and often forms the subject of complaint via the Internal Complaints Procedure and to the Scottish Prisons Complaints Commissioner.

WORK, EDUCATION EARNINGS AND RECREATION

4–42 Subject to the provisions of Pt 9 of the 2006 Rules, every adult convicted prisoner shall be required to work in prisons. The Rules requiring prisoners to work do not apply to untried prisoners, civil prisoners, or to young prisoners.

As soon as practicable after a prisoner's reception into custody, the governor shall obtain reports about that prisoner's particular needs and wishes concerning work and education, following which he shall, in consultation with the prisoner, determine a programme of work, educational activities and counselling for the prisoner with the objective of improving the prospects for the prisoner's successful resettlement in the community, and the prisoner's morale, attitude and self respect. In terms of r.82(2) no prisoner shall be required to work or to do work which is of a particular class, at any time when excused from working or from doing any particular class of work by a medical officer on medical grounds, or by the governor on any other grounds. Rule 82(3), however, specifically provides that a prisoner shall be excused from the requirement to work at a time when he or she is undertaking an educational class arranged in terms of r.86, or undertaking counselling provided in terms of r.87.

Except with the authority of the governor, no prisoner is required to work in the service of another prisoner or in the service of an officer.

In terms of r.83, no prisoner shall be required to work or take **4-43** part in educational class arranged in terms of r.86 in lieu of work for more than forty hours per week, excluding meal breaks. Every prisoner is entitled to a minimum of one day a week as a rest day on which he or she shall not be required to work or take part in educational class in lieu of work. Where a prisoner has declared himself to belong to a religious denomination, he shall be entitled to take the rest day on the recognised day of religious observance, and shall not be required to work or take part in educational class on such other days in the year as are recognised days of religious observance for his denomination, and are so specified in a direction made by Ministers.

In general, prisoners are required to work in association with other prisoners, except where an order has been made removing the prisoner from association with other prisoners, in terms of either r.94, r.114(2) or he is under cellular confinement in terms of r.119(1)(d).

SECURITY AND CONTROL

These are found in Pt 10 of the Rules, containing rr.92–120. Rules **4-44** 106–120, governing prison discipline, in particular searching of prisoners, drug and alcohol testing, and governor's punishments are dealt with in the next chapter. Among the provisions contained within this part of the Rules are some of the most far reaching and controversial of all the Prisons Rules.

Rule 92 provides that the governor shall be responsible for the supervision of the whole Prison, and the control of prisoners confined therein. In terms of r.92(2), "The Governor shall as far as practicable visit and inspect daily those parts of the Prison where prisoners are employed or accommodated." In practice, this function is often delegated to a Hall Governor, rather than the governor of the prison itself.

Rule 92 provides that, in the control of prisoners, an officer shall seek to influence by example and leadership, and to enlist the willing cooperation of prisoners. This rule encapsulates the vast changes that have occurred within the Scottish prison system over the course of the past five decades. It is simply impossible to imagine a similar provision having been considered by the draftsmen of the 1952 Rules. Rule 93(2) provides that an officer in dealing with a prisoner shall not use force unnecessarily, and when the application of force with a prisoner is necessary, no more force than is necessary shall be used. Rule 93(3) states that "No officer shall act in a manner deliberately calculated to provoke a prisoner". Rule 94 provides the criteria whereby the governor may order the removal of a prisoner from association. This is inevitably one of the most controversial powers available to a governor. Rule 94(1) provides "Where it appears the Governor desirable for the purpose of:

    (a) maintaining good order and discipline;
    (b) protecting the interests of any prisoner; or
    (c) Ensuring the safety of other persons,

4–45 the governor may order in writing that a prisoner shall be removed from association with other prisoners, either generally or during any period the prisoner is engaged or taking part in a prescribed activity."

In the event that the governor makes an order in terms of para.1 in relation to prescribed activity, r.94(2) states that the governor may specify only one prescribed activity in the order. Prescribed activities are defined by r.94(3) as either work undertaken in terms of r.82, educational classes undertaken in terms of r.86, counselling provided in terms of r.87, participation in activities and spending time in the open air in accordance with r.89, recreational activities, or attendance at any religious service or meeting which the prisoner would otherwise have been entitled to attend in terms of r.46(1).

In the situation where a governor makes an order in terms of this Rule, he is obliged to specify in the order whether the removal from association is in general, or in relation to prescribed activity, and if the removal is in relation to prescribed activity, the governor must specify to which activity the order relates. Rule 94(4)(c) obliges the governor to specify in the order the reasons why the order is made, the record in the order the date and time it is made, and to explain to the prisoner the reasons why the order is made and provide the prisoner with a copy of a written order. The maximum period of removal from association is governed by r.94(5). A prisoner shall not be subject to removal for a period in excess of 72 hours from the time of the order, except where the Scottish Ministers have granted written authority on the application of the governor to extend that period, prior to the expiry of the 72 hour period. In the event of authority being granted by the Scottish Ministers under r.94(5), r.94(6) specifies that such authority shall have effect for a period of one month commencing from the expiry of a 72 hour period mentioned above, but the Scottish Ministers may, on subsequent application from the governor, renew the authority for a further period of one month commencing from the expiry of the previous authority. The governor retains the power to cancel an order in terms of r.94(1) at any time if he considers it appropriate to do so, or to vary such order to restrict its effect. It is competent in terms of r.94(7)(iii) for the governor to vary the order on more than one occasion, and the governor is also obliged to cancel any order made for removal from association if a medical officer advises on medical grounds that the governor should do so.

The governor may allow a prisoner who has been removed from association to associate with other prisoners who have been removed from association under the same Rule, for the purpose of engaging or taking part in a prescribed activity.

If a prisoner is moved by the Scottish Ministers from one prison **4-46** to another in terms of s.10 of the 1989 Act as amended, any order made in term of this Rule shall cease to have effect, although the governor of the receiving prison retains the power to make a new order under r.94(1) immediately on receipt of the prisoner to his establishment. Thus, if a prisoner's disruptive behaviour in one establishment has been of such a nature that the governor considers that he requires to be removed from association, and Scottish Ministers then consider it necessary, for the preservation of good order and discipline, for him to be moved to a different establishment, and order for removal from association in terms of r.94 for 72 hours may be made immediately upon the prisoner's receipt in the new establishment, and they thereafter be extended by Scottish Ministers in terms of this Rule. Providing the provisions of r.94 are complied with by governors and Ministers throughout, it is therefore possible for a prisoner to spend several months in several different establishments removed from association for the preservation of good order and discipline within the prison system. It is therefore not surprising that many prisoners removed from association in terms of these Rules avail themselves of their rights under the prisons' internal complaints procedure, to complain to the Visiting Committee or the Scottish Prisons Complaints Commissioner, and ultimately, to seek judicial review of the decisions of Scottish Ministers.

PROHIBITED ARTICLES

4–47 A very common alleged breach of Prison Rules relates to the possession of permitted articles. In terms of r.95, no prisoner shall have in their possession or conceal or deposit anywhere within the Prison and prohibited article. Rule 95(2) provides that a prisoner may be permitted to receive alcoholic liquor or controlled drugs under the written order of medical officers specifying the quantity and description of the liquor or drugs to be given and the name of the prisoner for whose use it is intended. In practise, the most common breaches of r.95 relate to prisoners being found in possession of prescription medication without authorisation, possession of mobile telephones or SIM cards, or occasionally possession of alcohol or weapons.

Rule 95(3) prohibits any person from conveying, by any means whatsoever, a prohibited article. The Rule specifically prohibits the articles being concealed or deposited in a place with a view of its coming into possession of a prisoner, an article being conveyed to a prisoner whether inside or outside a prison, or the article being conveyed or thrown into a prison or concealed or deposited in a prison. In practice it has not been unknown, particularly in open prisons, or in the case of prisoners holding low supervision status attending outside work placements, for prohibited articles to be left for them or deposited at specified "drop off" points within the prison's perimeters. The governor detains the right to seize and retain any prohibited article found in the possession of a prisoner, a prison visitor, or conveyed or thrown into or concealed or deposited in the prison in contravention of this rule. Again, this is a matter in which the use of intelligence has often proved controversial. On occasions, packages are found within the precinct of the prison, following a report that a delivery is to be made to or on behalf of a specific prisoner, and these articles, when found, seized and detained. Inevitably, where such an article is not found within the possession of a prisoner, the quality of the intelligence is very often the subject of lengthy debate.

Rule 96 prohibits the possession by a prisoner of "unauthorised property". The distinction here is that prohibited articles, forbidden in terms of r.95 are article, the possession of which has been specifically prohibited either by the Rules themselves or by written intimation from the governor, while r.96 covers a prisoner having in their possession any property which the prisoner has not been authorised to possess or keep in terms of the Rule or by any officer. Given the wide discretion available to governors in terms of r.49 as to what articles may be retained within prison, the distinction is of some significance. However, r.96 is broadly in the same terms as r.95, and specifically forbids a prisoner from having in their possession or concealing or depositing within a prison any property which they are not authorised to possess or keep in terms of the Rules. In addition, however, r.96(2) specifically provides that no prisoner shall have in his or her possession any property in a part of the prison which he or she has been authorised to possess only in some other part of the prison. Thus, if it is permissible for an article to be retained within a prisoner's cell, it may not be permissible for the same article to be taken to the prisoner's place of work, or to any other part of the establishment. Again, there is a blanker provision in terms of r.96(3) of any person bringing any article into the prison, except where in terms of r.96(4) the governor has authorised a person to convey such article into the prison, deposit in the prison, or to convey it to a prisoner whether inside or outside a prison. "Property" in terms of this Rule does not include a letter of package addressed to a prisoner and sent to the prison by means of the postal service or otherwise (this is governed by r.96(4)(b)) once again the governor has the right to seize and detain any property which a prisoner is not authorised to possess.

In line with the new restrictions upon smoking in public places, **4-48** r.96(6) specifies that no prisoner (other than untried and civil prisoners) shall be allowed to have any tobacco in his or her possession except as a privilege granted by virtue of r.49, and provide that the prisoner is at least 16 years old. In practice, even in the health conscious early years of the 21st century, the majority of prisoners continue to smoke tobacco, and such a privilege is very often granted.

RESTRAINTS

The use of physical restraints is governed by rr.97 and 98. These **4-49** govern the limited situations in which it is lawful for the governor to order that a prisoner be placed under restraint by means of a body belt. In terms of r.97(2) the governor may order that a prisoner be placed under a restraint where it appears it is necessary to do so in order to restrain a prisoner (a) who threatens to injure or is in the course of injuring him or herself or other persons, (b) who threatens to damage or is in the course of damaging property or (c) who threatens to create or is in the course of creating a disturbance. Where the governor makes an order for restraint by means of a body belt, notice of the order shall be given by the governor to a medical officer as soon as possible, and on receipt of a notice in terms of this Rule, the medical officer shall inform the governor whether he or she concurs in the order. If the medical officer does not concur in the order, then r.97(4) obliges the governor to order the restraint to be removed immediately. In terms of r.97(5) a medical officer may order that a prisoner be placed under restraint if satisfied that it is necessary to do so to prevent self injury, and where an medical officer makes such an order, the medical officer shall give Notice of the order to the governor as soon as possible. It follows from the above, that the use of a restraint can never be used as a punishment within prisons.

Rule 98 provides that a prisoner shall not be placed under a restraint for any longer than is necessary, and further that a prisoner shall not be placed under a restraint for a period of more than 24 hours except with the authority of the Scottish Ministers. Where authority is given for continuous use of a restrain, such authority shall state the grounds for the continued use of restraint, and the time which it may be continued to be used, and shall require a medical officer to visit the prisoner at regular intervals (the regularity of these intervals is not specified within the Rule). The manner in which restraints are to be applied, and when applied are to be removed, may be specified in a direction by the Scottish Minister. While there is no obligation of a medical officer to visit at any specified intervals, it is obligatory, in terms of r.98(4) for a prisoner under restraint to be visited by an officer at least once in every 15 minutes during the period that the prisoner is under restraint. A medical officer must examine the prisoner immediately following the placing of restraint, and immediately following the removal of the restraint, unless such removal is for a temporary purpose. Rule 98(6) obliges the governor to record particulars of every case of a prisoner placed under restraint, and to give notice to the Scottish Ministers of these particulars.

TEMPORARY CONFINEMENT IN A SPECIAL CELL

4–50 Rule 99 authorises the governor to order a temporary confinement is a special cell of any prisoner who is refractory or acting in a violent manner. Once again, confinement in a special cell shall not be by way of punishment, nor shall it be for any period longer than necessary, and in any event for no longer than a continuous period of 24 hours. Where an order for temporary confinement in a special cell is made, notice of this shall be given to the medical officer as soon as possible, and the governor is obliged, in terms of r.99(3)(b) to record the particulars of the case. During the temporary confinement, the prisoner shall be visited by an officer at least once every 15 minutes, and the prisoner shall be visited by a medical officer where he has been so confined for a continuous period in excess of 15 hours.

It should be noted that there are additional powers for temporary confinement to a cell in terms of r.100. In terms of this Rule an officer may cause a prisoner to be temporarily confined in a cell or room at a time when other prisoners detained in the same part of the prison or prisoners in general are permitted to be in association, if the officer is of the opinion that the prisoner is acting in a disobedient or disorderly manner, and that temporary confinement is appropriate for the controlling of such behaviour and is in the prisoner's best interests, or, by reason of the prisoners emotional state, it is desirable and in the prisoner's interests for him to be temporarily confined to a room. The maximum period of confinement in terms of r.100 is one hour, and once the officer has exercised the power conferred upon him by this Rule, he is obliged to inform the supervising officer of that fact orally as soon as reasonably practicable. In the event that the officer is of the opinion that the prisoner remains disobedient or disorderly at the expiry of a one hour period, then the officer shall forthwith report any suspected breach of discipline in accordance with r.114.

ADMISSION AND SEARCHING OF VISITORS

Again, this is an area which has caused a great deal of controversy **4–51** amongst prisoners, and in respect of which a considerable number of complaints are made both through the internal complaints procedure and to the Scottish Prisons Complaints Commissioner. When any person seeks to enter a prison as a visitor, an officer may ask the visitor to state his or her name and address and the purpose of their visit, and to deposit for the duration of the visit any article in the visitor's possession which the officer considers may be prejudicial to security, good order or safety. Rule 101(2) now specifies that no visitors shall smoke in any building which forms part of a prison. Again this is a significant change for the position prior to March 2006.

Where the visitor is a journalist, author or media representative, it is the visitor's duty to immediately inform an officer of their wish to visit a prison in accordance with r.73. Where a former journalist, author or media representative seeks to enter prison for the purpose of visiting a prisoner who is a friend or relative, and where such a visit is on a personal basis and not for professional or vocational purposes, it is the duty of the visitor to inform an officer of that fact on arrival. Rule 101(5) provides for three situations which an officer may refuse him as a visitor and may remove the visitor from the prison. Firstly, the officer has the power to do so if a visitor fails to state their name and address and the purpose of their visit or fails to deposit any article which the officer considers to be prejudicial to security. Secondly, where the visitor refuses to give consent to a search in terms of r.102 or having given consent is obstructive in the course of the search, and thirdly, if the officer has reasonable grounds for suspecting that the visitor has in their possession or concealed about their person any article which is not authorised to be conveyed into the prison or which may be prejudicial to security, good order or discipline. In any situation where an officer refuses admission to a visitor, it is the duty of the officer to record particulars of the matter including the reasons for such refusal. Rule 102 authorises an officer to ask a visitor to consent to a search or searches of their person, any other personal possessions, and their open mouth (without the use of force or instruments) and, where the visitor is in charge of any vehicle which they intend to take into any area forming part of the prison premises, that vehicle. Where the visitor has consented to such a search taking place, r.102(2) provides that the search may take place prior to the admission to the part of the prison where the visit is to take place, and where the governor considers that the visitor has failed to comply with the provisions of r.101 or, where it is considered that the terms of any undertaking mentioned in the Rules has taken place or has been a contravention of any restrictions in terms of visiting, the governor may authorise a search whilst the visitor is in the prison.

Where the visitor has given consent to a search in accordance with r.102(10)(c), their vehicle may also be searched prior to the visitor's leaving the prison. Where a visitor is searched in terms of r.102, except in the case of examination of the prisoner's open mouth, the officer carrying out the search shall be of the same sex as the visitor and the search shall be carried out as expeditiously and decently as possible. The only articles of clothing that a visitor may be ordered to remove are outer coats, jackets, headgear, gloves and footwear. Searching a visitor's personal possessions may be carried out by use of equipment involving "(1) The application of a suction device or a swab on or to such possessions or such vehicle or anything in it in order to collect particles from their surface; and (2) The analysis of such particles for the purpose of ascertaining where anything consists of a controlled drug or an explosive substance". Metal detectors may be used as well, and the procedures and conditions in respect of the carrying out of searches are such as may be specified in a direction by the Scottish Ministers.

4–52   In the modern era, it is well known that there are numerous methods whereby drugs are admitted into prison, and the 2006 Rules are specifically designed to afford the Prison Authorities as many methods as possible to search visitors who are believed or suspected to be involved in the introduction of controlled drugs into prisons. It is of course well known that a considerable number of persons are prosecuted each year for the admission or attempted admission of drugs into prison, and it has long been recognised that visitors to prison are one of the most common sources of the introduction of illicit drugs into prison.

Where in the course of a search in accordance with this Rule, an officer finds any prohibited article, the officer may seize and detain the article. Where a search is carried out under s.41(2A) of the 1989 Act, the officer carrying out the search shall be of the same sex as the visitor, where the visitor is under the age of 16 the search shall be carried out in the presence of an accompanying adult, and, except in that situation, the search shall be undertaken out with the sight of any prisoner, any other visitor or officers who are not of the same sex as the visitor, and the search shall be carried out as expeditiously and decently as possible.

REMOVAL OF VISITORS

In terms of r.103 an officer may terminate a visit and remove a **4-53** visitor from the prison where the officer either has reasonable grounds for suspecting that the visitor has in their possession or is taking out or attempting to take out any article which the governor has not authorised the visitor to take into the prison or any article which may be prejudicial to security, good order or discipline, or where he considers that the visitor's conduct is prejudicial to security, good order or safety or that it is otherwise necessary to terminate the visit in the interests of security, disciple or the prevention of disorder or crime, or the officer has reasonable grounds for suspecting that the visitor has failed to comply with r.101(3) or (4) (visits by journalists or former journalists) or, where an undertaking has been given by the visitor in terms of rr.63, 64 or 73, and the officer considers that the terms of the undertaking have been breached. In addition to this, any visitor who smokes in breach of r.101(2) may be removed from prison in terms of r.103(1)(b). An officer who terminates a visit in terms of this Rule shall record particulars of the matter including the reasons for termination.

Persons providing contracted out services to a prison, their lockers, motor vehicles and their property, may be searched in terms of r.104. Again, the same rules as in r.102 authorising the use of swabs and metal detectors in carrying out searches apply, and once again, r.104(3) and (4) provide that any such search may be carried out by use of reasonable force, must not include strip-searching, shall be carried by officers of the same sex as the person being searched, and shall be carried out expeditiously and decently and outwith the sight of any other person.

VIEWING OF PRISONS

4–54 This is governed by r.105, which provides that "No person shall be permitted to view a prison unless authorised by any enactment or by the Governor or the Scottish Ministers". Where authorisation to view is granted, no person viewing the prison is permitted to take a photograph, or make any film, sound recording or sketch or communicate with a prisoner unless authorised by any enactment or by the Governor or Ministers. In addition, a person viewing the prison is not permitted to take a photograph or make a film of a prisoner or an officer without obtaining their prior consent. In practice, other than in times of particular public concern, very few requests are ever made by media organisations or similar to view prisons.

VOTING RIGHTS

4–55 In terms of s.3 of the Representation of the People Act 1983, convicted prisoners are prohibited from voting in any parliamentary or local elections, including elections to the European Parliament. This principle has existed in its present form since the Forfeiture Act 1870, and is based upon the principle that the right to vote is one of the rights lost by a citizen upon their incarceration (although currently) it does not apply to fine defaulters or those sentenced for contempt of court. Remand prisoners and unconvicted mental patients are permitted to vote, in terms of the Representation of the People Act 2000. The majority of European countries either do not disenfranchise prisoners, or restrict their voting rights in certain restricted ways. In the UK, the Home Secretary described the policy in February 2001 thus:

> "By committing offences which by themselves or taken with any aggravating circumstances including the offender's character and previous criminal record require a custodial sentence, such prisoners have forfeited the right to have a say in the way the country is governed for that period. There is more than one element to punishment than forcible detention. Removal from society means removal from the privileges of society, amongst which is the right to vote for one's representative."

Given the amount of public money spent annually on prisons within the United Kingdom, some might observe that it seems a little anomalous that those who use these resources have no say in how the money is spent, but successive Governments have proved resistant to the notion of permitting prisoners, whatever sentences they are serving, the right to vote.

This was challenged in *Hirst v United Kingdom, No. 2)* [2004 **4–56** ECHR 122]. In the case the court held that a blanket ban on all convicted prisoners being entitled to vote was contrary to the ECHR, observing "As regards the purpose of enhancing civic responsibility and respect for the rule of law, there is no clear, logical link between the loss of vote and the imposition of a prison sentence, where no bar applies to a person guilty of crimes which may be equally anti-social or "uncitizen-like" but whose crime is not met by such a consequence."

Following this decision, further legislation is proposed that will permit some convicted prisoners to vote. It is expected that this legislation will be in force in time for the next U.K. Parliamentary Election, but not by the date of the Scottish Parliamentary election in May 2007.

Again, it came as little surprise when a serving prisoner sought to challenge the denial of the right to vote in the Scottish Parliamentary elections. This matter came before the Court of Session in January 2007 in *Smith v Scott*, [2007] CSIH 9, *unreported*, in which a serving prisoner challenged the refusal by the Electoral Registration Officer for Clackmannanshire, Falkirk and Stirling to permit his name to be entered onto the Register of Electors. The Inner House, following the decision in *Hirst,* and noting certain concessions made by the Advocate General, formally declared that s.3(1) of the Representation of the People Act was incompatible with the Convention. The effect of this decision on the 2007 Scottish Parliamentary elections is not known at the time of writing. A number of separate petitions were lodged by disgruntled would-be voters, upon which the court adjudicated in the period leading up to the date of the election.

CHAPTER 5

TESTING FOR DRUGS AND ALCOHOL, SEARCHING OF PRISONERS AND DISCIPLINARY OFFENCES

SEARCHING OF PRISONERS

5–01 Of all the areas of day to day life in prison, the issue of searching prisoners, and of testing for drugs and alcohol, is probably the most controversial. It has been a fact of life since the earliest writings on prison conditions, that prisoners have been able to obtain access to items from the outside, to which they are not entitled. Whenever a group of people is forbidden to possess something they want, human nature dictates that many of them will devote a great deal of time and effort to obtaining it. Equally, those charged with the preservation of order and discipline will be exercising their best endeavours to ensure that rules are complied with.

There is no doubt whatsoever that prisoners constantly seek new ways to subvert the rules by introducing forbidden articles, most commonly drugs, from outside. Many prisoners are released on a daily basis to attend outside work placements from top-end conditions, or are permitted weekend home leaves from open conditions, and many are either tempted or pressurised into bringing back illicit articles. Given the level of trust afforded to prisoners on placement, and the ease with which items such as drugs may be concealed, it would be surprising if prisoners were not found to be introducing forbidden articles. The 1989 Act was amended by the insertion of a new s.41A by virtue of the Criminal Justice and Public Order Act 1994, which provided that "an authorised employee at a prison shall have the power to search any prisoner for the purpose of ascertaining whether he has any unauthorised property on his person". In terms of s.41A(4), the governor of a prison shall take such steps as he considers appropriate to notify to prisoners the descriptions of employees who are for the time being authorised employees, as the definition of "authorised employee" excludes officers themselves (s.41A(5)).

In general, searches continue to be carried out by officers, and the 2006 Rules now provide specific guidance as to how and in what circumstances officers may search prisoners. These are to be found in Rule 106

Rule 106(2) provides that a search of a prisoner may take the **5–02** form of:

> "(a) an examination of the prisoner's person and clothing but without removal of the clothing;
> (b) the removal and examination of the prisoner's clothing;
> (c) the visual examination of the external parts of the prisoner's body following removal of the prisoner's clothing; or
> (d) the visual examination of the prisoner's open mouth without the use of force or any instrument."

A search of a prisoner shall be carried out only by an officer who is of the same sex (except in the case of a search mentioned in para.(2)(d), where Ministers have by direction specified other conditions), and as expeditiously and decently as possible.

In the case of a strip search as type mentioned in para.(2)(b) and (c), this must be undertaken by two officers of the same sex, and outwith the sight of any other prisoner.

Rule 106(4) confers an unfettered discretion on the governor in **5–03** respect of searching prisoners as he considers necessary, although the power to search conferred by this rule shall not be construed as authorising the physical examination of a prisoner's body orifices, unless such examination has been specifically authorised by Ministerial direction. The fact that this rule refers to searches taking place as the governor considers *necessary* does not appear to preclude occasional random searches. In practice, the majority of searches will be based upon intelligence reports or reasonable suspicion (for example, where a prisoner's actings and demeanour are concerning), particularly if there are suggestions that a particular inmate is involved in the introduction of prohibited articles. It might be argued that searching a prisoner, particularly if the search involves the removal of clothing, could be a breach of the prisoner's rights under Art.8 of the Convention, although the provisions of Art.8.2, permitting interference by a public authority into the right to private life "for the prevention of disorder or crime ... or for the protection of the rights and freedoms of others" would seem to provide a clear answer to this. However, there is no doubt that prisoners will continue to exercise their rights under the internal complaints procedure and beyond, to seek to challenge the lawfulness of some searches.

DRUG TESTING

5–04 The notion that prisoners would consume controlled drugs in custody would have seemed absurd to the draftsmen of the 1952 Rules. Indeed, even twenty years ago, by which time the number of inmates serving sentences for drugs offences had become significant, the notion of Mandatory Drug Testing of inmates was not generally considered. However, by at least the early to mid-1980s it was clear that a number of prisoners had access to, and were using, controlled drugs, particularly cannabis. There is some anecdotal evidence to suggest that, in the early part of that period, a blind eye might sometimes be turned to illicit cannabis use, perhaps on the basis that prisoners under the influence of cannabis were less likely to become violent or aggressive towards staff. When the 1989 Act first reached the statute book, s.41 made it an offence for any person to introduce into a prison "any letter, tobacco, spirits or other article not allowed by the rules". The notion of prisoners possessing and consuming illicit drugs in custody does not seem to have occurred to the parliamentary draftsmen. Times have clearly changed massively since 1989. Within a fairly short time of the Act coming into force, both internal and public concerns grew over both the number of drug addicts being sent to prison, and the apparent ease with which drugs seemed to be admitted to prisons. It became widely known that drugs were being used in prison, and the absence of any form of procedure to test inmates who appeared to be under the influence of drugs became a concern to prison management. It was clear that compulsory drug testing of prisoners would be necessary.

Section 41B of the 1989 Act, inserted in 1994, and subsequently amended by the Management of Offenders (Scotland) Act 2005, now provides that:

> "(1) If an authorisation is in force for the prison, any officer of the prison may, at the prison, in accordance with rules under Section 39 of this Act, require any prisoner who is confined in the prison to provide a sample of urine or saliva for the purpose of ascertaining whether he has any drug in his body.
>
> (2) If the authorisation so provides, the power conferred by subsection (1) above shall include power to require a prisoner to provide a sample of any other description specified in the authorisation, not being an intimate sample, whether instead of or in addition to a sample of urine or saliva."

The definition of "drug" for the purposes of this section encompasses any substance defined as a controlled drug in the schedules to the Misuse of Drugs Act 1971.

The internal rules governing the procedure for carrying out drug **5–05** testing were introduced in the 1994 Rules, and are now to be found in r.107 of the 2006 Rules, which apply where an officer, acting under the powers conferred by s.41B of the 1989 Act, may require a prisoner to provide a sample for the purpose of ascertaining whether he or she has any controlled drug in his or her body. In this rule "sample" means a sample of urine or any other description of sample specified in the governor's authorisation for the purposes of the Act.

When requiring a prisoner to provide a sample, an officer must, so far as is reasonably practicable, inform the prisoner that he or she is being required to provide a sample in accordance with s.41B, and that a refusal to provide a sample may lead to disciplinary proceedings being brought against the prisoner.

There is therefore a clear distinction between the methods of testing for drugs in prison and the provisions of the Misuse of Drugs Act 1971, which criminalise the unlawful possession of controlled drugs, but do not make it an offence in itself to have a controlled drug within the body. The reasoning behind this seems clear. Within a closed prison environment, the period of "possession" as defined by s.5(2) of the Misuse of Drugs Act is likely to be swift and transient, with prisoners rarely taking the risk of leaving any form of controlled drug in a cell or other place liable to be searched at any time. Proof of drugs within a prisoner's urine creates a presumption that the prisoner has recently consumed a controlled drug.

Schedule 1, para.(y) of the 2006 Rules states that a prisoner shall **5–06** be guilty of a breach of discipline if he "administers a controlled drug to him or herself or fails to prevent the administration of a controlled drug to him or herself by another person (but subject to rule 117(6))".

Rule 117(6) provides that it shall be a defence for a prisoner charged with a breach of discipline contrary to paragraph (y) of Sch.1 to show that:

"(a) the controlled drug had been, prior to its administration, lawfully in the prisoner's possession for the prisoner's use or was administered to the prisoner in the course of a lawful supply of the drug to the prisoner by another person;

(b) the controlled drug was administered by or to the prisoner in circumstances in which the prisoner did not know and had no reason to suspect that such a drug was being administered; or

(c) the controlled drug was administered by or to the prisoner under duress or to the prisoner without consent in circumstances where it was not reasonable for the prisoner to have resisted."

5–07 The physical mechanism by which such a sample may be obtained is specified in detail in r.107(4)–(8), which provide:

"(4) An officer shall require a prisoner to provide a fresh sample, free from any adulteration.

(5) An officer requiring a sample shall make such arrangements and give the prisoner such instructions for its provision as may be reasonably necessary in order to prevent or detect its adulteration or falsification.

(6) A prisoner who is required to provide a sample may be kept apart from other prisoners for a period not exceeding one hour to enable arrangements to be made for the provision of the sample.

(7) A prisoner who is unable to provide a sample of urine when required to do so may be kept apart from other prisoners until he or she has provided the required sample, save that a prisoner may not be kept apart under this paragraph for a period of more than 5 hours.

(8) A prisoner required to provide a sample of urine shall be afforded such degree of privacy for the purposes of providing the sample as may be compatible with the need to prevent or detect any adulteration or falsification of the sample; in particular a prisoner shall not be required to provide such a sample in the sight of a person of the opposite sex."

Every prison in Scotland now has its own Drug Testing Unit. When a sample has been taken, it will be sent for analysis. At present, the contract for drug testing in Scottish prisons is held by JMJ Laboratories in Abergavenny, and they carry out all sample analysis. Each sample is divided in two, individually bottled, and given a unique identification number. The initial laboratory screening test will simply advise whether the sample is positive or negative for the presence of benzodiazepines, buprenorphine, amphetamines, methadone, cocaine, LSD, opiates, barbiturates, or cannabinoids. Should the sample prove positive for any one or more of these drugs, and the result not be consistent with the consumption of prescribed medication, then the prisoner may request that a confirmation test is carried out. At that stage the sample is subjected to GCMS (Gas Chromatography/Mass Spectroscopy) testing, which can identify both the precise chemical compound within the urine, and the level of toxicity, in terms of microgrammes per hundred millilitres.

There are a number of circumstances in which a prisoner may be **5–08** selected to attend for drug testing. A number of prisoners will be selected at random by computer, and required to undertake a drug test without warning. Such tests are commonly called Mandatory Drug Tests. Failure, without reasonable excuse, to provide a sample when required is itself a breach of discipline. Current SPS policy is that 10 per cent of all inmates should be tested each month, and thus every prisoner in custody for more than a year can expect to be tested at least once. In addition, testing can be ordered on the basis of reasonable suspicion, where an officer has reasonable grounds to suspect, from his own observations, that a prisoner is under the influence of drugs.

The practice of drug testing is regularly reviewed, and present policy in Scotland is not to regard the failure of a drug test as a disciplinary offence deserving of punishment, but as an opportunity for a prisoner with ongoing or potential drug misuse issues to seek assistance in addressing any substance misuse problem. Where it is felt that intervention from drug services is necessary, then the prisoner may opt to go onto either voluntary drug testing or a frequent test programme, both of which are designed to ensure regular monitoring of the prisoner, in order that only prescribed medication is being taken. Commonly, prisoners who have a history of heroin misuse, who are selected for a methadone programme, will be placed on a frequent test programme, in order that any illicit drug use is swiftly discovered.

One consequence of present policy is that drug tests are now carried out as part of the risk assessment process. Where a prisoner is being considered for progression to a different work party, to a situation where a greater degree of trust is required, for onward progression to the open estate, or where they are being considered for release on temporary licence, then they may be tested at that stage, and the result of the test will be considered a part of the whole process of risk assessment.

The ECHR implications of a Mandatory Drug Test failure, and **5–09** its potential consequences in respect of a prisoner's eligibility for parole, were considered by the Outer House in *Matthewson v Scottish Ministers*, 2001 GWD 23–875, in which the petitioner sought, unsuccessfully, to argue that the charge of breach of discipline that followed from a failed drug test fell to be treated as a "criminal charge" for the purposes of Art.6, and drew attention to the possible consequences in respect of the refusal of parole in the event of the charge being proven. While the judge held that the governor had been in error in declining to afford the prisoner the opportunity of legal representation, he observed that the proceedings before the governor did not, in themselves, involve the determination of a criminal charge. The court further held that proceedings before the parole board, in which the sole issue related to the determination of risk of a convicted prisoner, did not involve the determination of a criminal charge, or the imposition of a penalty or punishment. It may be noted that the Divisional Court had come to the same view in respect of an English determinate sentence prisoner in *Greenfield v Secretary of State for the Home Department*, (February 22, 2001, unreported), and that the English courts had further held in *R (Carroll) v Secretary of State for the Home Department*, (February 16, 2001) that a charge of refusal to obey a lawful order brought against a life prisoner did not engage Art.6.

Prisoners, not surprisingly, are constantly seeking to discover new ways to subvert the drug-testing process, and prison staff and scientific laboratories are constantly developing their own strategies against subversion. The increasing sophistication and accuracy of GCMS testing makes it ever more difficult for a prisoner to blame a positive test for opiates on illicit consumption of a prescription pain-killer, as confirmation testing can now identify the precise drug type or subtype. For some time, there was a tendency for prisoners to drink large quantities of water shortly before drug testing, in order that their urine would be considerably more dilute. This would have the effect of materially altering the levels of creatine (a naturally occurring organic acid, synthesised in the liver) within the urine, and recent testing includes analysis of creatine levels. If the figures are found to be outwith the standard tolerance bands, the sample is recorded as demonstrating an abnormal result for creatine, and is treated as an invalid sample.

In recent years, a number of prisoners have been found in possession of bottles of "clean" urine — a practice seems to have developed of prisoners who do not misuse drugs selling or trading their drug-free urine, in order that, when a prisoner is called to take a mandatory drug test, they will be able to provide a clean sample. The attempt to use the contents of the bottle requires an element of sleight of hand, and prison staff will be vigilant during the testing process checking to see whether there is any evidence of an illicit bottle being smuggled in. Once more, testing has developed to the extent that urine samples are now checked for temperature (urine retained outwith the human body will be considerably colder) and if the sample is found to be below the appropriate range, it will be treated as invalid. Where a bottle of urine is found in a prisoner's possession, it tends to give rise to the inference that it was retained for the purpose of subverting urine testing. One prisoner in open conditions recently inventively, if not entirely credibly, maintained that there was in fact no sinister inference to be drawn from his possession of a bottle of urine; he suffered from a skin rash and was applying an ancient Indian Ayurvedic remedy, by using the urine to dab onto the affected areas to reduce the inflammation.

Prisoners of course become aware very quickly of developments **5–10** in the field of forensic science. One of the principal reasons for the increase in opiate use and decrease in popularity of cannabis over the last two decades is the knowledge that most opiate drugs are processed through the body and absent within around 24 hours, while traces of cannabinoids can be found in the system for up to 28 days after it was last consumed. In one English prison, an inventive inmate placed a large piece of cannabis resin into the hall tea-urn, and then tea was served to all the prisoners, who had of course drunk the tea before the hidden cannabis was discovered. The result of this was that all prisoners who had consumed the tea would test positive for cannabinoids, and therefore tests for cannabinoids for the next four weeks within that hall were automatically invalidated, as innocent contamination could not be ruled out, and as such a defence analogous to that provided by r.117(6) was available to all the unlucky inmates, at least for four weeks after the contamination of the tea-urn.

The increasing use of modern scientific methods has tended to lessen the prospects of successful challenge of a positive test result on the basis of error in analysis. The chain of custody procedures must be followed exactly, in order that there is no gap in the process whereby the sample leaves the prison, arrives at the laboratory, and the analysis is then returned. Should there be any gap in the chain, or should dates and numbers on samples and analysis certificates not correspond exactly, then the test process will be invalid and the governor would be obliged to dismiss the allegation at the Orderly Room hearing.

There are therefore, given the ready availability of drugs in many parts of the Scottish prison system, a large number of drug test failures reported. These will often have serious consequences, particularly for long term prisoners approaching their parole qualifying date, or who have recently progressed to open conditions and are therefore entitled to home leaves. If any of these prisoners are serving sentences for drug offences, or have a history of drug misuse in the community or in the early part of their sentence, the consequences of a drug test failure in terms of delaying their liberation can clearly be devastating. Home leaves or outside placements may be cancelled, and a second failure in open conditions will generally result in consideration being given to an immediate return to closed conditions. It is not therefore surprising that many prisoners wish either to challenge the result, blame it on innocent contamination, or plead mitigating factors. Prisoners are of course entitled, at their own expense (in practice, at the expense of the Scottish Legal Aid Board), to obtain their own independent analysis of the urine sample alleged to contain traces of controlled drugs. In practice, different results from two laboratories are virtually unknown. From many prisoners' own representations, it seems that within a short time of nursing officers leaving prison on Friday afternoons, an epidemic of toothache sweeps the open estate, curable only by the fortuitous offer of opiate-based medication by a charitable fellow inmate, resulting in the unfortunate prisoner (who often has a proven history of drug use either in the community, in prison or both) returning a positive test at the start of the following week. Very often it is then argued by the prisoner that he was unaware of the precise nature of the medication taken, and thus the contamination was innocent.

5–11   It must perhaps be recognised that drugs are prevalent throughout all parts of society, and the prospect of their eradication seems unlikely in the foreseeable future. Given the number of prisoners who abused drugs immediately before their imprisonment, and the fact that these are inevitably sourced from those who are willing to flout the law, there is no doubt that prisoners will continue to seek to access drugs during their sentence, and that drugs will, on occasion, be received by prisoners, despite the best efforts of staff and others to prevent this. There are many methods used to smuggle drugs into prisons. Video cameras in the visit area of most prisons has enabled staff to spot a number of suspicious transactions taking place during visits, and visitors are not permitted to bring in foodstuffs from the outside, lest packaging has been tampered with. In some prisons, packages are thrown over walls, although this method is not notable for its subtlety, nor for its success in avoiding detection. Some prisoners on outside placements have been found, on their return, to have secreted packages of drugs internally (placing packages into a balloon that is inserted into the rectum is a fairly common method), and in one recent case, unfortunately it emerged that a prisoner's law agent had supplied drugs into a closed establishment during the course of a legitimate legal visit. Courts will generally regard any breach of s.41 involving the introduction of drugs very seriously, and custodial sentences for those who supply or attempt to supply drugs into prison remain the norm, even when it is stated in mitigation that the supplier was under duress at the time.

ALCOHOL TESTING

In more recent times, the number of prisoners testing positive for **5–12** alcohol is considerably lower than those providing positive drug samples. However, there are three common situations in which prisoners can access alcohol whilst in custody.

The brewing of "hooch", by fermenting vegetable matter from the kitchens in the prisoner's own cell, while carrying obvious risks in terms of detection, and requiring the use of a bulky object such as a bucket, is still occasionally discovered. More commonly, alcohol is sourced on outside placements or on home leaves. The power to test prisoners for alcohol is now to be found in s.41C of the 1989 Act, inserted with effect from January 1, 1998, by the Crime and Punishment (Scotland) Act 1997, which provides that "if an authorisation is in force for the prison, any officer of the prison may, at the prison, in accordance with rules under section 39 of this Act, require any prisoner who is confined in the prison, and whom he reasonably believes to have taken alcohol, to provide a sample of breath for the purpose of ascertaining whether he has any alcohol in his body". Authorisation for the taking of such samples must be granted by the governor (s.41C(2)), and the procedure for carrying out such testing is specified in r.108 of the 2006 Rules.

This rule provides that where an officer, acting under the powers conferred by s.41C requires a prisoner to provide a sample for the purpose of ascertaining whether a prisoner has any alcoholic liquor in their body, he shall, so far as is reasonably practicable, inform the prisoner of the requirement to provide a sample in accordance with s.41C, and that a refusal to provide a sample may lead to disciplinary proceedings being brought against the prisoner.

In terms of r.108(2), "sample" means a sample of breath or any **5–13** other description of sample specified in the authorisation by the governor for the purposes of s.41C. If breath testing cannot be carried out, and the governor holds authorisation from Ministers to do so, he may authorise staff to require the prisoner to provide a urine sample.

An officer shall require each prisoner tested to provide a fresh sample, free from any adulteration, and r.108(5) obliges him to "make such arrangements and give the prisoner such instructions for its provision as may be reasonably necessary in order to prevent or detect its adulteration or falsification". A prisoner who is required to provide a sample may be kept apart from other prisoners for a period not exceeding one hour to enable arrangements to be made for provision of the sample.

Where a urine sample is ordered rather than a breath sample, and a prisoner is unable to provide a sample of urine when required to do so, he may be kept apart from other prisoners until the required sample has been provided, save that a prisoner may not be kept apart under this paragraph for a period of more than five hours.

5–14   Rule 108(8) states that "A prisoner required to provide a sample of urine shall be afforded such degree of privacy for the purposes of providing the sample as may be compatible with the need to prevent or detect any adulteration or falsification of the sample; in particular a prisoner shall not be required to provide such a sample in the sight of a person of the opposite sex."

In practice, the power to test prisoners is most commonly exercised where a prisoner returns to prison from an outside work or college placement, or a home leave period, during which they have been entrusted to comply with the conditions of their temporary release licence, which expressly prohibits the use of alcohol, and on the point of their return an officer has reasonable grounds to suspect that they have consumed alcohol. Occasionally prisoners do attempt to smuggle bottles of spirits into custody, but in the modern era, when drugs can be introduced internally in large quantities, it is rarer, though not unheard of, for prisoners to attempt to smuggle in bulky bottled items.

OFFENCES AGAINST PRISON DISCIPLINE

5–15 Part 11 of the 2006 Rules covers the whole area of breach of prison discipline, the offences against the rules, and the punishments therefor. Rule 113 specifies that "breach of discipline" shall be interpreted in accordance with Sch.1 of the 2006 Rules. This schedule lists all the disciplinary offences, as follows:

BREACHES OF DISCIPLINE

5–16 "A prisoner shall be guilty of a breach of discipline if he or she—

(a) commits any assault;

(b) detains any person against his or her will;

(c) denies access to any part of the prison to any officer or any person (other than a prisoner) who is at the prison for the purpose of working there;

(d) fights with any person;

(e) intentionally endangers the health or personal safety of others or, by his or her conduct, is reckless whereby such health or personal safety is endangered.

(f) intentionally obstructs an officer in the execution of his or her duty or any person (other than a prisoner), who is at the prison for the purpose of working there, in the performance of his or her work;

(g) escapes or absconds from prison or from legal custody;

(h) fails—

    (i) to return to prison when he or she should return after being temporarily released under Part 15 of these Rules; or

    (ii) to comply with any condition upon which he or she is so temporarily released;

(i) have—

    (i) in his or her possession, or concealed about his or her body or in any body orifice, any article or substance which he or she is not authorised to have or a greater quantity of any article or substance than he or she is authorised to have; or

    (ii) in his or her possession whilst in a particular part of the prison any article or substance which he or she is not authorised to have when in that part of the prison;

(j) sells or delivers to any person any article which he or she is not authorised to have;

(k) sells or, without permission, delivers to any person any article which he or she is allowed to have only for his or her own use;

(l) takes improperly any article belonging to another person or to the prison;

(m) intentionally or recklessly sets fire to any part of a prison or any other property, whether or not that property belongs to him or her;

(n) destroys or damages any part of a prison or any other property, other than his or her own;

(o) absents his or herself from any place where he or she is required to be or is present at any place where he or she is not authorised to be;

(p) is disrespectful to any officer, or any person (other than a prisoner) who is at the prison for the purpose of working there, or any person visiting a prison;

(q) uses threatening, abusive or insulting words or behaviour;

(r) intentionally fails to work properly or, being required to work, refuses to do so;

(s) disobeys any lawful order;

(t) disobeys or fails to comply with any rule, direction or regulation applying to a prisoner;

(u) inhales any substance, or the fumes of any substance, which is—

    (i)   a prohibited article;

    (ii) an article which he or she is not authorised to possess or keep in terms of these Rules or by any officer; or

    (iii) an article which he or she is so authorised to keep or possess but not for the purpose of inhaling or inhaling the fumes thereof;

(v) smokes in an area of a prison where smoking is not permitted by virtue of rule 31;

(w) consumes, takes, injects, ingests or conceals inside a body orifice any substance which is a prohibited article;

(x) commits any indecent or obscene act;

(y) administers a controlled drug to him or herself or fails to prevent the administration of a controlled drug to him or herself by another person (but subject to rule 117(6));

(z) fails, without reasonable excuse, to open his or her mouth for the purpose of enabling a visual examination in terms of rule 106(2)(d); or

(aa) attempts to commit, incites another prisoner to commit, or assists another prisoner to commit or to attempt to commit, any of the foregoing breaches."

5–17   It will be noted that Sch.1, para.(y) must be read subject to the provisions of r.117(6), which provide for certain defences in respect of charges involving the administration of controlled drugs. That Rule states—

"It shall be a defence for a prisoner charged with a breach of discipline contrary to paragraph (y) of Schedule 1 to show that—

(a) the controlled drug had been, prior to its administration, lawfully in the prisoner's possession for the prisoner's use or was administered to the prisoner in the course of a lawful supply of the drug to the prisoner by another person;

(b) the controlled drug was administered by or to the prisoner in circumstances in which the prisoner did not know and had no reason to suspect that such a drug was being administered; or

(c) the controlled drug was administered by or to the prisoner under duress or to the prisoner without consent in circumstances where it was not reasonable for the prisoner to have resisted."

PROCEDURE WHERE BREACH OF DISCIPLINE IS ALLEGED

Rule 114 obliges every suspected breach of discipline to be reported **5–18** forthwith in writing to the governor by the officer to whose notice it has come. Inquiry into disciplinary charges is governed by rr.115–117. Rule 115(1) provides that where a prisoner is to be charged with a breach of discipline, the charge shall be brought as soon as possible and in any event, save in exceptional circumstances, within 48 hours of the discovery of the act or omission giving rise to the charge. Written notice of the charge is obligatory in terms of r.115(2), and such notice must give the prisoner a minimum of two hours notice. There is a specific exception in the case of an untried prisoner reported for an alleged breach of discipline on the date before the prisoner's trial is due to commence, or on the day of (or any day during) the trial. In that situation, the officer concerned may delay bringing a charge in accordance with the above rules until the relevant criminal proceedings are concluded and, where the prisoner is sentenced to imprisonment, the officer must bring the charge no later than 48 hours after the time at which sentence is passed.

Rule 116(1) provides that, every charge of breach of discipline shall be inquired into by the governor not later, save in exceptional circumstances, than the next day after it is brought or, where the next day is a Sunday or a public holiday, the day after that Sunday or public holiday. This is, however subject to the provisions of para.(4), which, mindful of the requirements of Art.6.3 of the ECHR, provides that—

> "Every prisoner against whom a charge is brought shall be given a full opportunity of
>
> (a) hearing the allegations made;
> (b) presenting his or her own case and, subject to paragraph (5), calling witnesses; and
> (c) subject to rule 117(3), cross-examining any other witnesses."

The governor must therefore be satisfied before commencing an **5–19** inquiry into any charge that the prisoner concerned has had sufficient time to prepare his or her case, and, if satisfied that the prisoner requires further time to prepare or that there exist other reasonable grounds for an adjournment, he must adjourn the inquiry, for such period of time as may be reasonably necessary. While the prisoner has a right to call a witness or witnesses of his choosing, the governor may, in terms of r.116(5), refuse to allow him to call any witness if, having discussed the matter with the prisoner, he or she is reasonably satisfied that the evidence which the witness is likely to give will be of no relevance or value in determining whether the charge is proven. A prisoner may choose to be seated or may stand during the inquiry.

Rule 116(7) provides that the governor may, on the application of a prisoner, permit him or her to be represented at the inquiry by a solicitor, an advocate or a barrister where in exceptional circumstances the governor considers such representation is necessary or desirable. Such requests are not uncommonly made, but are in practice very rarely granted, although it may be observed that there will be occasions on which matters of substantive law may arise in such hearings. Of course, an aggrieved prisoner in such a situation may of course seek legal advice subsequent to the hearing, and may thereafter choose to pursue his grievance through the routes described elsewhere.

It is not necessary for the adjourned hearing to proceed before the same person as granted the adjournment, by virtue of r.116(8), unless evidence had been led prior to the hearing being adjourned, in which case that rule does not apply, and another person holding authority in terms of para.(8) to adjudicate may desert the charge, but authorise any officer to bring a new charge in relation to the same suspected breach of discipline.

5–20   In adjudication upon any charge of breach of discipline, the governor shall be entitled to take into account any evidence, in whatever form, at the inquiry into any charge of breach of discipline, subject to the proviso that he may only take into account the evidence of any person who has not given oral evidence at the inquiry if the prisoner concerned agrees.

Rule 117(3) provides for certain special provisions in relation to any inquiry into a charge of a breach of discipline contrary to para.(v) or (x) of Sch.1. Again, this appears to be a drafting error, and I presume that the rule is meant to refer to paras (w) (consuming, ingesting or concealing a prohibited article) and (y) (administering or failing to prevent the administration of a controlled drug). In these cases, the governor may take into account written evidence of any person (other than an officer or employee) relating to an analysis of a sample required to be provide in accordance with r.107 or 108 which was carried out by that person, without requiring the attendance of the analyst, if the prisoner has been afforded the opportunity to make representations why the person should give oral evidence, and, having heard the prisoner, the governor is satisfied that the evidence is relevant and admissible and that there is no sufficient reason why the person need give oral evidence.

The burden of proof is specified in r.117(4) as the criminal standard, namely whether the charge has been proven beyond any reasonable doubt. If the governor finds a prisoner guilty of a breach of discipline, he must afford the prisoner an opportunity to make a plea in mitigation before considering whether to impose a punishment in terms of r.119.

There are somewhat complex provisions contained in r.118 to **5–21** cover the situation where a report under r.114(1) is made against a young offender shortly before his reception into prison, empowering the governor of the receiving establishment to investigate and adjudicate upon the report. In addition, where a prisoner provides a positive drug test but it cannot be established whether the drugs were taken in one or other establishment, although he was detained in prison throughout the period during which the drug might have been administered, the receiving governor may adjudicate upon the report. Rule 118(4) further provides that where the prisoner was untried throughout the whole period of the alleged drug consumption, but has since been sentenced to imprisonment, the governor of the receiving prison may adjudicate, irrespective of whether the controlled drug was ingested in his establishment or not.

REMOVAL FROM ASSOCIATION

It should further be noted that prison staff have certain specific **5–22** powers in terms of r.114 to remove a prisoner from association with others prior to the determination of a charge. Subject to paras (3) and (4), where any officer has reasonable grounds for suspecting that a prisoner has committed a breach of discipline the officer may, if he considers it appropriate, remove the prisoner from association with other prisoners in general pending the making of a report and the adjudication of the charge.

Paragraph (3) directs that "a prisoner shall not be subject to such removal for a period in excess of 72 hours from the time of the removal except where there are exceptional circumstances and, on the application of the governor, the written authority of the Scottish Ministers has been obtained prior to the expiry of the 72 hour period."

Rule 114(4) governs the granting of such authority by Ministers. Such authority shall have effect for a period of one month commencing from the expiry of the 72 hour period above, but Ministers may, on a subsequent application of the governor, renew the authority for further periods of one month commencing from the expiry of the previous authority. The authority to remove a prisoner from association ceases to have effect when the charge has been adjudicated.

5–23   The power to remove a prisoner from association has long been controversial, and it came as little surprise when, following the coming into force of the Scotland Act, after which it became unlawful for public bodies to act in a manner contrary to the ECHR, that a number of prisoners sought to challenge the lawfulness of this power. Between 2002 and 2004 five separate petitions for Judicial Review were raised, contending that the periods of segregation imposed under the previous r.80 (effectively in the same terms as the present r.114) were unlawful. These actions have been conjoined, and are, at the time of writing, proceeding in the Court of Session. A number of preliminary please have been tabled by both sides, and on November 3, 2006 the Inner House ruled on these in *Somerville, Cairns, Ralston, Blanco and Henderson v The Scottish Ministers*, [2006] CSIH 52 (unreported). The court ruled that actions of prison governors in respect of removal from association are, for the purposes of s.57(2) of the Scotland Act 1998, Acts of the Scottish Ministers, and further, following a long and detailed analysis of the constitutional dimensions of the interrelationship between the Scotland Act and the Human Rights Act, that the prescriptive period for the raising of such actions is, in terms of s.7(5) of the Human Rights Act, one year from the date of cessation of the period of removal.

Full argument on the merits of the case is likely to be heard some time during 2007.

GOVERNOR'S PUNISHMENTS

5–24   These are detailed in r.119. As stated previously, the award of additional days loss of remission, by the governor, at a hearing within the prison, based often on the evidence of prison staff, was virtually impossible to justify in terms of Art.6.1 of the ECHR, and such punishment has now disappeared from the 2006 Rules. The punishments now permitted in terms of r.119(1), are:

"(a) a caution;
(b) forfeiture of any privileges granted under the system of privileges applicable to a prisoner for a period not exceeding 14 days;

- (c) stoppage of or deduction from earnings for a period not exceeding 56 days and of an amount not exceeding one half of the prisoner's earnings in any week (or part thereof) falling within the period specified;
- (d) except in the case of a young prisoner, cellular confinement for a period not exceeding 3 days;
- (e) in the case of an untried prisoner guilty of escaping or attempting to escape, forfeiture of the entitlement to wear their own clothing under rule 25 for any period as may be specified;
- (f) in the case of an untried prisoner or a civil prisoner, forfeiture of any or all of the entitlements referred to in rules 48, 49 and 54 for any period as may be specified; or
- (g) forfeiture of the entitlement to withdraw money in terms of rule 53(3) for any period not exceeding 14 days.

Where a prisoner is found guilty of more than one breach of discipline arising out of an incident, all punishments other than cellular confinement may be ordered to run consecutively. Where the governor awards a punishment of cellular confinement, the governor must inform the medical officer as soon as possible, and the prisoner will serve the period of confinement in accordance with the provisions of, and subject to any conditions imposed by any direction made by the Scottish Ministers.

Rule 120 allows the governor to impose "suspended punishments". He or she has power to direct that the punishment shall not take effect unless, "during such period of the prisoner's sentence as shall be specified in the direction (not being more than six months (or three months in the case of an untried prisoner) from the date of the direction), the prisoner commits another breach of discipline and a direction is given under paragraph (2)."

In terms of para.(2), where a prisoner is found guilty of a breach of **5–25** discipline committed during the period specified in a direction as specified above, then the governor dealing with the breach may either direct that the suspended punishment shall take effect, reduce the period or the amount of the suspended punishment and direct that it shall take effect as so reduced, vary the original direction by substituting a period expiring not later than six months from the date of variation, or make no direction with respect to the suspended punishment. In practice, the sanction of suspended punishments is regularly used in respect of first time drug test failures in open conditions, where the failure itself would not necessarily merit a return to closed conditions, providing the prisoner can provide some evidence that he can otherwise comply with the requirements of his enhanced status.

CHAPTER 6

HOW TO BE RELEASED FROM PRISON: PART ONE — APPEALS, DAY RELEASE, COMPASSIONATE RELEASE, HOME DETENTION CURFEWS AND RELEASE OTHER THAN ON LICENCE

It is almost universally known that when a person receives a sen- **6–01** tence of imprisonment, they do not spend every single hour of every day from the date of commencement of the sentence until its conclusion in custody. There are a great many situations in which someone who has been sentenced to a period of imprisonment may lawfully be found within the community before their sentence end date. Many of these are in terms of the "early release" provisions of the 1993 Act, which currently govern release as stated in Chapter Two, and which are scheduled for significant amendment in the near future. The current law, and its proposed amendment, will be addressed in detail later in this chapter. However, there are a number of situations in which a convicted prisoner may lawfully leave the establishment before the last day of their sentence.

APPELLANTS

One that should not be forgotten is that a person may have spent **6–02** many months, perhaps even many years, in prison before their conviction and/or sentence is quashed. The right to appeal against conviction and sentence is found in s.106 (solemn procedure) and s.175 (summary procedure) of the Criminal Procedure (Scotland) Act 1995. The practices and procedures of the appeal system do not fall within the remit of this book, but it will be noted that the right to appeal is no longer automatic, but now requires the leave of the High Court of Justiciary in terms of s.107 or s.180, for solemn and summary appeals respectively. In respect of any solemn appeal against conviction, in terms of s.118 the High Court has the power to affirm the verdict of the trial court, set aside the verdict of the trial court and quash the conviction, set aside the verdict of the trial court and substitute therefor an amended verdict of guilty that could competently have been returned by the trial jury, or set aside the verdict of the trial court, quash the conviction and grant authority to bring a new prosecution. The summary provisions in s.183 of the Act are broadly analogous.

While bail is competent pending determination of an appeal, and is customarily granted in respect of appeals against conviction in summary procedure, where the sentence would otherwise often have been served before the hearing of the appeal, it is relatively rare for those receiving a long-term sentence to be admitted to bail pending determination of their appeals, particularly since the prosecution has had a right to be heard on the matter of bail since June 27, 2003 (Criminal Justice (Scotland) Act 2003, s.66). It is therefore common for many prisoners to remain in custody for many months, and sometimes in excess of a year, before their case is finally disposed of. While they are serving prisoners, their status as appellants means that they cannot be compelled to undertake prison work or offender programmes, as discussed previously.

Where an appellant's conviction is quashed, and no retrial is ordered, he is free from any further question in respect of the original offence, and returns to society a free individual. This has, of course, caused considerable difficulties for many appellants who have, on the quashing of their convictions, found themselves returned to the community from closed conditions, without having undertaken any form of preparation for release by way of outside placement or home leaves. Unlike those who are released on licence, in respect of whom compulsory measures of supervision are put in place in time for their release, successful appellants have no statutory right to receive any assistance in the securing of accommodation or employment, or to be assessed for any relevant form of addictions counselling, as they, being innocent in the eyes of the law, cannot be placed under any compulsory measures. Not surprisingly, many who have been released after several years in custody have struggled to readjust to life in the community.

6–03   It should perhaps also be noted that where an appeal is partially successful, to the extent that a sentence is substantially reduced, similar difficulties may arise. For example, an appellant convicted on indictment of assault and robbery and assault may have received concurrent sentences of seven years and three years. He is eligible for consideration for parole after three years six months, and entitled, in terms of the 1993 Act, to release on licence after four years eight months. Under normal circumstances, he would not expect to be in open conditions until he were in the last year before his parole qualifying date. If his appeal is determined after twenty months, and only his appeal against conviction for the more serious offence succeeds, the longer sentence is quashed. As he has served more than eighteen months of his three year sentence, again he falls to be released immediately.

Until relatively recently, it was rare indeed for appeals against conviction to take more than a few months to be determined, and the decision of the High Court exercising its appellate function was final and not subject to review. Until April 1999, s.124 of the 1995 Act continued the previous provisions that precluded any review of a final interlocutor of the High Court, save in the very rare cases where the Secretary of State, on the consideration of any conviction, elected to refer the whole case to the High Court for them to hear and determine the case of new. In the event that the Secretary of State declined to refer such a case, it was not competent for the aggrieved prisoner to have his case heard of new (*Windsor v HM Advocate*, 1994 S.C.C.R 59).

Concern continued to grow for several years over the lack of independent scrutiny of potential miscarriages of justice, particularly given the limited grounds upon which a "fresh evidence" appeal could be lodged, until eventually the Crime and Punishment (Scotland) Act 1997 inserted a new Part XA into the 1995 Act, setting out the powers and duties of the Scottish Criminal Cases Review Commission (SCCRC), which came into effect on April 1, 1999. The powers and duties of the Commission, whose independence from the Crown is guaranteed by s.194A(2), are set out in full in the new ss.194A-L of the 1995 Act, and the finality of interlocutors of the High Court is expressly subject to the powers of the SCCRC. The Commission may refer a case to the High Court if they believe both that a miscarriage of justice may have occurred, and that it is in the interests of justice that a referral may be made.

In practice, many such referrals are not made until many years **6–04** after the original conviction, particularly when detailed investigation requires to be undertaken into alleged new lines of evidence. For example, in *Campbell and Steel v HM Advocate*, 2004 SLT 397, the High Court's final determination quashing the appellants' convictions for multiple murder by fireraising was issued in April 2004, the appellants having been convicted in October 1984. While the appellants in that case had been fortunate enough to have spent a proportion of that period at liberty before their convictions were quashed, the appellants in *Allison and Johnston v HM Advocate* (High Court, HCJAC30, March 17, 2006, presently unreported) had spent the full ten years since their convictions for murder in custody, before being released directly from closed conditions. While persons acquitted in this manner do of course retain certain rights in respect of obtaining recompense through the civil courts, the lack of structured support on release for those acquitted after many years in custody remains a concern.

TEMPORARY RELEASE

6–05 There are a number of situations in which prisoners are permitted to be outside the prison itself while serving their sentences. The most restrictive of these is Special Escorted Leave (SEL), which is governed by r.111. Such leave means leave of absence from the prison of a prisoner for the purpose of being escorted to their home or other approved place for a visit not exceeding two hours, excluding travelling time.

The prisoner may apply for inclusion on the SEL scheme, and on his application, the governor may grant special escorted leave if he or she is of the opinion that, having regard to the relevant criteria applicable to the granting of such leave and to any operational requirements, it is appropriate to do so.

To qualify for admission onto the SEL scheme, a prisoner must be either a life prisoner or serving a sentence for a term of more than one year, have been for at least three months prior to commencement on the scheme assigned low supervision level, and if serving a sentence for a term of more than one year, have served at least one third of his or her sentence. In practice, prisoners do not receive SELs until they have progressed to a National Top-End facility, for which the holding of a low supervision level is a prerequisite. Generally, a prisoner requires to spend eight weeks in top-end conditions demonstrating his suitability for outside leaves before he or she takes their first SEL, although this period may be reduced in exceptional circumstances. Where a prisoner has been downgraded, a further period of acclimatisation and good behaviour (normally passing a drug test is required) is expected before he may resume escorted leaves.

6–06 In terms of r.111(4), Scottish Ministers may specify by direction the prisons, categories of prisons, or parts of prisons to which this rule applies, the manner in which the governor shall consider an application for special escorted leave, the criteria about which the governor must be satisfied before he or she may grant such leave, the conditions which may be imposed in relation to any approval of such an application, and the timing and duration of special escorted leave and the frequency with which it may be granted to an eligible prisoner. In general, a prisoner will take no more than six SELs per year, and it is only in very unusual circumstances that two such leaves will be authorized within a month of each other.

There are similar provisions in r.112 to cover the discretionary granting of escorted day absences from prison, for a period not exceeding one day, to enable a prisoner to visit a near relative who, it appears to the governor, is dangerously ill, to attend the funeral of a near relative, or to attend at any place for any other reason where the governor is of the view there are exceptional circumstances.

The granting of escorted day absences must follow the written application of a prisoner, but the governor retains an unfettered discretion whether to grant such leave or not. Before granting permission for such leave, and bearing in mind operational requirements within the establishment before deciding whether to grant leave or not, the governor must be satisfied that the purpose of the application is genuine and appropriate.

Where the governor grants escorted day absence, the prisoner **6–07** concerned must be escorted by an officer or officers throughout his whole period of absence from the prison.

Rule 112(4) authorises the Scottish Ministers to specify in a direction—

"(a) the criteria about which the Governor must be satisfied before granting leave of absence for the purpose specified in paragraph (1)(a);

(b) the persons who are to be treated as near relatives of the prisoner; and

(c) the proceedings, services or ceremonies which a prisoner may attend for the purpose specified in paragraph (1) (b)."

WORK PLACEMENTS

Rule 84 provides that the governor shall provide a fairly wide and **6–08** varied range of work for prisoners, which, so far as reasonably practicable, takes into account the interests and need of prisoners to obtain skills and experience which will be of use to them after their release, and the operational requirements of the prison. Such work may include vocational training, work placements outside the prison, and voluntary work outside the prison. It goes without saying that permitting a prisoner to carry on unsupervised work outside the prison itself is a very important step in the prisoner's progression, and should only be granted to those whose behaviour indicates that they will not abuse such a trusted privilege.

Permission to allow a long-term prisoner access to the community on work placement is dependent upon the prisoner attaining and retaining his low supervision status, and remaining free from misconduct reports. It is manifestly a privilege only granted to those who are assessed as presenting a low risk to the public, and Scottish Ministers therefore take an active role in considering the case of any prisoner who is proposed by local prison staff for consideration of an outside placement. The issuing of a First Grant of Temporary

Release, allowing access to the community on an outside work placement is a vitally important step in the progression of a life sentence prisoner. As current sentence planning guidelines propose that life prisoners should be on outside placement for a full year without adverse incident before progression to the Open Estate, its importance is obvious.

Each prison that sends prisoners out into the community will have a number of dedicated placement managers on their staff. Once local management consider that a prisoner is ready for onward progression (in general, a year's successful completion of Special Escorted Leaves and absence of any evidence of drug misuse will be expected), an application will be sent to the Justice Minister. This is submitted in writing, and sets out in detail why staff consider the prisoner suitable. The grant of temporary release remains entirely at the discretion of the Minister. In general, it will be at least four to six weeks before the Ministerial decision is returned.

Good behaviour in custody is of course expected during this period. Rule 84(3) provides that Ministers may, in relation to such work placements, specify by direction the groups or categories of prisoners who may be allowed to undertake such work, the circumstances in which such work may be provided to any eligible group or category of prisoners, and the conditions which are to apply to any prisoner or group of prisoners undertaking work outside the prison. In practice, outside work placements are most commonly granted to life sentence prisoners who have attained low supervision status, have successfully completed six SELs, have provided two consecutive negative drug tests, and where there are no apparent concerns arising from the nature of the index offence. Not surprisingly, there are a number of placements where contact with the public is a requirement of the placement, where sex offenders are not considered suitable.

In general, where the placement is work-based, such as a shop, rather than a college placement, the prisoner will start by attending one day per week and then, if his behaviour merits it, this will increase to three and then five days per week. Any breach of temporary licence conditions, any specific concern reported by the placement supervisor, or any internal breach of prison discipline resulting in an adverse finding in the Orderly Room may result in his being removed from the placement.

HOME LEAVES

The next stage in progression towards release for long term pris- **6–09** oners holding low supervision status is by way of home leaves. These are only available at present from the two establishments forming the Open Estate, namely Castle Huntly and Noranside, although in very exceptional circumstances prisoners whose health precludes transfer to open conditions have been permitted to take home leaves from top-end conditions. It should be noted that such permission is granted less than once per year on average, and requires the existence of compelling medical reasons. When a prisoner progresses to the open estate, there is generally a waiting period of some four weeks before he or she commences taking home leaves, again this period being designed to ensure, so far as possible, that the prisoner is ready to commence taking overnight leaves in the community.

Unless a low supervision prisoner is disqualified in terms of r.145 from being considered for temporary release by virtue of being either an appellant, subject to proceedings under the Extradition Act 2003, in the opinion of a medical officer, suffering from mental disorder, or in the opinion of a medical officer, otherwise unfit, r.140 provides that he or she may be considered for "short leaves" meaning temporary release for the purpose of enabling the prisoner to visit his or her home or other approved place for a period not exceeding seven nights excluding travelling time, and "winter and summer leave", meaning temporary release for the purpose of enabling the prisoner to visit his or her home or other approved place for a period of up to five nights, excluding travelling time, during the winter or summer. Customarily, the winter leave is always taken at Christmas. Prisoners must apply to the governor for such leave. In terms of r.140(2), the granting of such leave is discretionary, with the governor requiring to be of the opinion that it is appropriate to do so. In practice, unless misconduct in custody is of a nature that would demonstrate breach of trust (including failing a mandatory drug test), or there is no suitable address available after enquiry into the suitability of any proposed address for home leave purposes has been carried out by the appropriate local authority social work department, such requests are granted.

In addition to the regular short leaves and winter and summer leaves, a low supervision prisoner serving a sentence of imprisonment for a term of four years or more, or a life prisoner, whose release date is within six weeks of its commencement, may be granted a "pre-release leave", in terms of r.141. The 2006 Rules state that the prisoner must not be disqualified from consideration by virtue of the provisions of r.146(1), although as this rule specifically applies to recall by Ministers of those who have breached licence conditions, I presume that this is in fact an error, and that the disqualification in question is that specified in r.145 as detailed above. "Pre-release leave" is defined as "temporary release of an eligible prisoner to enable the prisoner to visit his or her home or other approved place for a period not exceeding three days and three nights for the purpose of assisting in the prisoner's preparation for release".

6–10   Again, in terms of r.141(2) the governor may grant the prisoner pre-release leave if he or she is of the opinion that, having regard to the relevant criteria applicable to the granting of such leave, it is appropriate to do so.

In addition to these provisions, r.142 provides that an eligible prisoner, who is not an untried or civil prisoner, and not subject to disqualification under r.145, may apply for "unescorted day release", meaning the temporary release of an eligible prisoner for a period not exceeding one day, including travelling time, who is, for the time being, assigned low supervision level for the purposes of enabling the prisoner, in preparation for eventual release:

> "(a) to develop further, or to re-establish, links with his or her family or community; or
> (b) to develop educational or employment opportunities."

This therefore applies to convicted prisoners, regardless of the length of sentence they are serving, and remains at the governor's discretion.

COMPASSIONATE RELEASE

6–11   In terms of s.3 of the 1993 Act, Ministers may at any time, if satisfied that there are compassionate grounds (which are not specified in the Act) justifying the release of a person serving a sentence of imprisonment, release him on licence. Where the prisoner is a long-term prisoner or a life prisoner, the Ministers must, in terms of s.3(2) consult the parole board unless the circumstances are such as to render consultation impracticable. Any release under this provision is expressly stated as not constituting "release" for the purpose of a supervised release order. It is not proposed that this system will change, in terms of the 2006 Bill.

Section 11(3)(a) of the Act provides that, where a short-term prisoner is released on licence in respect of these provisions, then that licence remains in force until the date on which, were it not for his release, he would have been released in terms of s.1(1), namely at the one-half point of his sentence.

In certain limited circumstances, a low supervision prisoner, but not a prisoner holding a higher supervision category, may, in terms of r.143, request an "unescorted day release" meaning the temporary release for a period not exceeding one day, excluding travelling time, of an eligible prisoner who is, for the time being, assigned low supervision level for the purpose of enabling the prisoner to visit any relative who it appears to the governor is dangerously ill, to attend the funeral of a near relative, to visit a parent who is either too old or too ill to travel to the prison, or to attend at any place for any other reason where the governor is of the opinion that the circumstances warrant it. Once again the exclusions in respect of untried prisoners, civil prisoners, and those disqualified in terms of r.145 apply.

RELEASE ON HOME DETENTION CURFEW

With effect from July 3, 2006, the 1993 Act provisions on the release **6–12** of both short-term and long-term prisoners have been substantially altered by the provisions of s.15 of the Management of Offenders (Scotland) Act 2005, which has inserted five new sections into the Act. Four of these sections govern the criteria by which prisoners may be released subject to curfew conditions. In terms of these new provisions, Ministers have the power to release certain offenders on licence at a date earlier than that on which they would have been returned to the community, subject to certain statutory requirements being met.

The new s.3AA of the 1993 Act provides that, subject to certain specified requirements, the Scottish Ministers may release on licence:

(a) a short-term prisoner serving a sentence of imprisonment for a term of three months or more; or
(b) a long-term prisoner whose release on having served one-half of his sentence has been recommended by the Parole Board.

However, such release cannot be granted until the prisoner has served whichever is the greater of one quarter of his sentence and four weeks of his sentence.

While release in terms of s.3AA may be directed in terms of very **6–13** short sentences, subs.(3) specifically provides that the power to direct release in terms of the Act "is to be exercised only during that period of 121 days which ends on the day 14 days before that on which the prisoner will have served one half of his sentence." The arithmetic is not necessarily straightforward, but the effect of this provision is, for example, that a prisoner serving two years shall not be eligible for consideration of release under these provisions until he has served eight months, while a prisoner serving three years shall not be considered for release under these provisions until he has served fourteen months. Subsection (6) specifically provides that Ministers may, by order, amend the time periods specified in the section or the categories of prisoner ineligible for consideration for such release, as detailed in subs.(5).

Section 3AA(4) specifically provides that "In exercising the power conferred by subsection (1) above, the Scottish Ministers must have regard to considerations of:

(a) protecting the public at large;
(b) preventing re-offending by the prisoner; and
(c) securing the successful re-integration of the prisoner into the community."

With the greatest of respect to those who drafted the legislation, this does appear to be somewhat of a statement of the obvious. It might be considered a little unusual for any government seeking the approval of the electorate, to enact legislation directing release of an offender into the community earlier than would otherwise be the case, without having expressly considered the effect of their policy upon public protection.

6–14   Another pragmatic consideration also seems to arise here, particularly in terms of short-term sentences imposed on summary complaint. Given that s.204 of the 1995 Act obliges sentencers not to impose a first sentence of imprisonment unless satisfied that no other means of dealing with the offender is appropriate, the court must have rejected the possibility of imposing a Restriction of Liberty Order before passing a sentence of imprisonment. If such an offender is to be considered an acceptable risk to return to the community after serving one quarter of their sentence, subject to curfew conditions, can it truly be said that the imposition of a prison sentence was necessary and in the public interest? Given that close to 50 per cent of all offenders sent to prison return there within two years, and given the disruption to family life and employment that can be occasioned even by a short sentence, should persons whose level of risk is acceptable for release after a quarter of a summary sentence be sent to prison at all, and if so, what is the purpose of their imprisonment? It has already been observed that most offence-focussed coursework is conducted over periods of several weeks, and such courses are customarily run perhaps two or three times per year, once there are sufficient prisoners available and suitable to undertake them. Where a prisoner is sentenced to six months or less, at present the chances of his being able to undertake any meaningful educational programme or course are somewhat minimal, and there is little evidence that such sentences operate in any rehabilitative manner, nor is there any solid evidence that short sentences act as a particular deterrent.

Release in terms of the statute is specifically precluded in respect of those serving extended sentences imposed under s.210A of the 1995 Act or supervised release orders made under s.209 of that Act (again, given that such sentences specifically include a requirement for additional supervision beyond that which would normally be imposed, this is hardly surprising), prisoners subject to a hospital direction imposed under s.59A of the 1995 Act or a transfer for treatment direction made under s.136(2) of the Mental Health (Care and Treatment) (Scotland) Act 2003 (asp 13), prisoners subject to the notification requirements of Pt 2 of the Sexual Offences Act 2003, or where the prisoner is liable to removal from the United Kingdom under the provisions of s.9 of the Act (which has been amended by substituting the word "entrant" for "immigrant", and inserting reference to s.10 of the Immigration and Asylum Act 1999).

In addition, there are provisions precluding recalled prisoners (the circumstances in which such recall may take place are discussed in a later chapter) from release in terms of this section. Where a prisoner has been released on licence under either the 1993 Act or the 1989 Act, but has been recalled to prison other than by virtue of s.17A(1)(b) of this Act (recall for breach of home detention, discussed later in this chapter), or before the date on which he would, but for his release, have served his sentence in full, has received a further sentence of imprisonment, or he has been released (whether or not on licence) during the currency of his sentence but has been returned to custody under s.16(2) or (4) of this Act (reimposition by the court of the "unexpired portion" of a previous sentence following a subsequent conviction), he may not be considered for early release in terms of s.3AA.

The provisions also do not apply to fine defaulters and persons **6–15** imprisoned for contempt of court (s.3AA(6)).

When Ministers grant a licence in terms of the section, such licence does not remain in force throughout the currency of the prisoner's sentence. Instead, it remains in force (unless revoked) until the date on which the released person would, but for his release under the section, fall to be released under s.1 of the 1993 Act. Thus, where the prisoner is a long-term prisoner recommended for parole at the one half-point of his sentence, and the parole board's recommendation is made four months or less before his Parole Qualifying Date (PQD), Ministers may release him under this section on licence up until the date on which he would have been granted parole. On his PQD, the curfew imposed in terms of the Ministers' licence comes to an end, s.1 of the 1993 Act takes over, and his release becomes subject to the licence conditions proposed by the parole board. In the case of a short-term prisoner liable to unconditional release at the halfway point of his sentence, the curfew requirement must therefore come to an end on that date on which he would otherwise have been released unconditionally.

Licence conditions imposed in terms of s.3AA rather than s.12 of the 1993 Act may now, in terms of the new s.12(2A) include a condition requiring that the person subject to it:

"(a) shall be under the supervision of a relevant officer of such local authority, or of an officer of a local probation board appointed for or assigned to such local justice area, as may be specified in the licence; and

(b) shall comply with such requirements as that officer may specify for the purposes of the supervision". Both these conditions remain a mandatory requirement of any long-term parole or non-parole licence imposed under Section 12."

6–16   Until the coming into force of the 2005 Act, Ministers' power to insert, vary or cancel a condition in a long-term prisoner's licence was restricted by s.12 of the 1993 Act. Such a condition could not be inserted, varied or cancelled unless it was in accordance with the recommendations of the parole board or was made after consultation with the Board (which included consultation with the board about the general implementation of certain proposals). Section 12(4A) now provides that the requirement for consultation, "does not apply in relation to a condition in a licence granted under s.3AA of this Act; but in exercising their powers under this section in relation to a long-term prisoner released on such a licence the Scottish Ministers must have regard to any recommendations which the parole board made for the purposes of section 1(3) of this Act as to conditions to be included on release." This does present as making the imposition of licence conditions in these circumstances a political, rather than a quasi-judicial one, and it remains to be seen what view the courts will take of the inevitable challenges that will follow the imposition of such conditions by Ministers.

Section 12AA governs conditions for persons released on licence under the new provisions. Licence conditions must include, in addition to any conditions considered necessary for the protection of the public in terms of s.12(a) the standard conditions (to be discussed in detail in Chapter 7); and (b) a curfew condition complying with s.12AB of this Act. "Standard Conditions" are defined as such conditions as may be prescribed as such by Ministers, which may be varied in respect of different classes of prisoner.

Section 3AA(4) of the Act (the obligation on Ministers to consider public protection, prevention of reoffending, and reintegration) applies in relation to the prescription of licence conditions, and to the specification, variation or cancellation of additional conditions in the same way as it applies in relation to the exercise of the power conferred by subs.(1) of that section (power to direct release).

Curfew conditions themselves are defined in, and governed by, **6–17** s.12AB, which provides that a curfew condition is a condition which:

"(a) requires the released person to remain, for periods for the time being specified in the condition, at a place for the time being so specified; and

(b) may require him not to be in a place, or class of place, so specified at a time or during a period so specified."

The curfew condition as detailed above may specify different places, or different periods, for different days but the minimum period in respect of which a condition such as is mentioned in paragraph (a) above is specified as being nine hours in any one day (excluding for this purpose the first and last days of the period for which the condition is in force). In practice, the bulk of curfews currently imposed in terms of Restriction of Liberty Orders imposed under s.245A of the 1995 Act are for 12 hours per day. Generally, the offender requires to remain within his home (if he or she is not the owner or tenant, then the consent of the householder is required) throughout the prescribed hours for every day of the set period. Obviously, the temptation to stray when subject to curfew is greater than that when an offender is in prison, particularly when past offending has occurred in situations of domestic stress, and it remains to be seen how this condition will operate in the real world. There is, however, some evidence from England that the majority of persons subjected to tagging do cooperate with such orders.

The power specified in para.(b) operates to preclude a perpetrator of domestic violence from returning to the home or workplace of an ex-partner, or a person convicted of racial abuse of a shopkeeper from returning to the shop. However, if the offender's behaviour was so flagrant as to make the court conclude that only a custodial sentence was appropriate, it might be considered a little surprising were Ministers to conclude, within a relatively short time, that such offender *both* presented an acceptable risk, suitable for release subject to Home Detention Curfew, *and* that such licence conditions as were to be imposed would require him to avoid certain specified places. Again, it remains to be seen how this will work in practice.

6–18 The arrangements for the installation and monitoring of remote monitoring devices, and of specification of which devices are approved by Ministers for the purpose of such monitoring found in s.245C of the 1995 Act also apply in relation to the imposition of, and compliance with, a curfew condition specified in terms of s.12AB(1).

Subsection 4 states that a curfew condition is to be monitored remotely and the Ministers must designate in the licence the name of a person who is to be responsible for the remote monitoring and must, as soon as practicable after they do so, send that person a copy of the condition together with such information as they consider requisite to the fulfilment of the responsibility. Such person will almost invariably be an appropriately qualified Criminal Justice Social Worker, employed within the appropriate team for the released prisoner's designated release area. The designated person's responsibility commences on their receipt of the copy licence including the curfew and remote monitoring conditions, but is suspended during any period in which the curfew condition is suspended and ends whenever the licence is revoked or otherwise ceases to be in force.

Section 12AB(6) provides that Ministers may from time to time designate another person to replace the person designated under subs.(4) above (or last designated under this subsection) to be responsible for the remote monitoring, and on such substitution taking place the new designated person assumes all the supervision responsibilities of the previous person. If a designation under subs.(6) above is made, the Ministers must, in so far as practicable, notify the person replaced accordingly.

6–19 Prisoners released in terms of s.3AA may be recalled to custody in certain circumstances, while subject to HDC conditions. The circumstances in which such recall may take place are found in the new s.17A of the 1993 Act, which provides that, where it appears to Ministers that a prisoner released on licence under s.3AA has failed to comply with any condition included in his licence, or his whereabouts can no longer be monitored remotely at the place for the time being specified in the curfew condition included in the licence, they may revoke the licence and recall the person to prison. Often the prisoner will have left his address, and his whereabouts may be unknown. In terms of s.17A(6):

"On the revocation under this section of a person's licence, he shall be liable to be detained in pursuance of his sentence and, if at large, shall be deemed to be unlawfully at large."

As the power of recall is given by statute only to Ministers, the requirements of Art.6.1 of the ECHR require that any recalled prisoner must be entitled to a fair hearing before an independent and impartial tribunal established by law. Therefore, any person whose licence is revoked for any of the above reasons, has the right, under s.17A(2), to be informed, on his return to prison, of the reasons for the revocation and of his right under para.(b) to make representations in writing with respect to the revocation to the Scottish Ministers.

Where the prisoner elects to avail himself of his right to make representations, he completes a pre-printed form within the prison, and submits it to Ministers, who must then, in terms of s.17A(3), refer his case to the parole board.

Section 17A(4) provides that "after considering the case the **6–20** Parole Board may direct, or decline to direct, the Scottish Ministers to cancel the revocation." Further, in terms of Section 17A (5):

"Where the revocation of a person's licence is cancelled by virtue of subsection (4) above, the person is to be treated for the purposes of section 3AA of this Act as if he had not been recalled to prison under this section."

While in other areas in which it operates, the statutory duty of the Parole Board is to assess a prisoner's level of risk, and to direct release where it is satisfied that the offender's level of risk is manageable within the community, it is clear that, in exercising its duties under s.17A, it has a rather different function, namely acting purely as an appellate body where a prisoner elects to challenge their recall. Where the circumstances of an alleged breach of HDC conditions are disputed, then the Board may convene a hearing as soon as possible in order to determine the outstanding issues. While it was proposed that, wherever possible, such hearings take place within seven days of the prisoner's recall, in the relatively small number of such cases to come before the Board (fewer than 20 have been heard as at the time of going to press) to date, periods of four weeks have not been uncommon before appeals have been determined. At present, appeals against recall are dealt with by way of a paper review by a quorum of the Board, whose function is not to determine the recalled prisoner's level of risk, but merely to "consider" the case, and direct Ministers to cancel the revocation of licence or not. Rule 14(1) of the Parole Board (Scotland) Rules 2001 dictates that the powers of the Board shall be exercised by a quorum of three members, and at present appeals against revocations of HDC are considered by three members, one of whom must be qualified to chair Tribunals.

Where the breach of HDC is denied, then the Board will firstly have to establish whether the alleged breach is proven. At present this is done by consideration of papers submitted from the receiving prison, which include details from the monitoring body of the alleged breach, together with the prisoner's explanation. Oral hearings are of course competent where any factual dispute cannot be determined by way of paper review, although the timescales involved are likely to make these fairly rare. It is proposed that, in future, certain parts of the work of the Parole Board may be undertaken by way of videoconferencing, and it may be that oral hearings in such appeals would be dealt with in this manner.

6–21   It further seems, from the terms of s.17A, that where a breach of HDC is admitted, the Board may not direct re-release even if, having regard to the types of risk factors with which it deals regularly, it is satisfied that the offender presents an acceptable risk. In practice, in a great many cases, the period between recall to custody and the prisoner's liberation date will be very short indeed, the facts in dispute will be in very narrow compass, and a great many recalled prisoners may elect not to request a hearing. The very small number of such cases referred to the Parole Board in the first eight months of the scheme seems to indicate that the right of appeal may be exercised rarely.

RELEASE ON LICENCE OF SEX OFFENDERS

6–22   As stated in Chapter Two, with effect from January 12, 2006, the Management of Offenders (Scotland) Act 2005 inserted a new s.1AA into the 1993 Act, providing that sexual offenders serving short-term sentences of six months and above shall be liable to licence conditions, and thus eligible for consideration of recall, during the currency of their period in the community. Release must be directed at the one-half point of the sentence.

Where the offender is, by virtue of the conviction in respect of which their sentence was imposed, subject to the notification requirements of Pt 2 of the Sexual Offences Act 2003 then release on licence is now mandatory, based upon the date of conviction, not upon the date of the offence, in terms of s.1AA (3). This section does not apply to any prisoner who had already been released in terms of the 1993 Act before the commencement date of these provisions. "Release" in this case means physical release from prison — where a prisoner has completed his first sentence, and is still serving a consecutive sentence, the "single-terming" provisions of s.27(5) come into force, and he falls within the ambit of the new provisions (s.1AA(5)).

The recall provisions of s.17 of the 1993 Act expressly apply to all prisoners released under this section, and s.1AA(6) states that:

> "(6) Where a prisoner is released on licence under this section, the licence (unless revoked) remains in force until the entire period specified in his sentence (reckoned from the commencement of the sentence) has elapsed".

This is, however, subject to the provisions of subss.(7) and (8). **6–23** Where the prisoner is serving two or more sentences, which, in terms of s.27(5) fall to be treated as a single term, his licence (unless revoked) remains in force until the relevant period (reckoned from the commencement of the single term) has elapsed.

The "relevant period" mentioned above is defined by subs.(8) as:

> "(a) the single term after deduction of half the number of days (if any) by which that term exceeds what it would be were there disregarded in determining it such terms (if any) as are imposed for a conviction other than one by virtue of which the prisoner is subject to the notification requirements mentioned in subsection (2)(b) above; or
>
> (b) if to disregard such terms as are so imposed would have the consequence—
>
> > (i) that there would not remain two or more terms to treat as a single term; or
> >
> > (ii) that though two or more terms would remain they would no longer be consecutive or wholly or partly concurrent, the single term after deduction of half the number of days (if any) by which that term exceeds the term imposed for the conviction, or as the case may be the terms imposed for the convictions, by virtue of which the prisoner is subject to those requirements."

This provision is, to put it mildly, not instantly comprehensible, but it appears to be designed to cover the situation where an offender receives consecutive sentences for sexual and non-sexual offences. Thus, where an offender receives sentences totalling two years for non-sexual offences, and a consecutive twelve month sentence for a notifiable sex offence, he is due for release after serving eighteen months in custody. It appears that the period during which he would be on licence would be six months. Where an offender receives a two year sentence for a sexual offence, and consecutive sentences of twelve months, he would likewise be due for release after eighteen months, but his period on supervision would be one of twelve months.

UNCONDITIONAL RELEASE OF SHORT-TERM PRISONERS

6–24 The law, as contained in s.1(1) of the 1993 Act has already been discussed in Chapter Two. Two particular recent developments have combined to increase political and public unease at the mandatory nature of the unconditional release provisions. As has been discussed previously, since 2001 the practice of governors awarding additional days by way of loss of remission had fallen into disuse, and the power to award a punishment of loss of remission does not appear in the 2006 Rules.

In addition, the statutory authority in s.196 of the 1995 Act now given to the practice of awarding discounts to those who plead guilty means that many, if not most, offenders tendering please by s.76 procedure will automatically receive a discount of between one-third and one-quarter of the "gross" sentence. Thus, when a sentencer considers the appropriate sentence to be one of five years, but the offender has tendered an early plea, the sentence is likely to be of the order of three years four months. Thus, instead of potentially serving forty months in custody, and being at risk of recall to custody to serve the entire balance of the sentence if he fails to cooperate with the supervision requirements of his licence, the offender is required to serve twenty months in prison, then is released unconditionally, and can only be returned to custody in the event of being convicted of another offence punishable by imprisonment during the period between his liberation date and his sentence end date, and only if the court so orders.

The cumulative effect of these provisions does tend to produce results that sometimes appear anomalous, and arguably contrary to the public interest. There is no incentive for the drug addict to seek help to address his addiction in custody, as he will be unconditionally released on the same date whether he is or is not drug free. A released prisoner actively seeking employment has no statutory right to engage with an agency experienced in job search advice for offenders. Supported accommodation may be appropriate, but not available on release. In effect, for prisoners serving short-term sentences, which manifestly will include a number of persons convicted on indictment for serious offences, assessment of their level of risk plays no part in determining their liberation date, and even those considered an unacceptable risk spent, at the very least, a few days or weeks in the community before being recalled, sometimes reoffending almost immediately upon release.

The position of release of long-term prisoners was also con- **6–25** troversial. The public, being generally unaware of the thinking behind release on licence, the existence of licence conditions, and of the power of recall, could not understand why someone sentenced to six years was returned to the community after four, and in some situations prisoners were being released who clearly presented an unacceptable risk in terms of reoffending, and were being returned to custody within a matters of weeks of chaotic behaviour in the community. The practical basis upon which such decisions are reached will be discussed in the next chapter.

It was therefore little surprise when the Scottish Executive commenced a consultation exercise in 2005, designed to devise a new set of provisions to govern the release and post-custody management of offenders, and with the express intention of devising a sentencing scheme that would be easier for the public to understand. The Sentencing Commission for Scotland, under the Chairmanship of Lord Macfadyen, published their report entitled "Early release From Prison and Supervision of Prisoners on Their Release" in January 2006, and their recommendations formed the basis for the Scottish Executive's policy document "Release and Post Custody Management of Offenders", published in June 2006. As sentencing practice falls outwith the ambit of this book, and as the Bill has not, at the time of writing, been published, and is not expected to become law until some time in 2007, I do not propose to describe the new proposals in detail. The proposals are, however, now designed to secure "end to end sentence management", based throughout on the principles of risk assessment, and once in force will alter significantly the structure of most Scottish prison sentences.

It is now proposed that sentence management will apply to all sentences of fourteen days and over, with sentences divided, at the point of imposition, into a custody part of a *minimum* of 50 per cent of the total sentence, during which offenders will be subject to continuous review, and a community part. This review will include an element of risk assessment, and the parole board will have the power, on referral from Ministers with a recommendation for continued detention, to direct that the offender remains in custody. Once the custodial part has been served, every offender will be on licence for the community part of their sentence, and will be subject to at least basic conditions of supervision and an obligation to be of good behaviour and keep the peace and therefore subject to recall.

The court will have the power to state that the minimum custodial part will be a period in excess of 50 per cent.

6–26   While this system may have its attractions in respect of offenders receiving their first short custodial sentences (although the practice of imposing short sentences on virtual first offenders on summary complaint has not always met with approval in the High Court (e.g. *McCulloch v Friel*, 1993 SCCR 7, *Duff v Stott*, 1999 SCCR 455, *McKenna v PF Glasgow*, September 12, 2002, HCJ 1313/02, unreported) the immediate attraction of a system based upon risk assessment in dealing with the serial offenders, mostly with alcohol and drug problems, who receive sometimes three or four short sentences a year, is not obvious. A significant proportion of the prison population consists of those recently released, who have either remained drug users during their sentence or have reverted to drug use on release. If such an offender pleads guilty on first appearance to, say, theft by shoplifting and receives a four month sentence, under the new proposals the court must specify that the offender serves at least two months, but perhaps longer, in prison. While that period will be long enough for a swift detoxification if so desired, the sentence will not be long enough to enable the prisoner to access specialist drug counselling, nor will the period in the community be one of sufficient length to allow effective use of drug counselling services. Such short sentences operate only to withdraw offenders from the streets, without engaging them in practical rehabilitation. They are often imposed because the court feels that there is no alternative, given the offender's past supervision failures and ongoing difficulties, and there may be little doubt that the offender poses a high risk of reoffending. This is likely to mean that sentences served by short-term prisoners will become longer, requiring the provision of a large number of extra prison spaces at public expense.

6–27   There will of course be many who may safely be released at the halfway stage, subject to a single licence condition to be of good behaviour and keep the peace, but those who practice regularly in the criminal courts are all too aware that the bulk of repeat offenders have particular difficulties and needs that do not lend themselves easily to a "quick fix". It may yet transpire that courts might elect, in such cases, to bring together a number of separate summary complaints for sentence on the same date, thus ensuring that, when a custodial sentence or sentences are imposed, they are of sufficient duration as to make both the custodial and community periods worthwhile in respect of sentence management, risk assessment, and community supervision. Certainly it does not seem an entirely prudent use of resources to engage in a comprehensive risk assessment of an offender serving a first custodial sentence of thirty days, whose supervision on licence will terminate within barely a fortnight of release. In addition, it remains far from clear how the parole board is to be engaged in this process as presently advised. Currently, in determining the level of risk of a determinate sentence prisoner, a quorum of the board is usually furnished with dossiers approximately three months before the prisoner's Parole Qualifying Date. Board members are generally given eleven days to scrutinize the dossier, to allow for any errors or omissions to be identified and attempts made to rectify them, and the minute setting out the board's decision is not ratified until fourteen days after consideration of the case. These time periods cannot realistically apply in respect of prisoners serving sentences measured in terms of days or weeks, and it is unclear what information will be contained in the dossiers of short-term prisoners, or when these will be issued and decided upon.

While the present definitions of "short-term" and "long-term", with an inviolable dividing line coming into force once the sentences imposed pass four years, were arbitrary and increasingly anomalous, the resource implications for the Executive and SPS in carrying out risk assessments of all prisoners serving over fourteen days (a group that will almost inevitably include several fine defaulters) seem incalculable, and it remains at this stage to be seen whether the Scottish Parliament will select the period presently proposed, or whether the risk assessment proposals will only operate in sentences somewhat longer than presently proposed.

The current statutory definitions of "short-term" and "long- **6–28** term" are intended to disappear, along with much of the 1993 Act, when the new sentencing provisions contained in the 2006 Bill become law. However, as they remain in force at the time of writing, their operation as they affect prisoners serving four years and more will be detailed in the next chapter, as will the proposed changes.

CHAPTER 7

PAROLE AND NON-PAROLE LICENCE

THE DEVELOPMENT OF THE PAROLE SYSTEM

7–01 The system of allowing convicted offenders some form of remission of sentence has existed since at least the era of transportation, when a "ticket of leave" could be granted to offenders, under the Royal Prerogative, as a reward for good conduct, allowing them to return early from the Colonies. When imprisonment replaced transportation as the principal form of punishment for serious offenders, release on ticket of leave was replaced by release on licence. That system was replaced in the 1930s by the development of the remission system. Remission was initially introduced as a reward for good behaviour, but evolved in practice into a system under which one third of any determinate sentence was automatically deducted at the outset: a deduction which could only be lost as a result of breaches of prison discipline. Section 20(1) of the 1952 Act provided that rules made under that Act may make provision whereby, in such circumstances as were prescribed by the rules, a person serving a sentence of imprisonment may be granted remission of such part of his sentence as may be so prescribed on the grounds of his "industry and good conduct". Rule 37 of the Prison (Scotland) Rules 1952, and r.35 of the rules governing Young Offenders Institutions provided that the maximum remission that could be granted to a convicted prisoner serving a determinate sentence was one third of the total sentence, with a minimum period of five days to be spent in custody. Remission could therefore apply to all sentences, including those for fine defaults.

In 1968 a system of parole was superimposed on the remission system, by virtue of Part III of the Criminal Justice Act 1967. Under s.60 of the 1967 Act (now repealed by the Criminal Justice Act 1991), a prisoner serving a determinate sentence was eligible for parole after serving one third of the sentence or twelve months, whichever was the longer. Parole was therefore available to all those serving over eighteen months, albeit for very short periods in respect of short sentences — for example, a prisoner serving two years was eligible for parole for the last four months of his sentence.

It may be remembered that, at that time, the maximum sentence that could be imposed in the sheriff court on indictment was two years. Parole was also a method by which prisoners sentenced to indeterminate sentences could be released from custody. Schedule 2 of the Act (also now repealed) set up the parole board, and specified its membership requirements. These are now to be found in Sch.2 of the 1993 Act, and provide that:

"The Parole Board shall include among its members—

(a) a Lord Commissioner of Justiciary;
(b) a registered medical practitioner who is a psychiatrist;
(c) a person appearing to the Secretary of State to have knowledge and experience of the supervision or aftercare of discharged prisoners; and
(d) a person appearing to the Secretary of State to have made a study of the causes of delinquency or the treatment of offenders."

With effect from the coming into force of the Custodial Sentences **7–02** and Weapons (Scotland) Bill, there will also be a statutory duty for the board further to include among its members "a person who the Scottish Ministers consider has knowledge and experience of assessment of the likelihood of offenders causing serious harm to members of the public", and "a person who the Scottish Ministers consider has knowledge and experience of (1) the way in which, and (2) the degree to which, offences perpetrated against members of the public affect those persons". Thus the parole board will in future be obliged to contain at least one member experienced in the risk assessment process, and one member with experience of crime upon its victims.

The system of parole for determinate sentence prisoners operated differently from that which applied to life sentence prisoners. Under s.61 of the 1967 Act, the Secretary of State was empowered to release on licence a prisoner serving an indeterminate sentence, but only if recommended to do so by the parole board, and only after consultation with the Lord Justice-General together with the trial judge, if available. In practice, after approximately four years of every life sentence, the prisoner's case was considered by the Pre-liminary Review Committee, which was an administrative body, comprising a number of members of the parole board, usually including the judicial and psychiatric members of the board. It recommended a date for the first formal review of the case. The Secretary of State then decided the timing of the first review in the light of the Committee's recommendation. At that point the case was considered by the Local Review Committee (LRC), which reported to the Secretary of State. Commonly, life sentence prisoners would be reviewed on a number of occasions before release would be recommended. If the LRC recommended the grant of a provisional release date, and the Secretary of State accepted the recommendation, the Lord Justice-General and the trial judge (if available) would be consulted. If they also considered release appropriate, the case would be referred to the parole board for its recommendation. The Secretary of State would then take the final decision.

This system clearly vested all control in the hands of the Secretary of State, with the board having a purely advisory function. At this time, recommendations for release were customarily in the form of a proposed forward date, to allow the prisoner to progress through conditions of increasing freedom, and usually to the stage of occupying the Training for Freedom Units, since abolished, that were attached to some establishments at the time. An adverse development would be referred to the Secretary of State, who could withdraw the proposed parole date. This system no longer applies to life prisoners since the coming into force of the Convention Rights (Compliance) (Scotland) Act 2001, and the present provisions governing life prisoners will be examined in detail in Chapter Eight.

7–03   Remission for determinate sentence prisoners operated in England and Wales in much the same way as in Scotland, evolving into a system of automatic remission of the final one third of the sentence (increased in 1987 to one half, in relation to prisoners serving sentences of twelve months or less). The legal framework of parole was identical to that in Scotland, being based on the same provisions of the 1967 Act. As in Scotland, prisoners serving determinate sentences were eligible for parole after one third of the sentence or twelve months, whichever was the longer. The system in respect of life prisoners developed in a markedly different manner, as will be seen later.

When the 1952 Act was replaced by the 1989 Act, the provisions governing release on licence were specified in ss.22–29, while post-release supervision was governed by ss.30–32. Schedule 1 contained the provisions as to the membership, terms of office and remuneration of members of the parole board and local review committees. By the time the 1989 Act came into force, the Secretary of State had already appointed a committee under the chairmanship of Lord Kincraig, whose remit was to review the arrangements for the early release of prisoners. Its report, *Parole and Related Issues in Scotland* Cm 598 was issued in 1989, and formed the basis for the Prisoners and Criminal Proceedings (Scotland) Act 1993. Even then, it was recognised that the system of remission was not easily understood by the public, and that the system then in force could give rise to anomalous results. Some who gave evidence suggested that the parole system be abolished altogether, but the committee rejected this, noting that the parole system enabled account to be taken of changes in prisoners' behaviour during their sentence, and that information could become available during the currency of an offender's sentence that would make it reasonable to return that person to the community without increasing risk to the public. The Kincraig Committee recommended that parole should be available to all prisoners serving sentences of five years or more, and that release should be granted at the one-half stage of all shorter sentences, with power of recall if the released prisoner reoffended during the latter half of the sentence. On investigation, it transpired that a very significant percentage of the sentences then being imposed by the High Court (since 1987 the maximum sentence available in the sheriff court had been increased to three years) were of the order of four years, and that was the cut-off point finally selected. The Act came into force in respect of all prisoners sentenced to imprisonment on or after October 1, 1993, with those already serving their sentences as at that date having their eligibility for parole governed by s.22(1) of the 1989 Act. Interestingly, parole licences granted in terms of s.22 were deemed to expire at the two-thirds stage of the sentence in terms of s.22(8).

The Criminal Justice Act 1991 had already reformed the law in England and Wales by the time the 1993 Act reached the statute book. In relation to prisoners serving determinate sentences of four years or more ("long-term prisoners"), the 1991 Act provided, in s.33(2) "As soon as a long-term prisoner has served two-thirds of his sentence, it shall be the duty of the Secretary of State to release him on licence". Section 35(1) provided: "After a long-term prisoner has served one-half of his sentence, the Secretary of State may, if recommended to do so by the Board, release him on licence." Under these provisions, therefore, a long-term prisoner was eligible for release on licence (subject to the recommendation of the parole board) after serving one half of his sentence, and was entitled to be released on licence after serving two thirds of his sentence. Thus, the provisions of the 1993 Act effectively followed the provisions enacted in England two years previously, these following the recommendations of the Carlisle Committee, which had reported to parliament the year before the Kincraig Committee.

The Kincraig Committee also recommended that prisoners be **7–04** granted access both to their dossiers, which were hitherto confidential, and to the precise text of the parole board's decision, which was previously sent to the prison, on the understanding that staff would be encouraged to counsel the prisoner who had been refused parole on the basis of a decision the prisoner could not himself see.

The 1993 Act adopted the majority of the Kincraig Committee's recommendations, apart from selecting four years as the point at which a prisoner was treated as a long-term prisoner, and clearly opened up the parole system to the prisoners themselves, while at the same time (although this does not seem even now to be fully appreciated) ensuring that prisoners remained subject to scrutiny and the sanction of recall throughout the entirety of their sentence.

It should of course be noted that, when the 1993 Act came into force, the final decision on whether to release a long-term determinate sentence prisoner continued to vest in a politician. The Board's functions remained advisory. As originally enacted, s.1(3) read:

> "After a long-term prisoner has served one half of his sentence the Secretary of State may, if recommended to do so by the Parole board under this section, release him on licence".

7–05 Thus, where the board did not recommend release, the prisoner would not be released, and where the board did recommend release, the Secretary of State was under no obligation to accept such a recommendation. The equivalent English provisions had been considered by the Court of Appeal in *Findlay v Secretary of State for the Home Department*, [1985] A.C. 318, in which the court had held that the Secretary of State was entitled to adopt a policy restricting the grant of parole, so long as the policy permitted consideration to be given to each individual case. In practice in Scotland parole was seldom granted at the halfway stage in cases where person had been sentenced to five years or more for offences of violence, drug supplying or sexual offences. The Secretary of State would in practice often agree with the board's recommendations, although in the type of cases specified above, parole was usually granted only where "exceptional circumstances" (which were never defined) existed. Prisoners had, at this stage, no legal entitlement to see the reasons for the board's decision, except when they had been recalled to custody in terms of s.28(3) of the 1989 Act, in which case the statute provided that the offender "shall on his return to prison be informed of the reasons for his recall and of his right to make ... representations [against the decision]".

Quite clearly, the cumulative effect of even the more open and liberal regime that had come into being after October 1993 still meant that a huge number of long-term prisoners still came to their liberation date without knowing why, and on what basis, they had not been considered suitable for parole, and indeed whether such decision had been made by the parole board or by the Secretary of State. Such practices were widely criticized in respect of their non-compliance with Art.5(4) of the European Convention on Human Rights, and of the recent jurisprudence of the European Court, and within a few years it was clear that the advisory function of the parole board and the determinative function of the Secretary of State could not stand. The first change came about in terms of the Prisoners and Criminal Proceedings (Scotland) Act 1993 (Release of Prisoners) Order 1995, which directed that, in respect of prisoners serving less than ten years who were sentenced after October 1, 1993, the word "shall" was substituted for the word "may" in s.1(3), thus providing the board with a directive function for the first time. The coming into force of the Scotland Act 1998, and in particular s.57(2), which provides that:

"A member of the Scottish Executive has no power to make any subordinate legislation, or to do any other act, so far as the legislation or act is incompatible with any of the Convention rights or with Community law"

clearly signaled the end of a regime in which politicians retained control over the length of prison sentences. This was recognised in the very early days of the Scottish Parliament, and thus the 1993 Act was radically altered by the Convention Rights (Compliance) (Scotland) Act 2001, which came into force on October 8, 2001. With some minor exceptions, the current practices of the parole board are those that were created by the 2001 Act.

THE PRACTICES OF THE PAROLE BOARD IN RESPECT OF DETERMINATE SENTENCE AND EXTENDED SENTENCE PRISONERS

Since the coming into force of the 2001 Act and the Parole Board **7–06** (Scotland) Rules 2001, which came into force on the same day, the parole board considers the cases of all children and young persons serving custodial sentences of whatever length (all children sentenced to a period of detention on indictment must be released on licence at the appropriate point of their sentence, on conditions determined by the Board), all long-term determinate sentence prisoners, whatever the length of their sentence (the Minister's right of veto over a board recommendation in favour of parole for those serving ten years or more was finally abolished in 2003, by which time it was virtually unused) and including extended sentence prisoners, excluding only those. who have opted not to be considered for parole (such persons requiring to sign a form or advise an officer that they wish to self-reject from consideration for parole). It further considers all cases where the board has refused parole at first instance and ordered a second review, cases of all determinate sentence prisoners who have self-rejected from consideration for parole and are approaching their statutory release date in terms of s.1 of the 1993 Act, requests to vary the dates of tribunals, and requests to vary specific licence conditions.

The number of cases referred to the board for first consideration of parole has shown a steady increase over the past decade, rising from 537 in 1996 to a peak of 764 in 2005. All these cases are dealt with by way of a review of the prisoner's dossier at one of the board's casework meetings, which take place in Edinburgh 48 times per year. Grounds for recall, re-release and transfer of supervision are also considered at these meetings.

While the quorum of the board is set at three in terms of r.14 of the 2001 Rules, present practice is that six members will sit at a casework meeting, dealing with between 25 and 40 cases on average. Any member of the board with personal knowledge of the prisoner cannot vote on that particular case, or even participate in its discussion. While there are occasional cases where the sentencing judge or sheriff, or the former defence agent or psychiatrist who prepared a report is sitting on the board, the most common reason for a member not to participate is that they interviewed the prisoner. In terms of r.15(3) of the 2001 Rules, the prisoner "shall be entitled to request an interview with the Board before it reaches a decision, and—

(a) where he or she does so; or
(b) where the Board considers it desirable to interview that person or any other person, the chairman of the Board may authorise one or two members of the Board to conduct such an interview and to make a report thereon to the Board."

7–07   While the Rules provide that the prisoner must request an interview, present practice is for the board to offer every prisoner an interview, which they may of course decline. In practice, when cases of life imprisonment for murder were considered by the full Board by paper review at casework meetings (at that time the board met in full session of at least 15 members, 24 times a year), interviews of life prisoners were usually carried out by two members. As all such cases have, since 2001, been heard by Life Prisoner Tribunals at which the prisoner is present and able to give evidence, life sentence prisoners no longer require to be interviewed, and interviews with determinate sentence prisoners are carried out by single members of the board, within the establishment in which the prisoner is situated. The interview report forms part of the dossier considered by the board, and the prisoner is entitled, should he so wish, to have a legal representative present. The interview must be carried out in accordance with the common-law principles of fairness and Art.6 of the ECHR. The prisoner must be advised that any information given to the member, of whatever nature, will be recorded. The interview is not an assessment process, and the board member must not express personal opinions about the prisoner. Where the prisoner is facing outstanding charges, the board's guidance manual indicates that, unless volunteering any information, the prisoner should not be questioned about outstanding charges. The interview, when completed in written form, is added to the dossier considered by the board (in most cases, it will be the most recent document), and the interviewing member takes no part in the discussion of the case.

When an offender receives a determinate sentence or sentences totalling over four years, Ministers will automatically calculate the halfway point of his sentence, his Parole Qualifying Date (PQD), the two-thirds point of the sentence, on which he falls to be released on non-parole licence, still referred to as his Earliest Date of Liberation (EDL), and the Sentence End Date (SED). Preparation of the parole dossier normally commences at least nine months before the PQD, and the dossier will normally be in the hands of the parole board in time to allow it to conclude its deliberations approximately twelve weeks before the PQD. However, it is not unknown for dossiers to be delayed beyond that date due to the non-availability of an essential part of the dossier, sometimes an external report, and sometimes (perhaps more surprisingly) because of the absence of a trial judge's report. Rule 5 of the 2001 Rules obliges Ministers, not later than two weeks after the date of the reference of the case to the board, to send to them and to the person concerned "a dossier containing any information in writing or documents which they consider to be relevant to the case, including, wherever practicable, the information and documents specified in the Schedule to these Rules."

Rule 6 of the 2001 Rules makes specific provision as to Ministers' duties where they consider that any written information or document contains "damaging information" that should not be sent to or disclosed to the prisoner. The two most common examples of this are where evidence of drug involvement, especially allegations of supplying are made, and the evidence is presented in such a way that the prisoner may well identify the source, or where the victim of domestic violence who does not wish her former partner back home discloses certain matters in confidence to a report writer that might be likely to lead to further violence. In these situations, r.6(2) provides that the Scottish Ministers or, as the case may be, the board shall not be required to send a copy of the damaging information to the prisoner, that the board may take such damaging information into account even although it has not been disclosed to the prisoner, but that the Ministers or the board must send the prisoner a written notice informing him or her that certain information which has been sent to or obtained by the board has not been sent to him or her because the Scottish Ministers or, as the case may be, the board considers that the disclosure of that information would be likely to be damaging on one or more of the grounds mentioned in r.6, and giving that person, but only so far as is practicable without prejudicing the purposes for which the information is not disclosed, the substance or gist of the damaging information. Where the decision is made by Ministers, they are obliged to send written notification to the chairman of the parole board.

7–08   Non-disclosure of sensitive information to the board, on the grounds of public protection, proved controversial in the English case of *Regina (Roberts) v Parole Board* [2005] UKHL 45, [2005] 3 WLR 152. The House of Lords, in the particular circumstances of that case, approved the appointment by the board of a specially appointed advocate to whom alone information from the Home Secretary should be disclosed. No similar case has yet arisen in Scotland, and the implications of the *Roberts* case will be discussed, with respect to tribunal cases, in Chapter Eight. In a significant number of cases, this sensitive information will be presented to the Board in the form of intelligence reports, redacted in such a way as to ensure that the source of the adverse intelligence cannot be identified, but the gist of the intelligence is clear, as is its rating. The use of such intelligence has long proved controversial. Until relatively recently, SPS operated a complex and unwieldy system of intelligence rating, in which the quality and reliability of the source was rated as either, A, B C or X, depending on previous assessments of reliability, while the quality of the evidence itself was rated as between 1 and 4, depending on a specific assessment of its reliability. This system therefore provided for sixteen possible assessments of the quality of intelligence, several of which involved such rare combinations of circumstances as to be unknown in practice, and others of which were virtually indistinguishable. Few tears were shed when this system was jettisoned in 2005, to be replaced by a system in which each specific entry is assessed as "Very Reliable", "Reliable", or "Not Reliable". While the Prison Service is, for obvious reasons, unwilling to disclose its intelligence gathering methods, they are stated to be of the same standards as those used nationwide by police forces.

THE PAROLE DOSSIER

The Schedule specifies that the dossier must include: **7–09**

1. A note of the prisoner's full name and date of birth
2. A note of the place where he is detained and of all the other prisons in which he has been detained
3. Details of his sentence or sentences and an indication of the circumstances of the offence or offences
4. A record of his previous convictions and sentences
5. (Tribunal Cases only) A copy of any appeal judgement by the High Court, and copies of the dossiers in connection with any previous referrals of his case since August 4, 1995
6. A copy of any report on the prisoner made while he was subject to a transfer direction under the Mental Health legislation
7. Up to date reports by those involved in supervising, caring for, or counselling the prisoner on his circumstances (including home background) and behaviour and on his or her suitability for release or, as the case may be, re-release on licence.

In current practice, a parole dossier, after specifying the prison- **7–10** er's personal and sentence details, commences with a copy of the indictment on which he was convicted, followed by a report from the sentencing judge (if available). It is mandatory for the judge to submit a report to the board when a prisoner receives a sentence of four years or more, although there is no set format for same, with the result that reports regularly vary in terms of the amount of information provided. Regrettably, where a prisoner receives consecutive sentences of, for example, eighteen months and three years on two separate indictments, and thus falls within the parole system, there is no duty on either sentencer to submit a report to the board. Similarly, when the total sentence imposed in terms of s.210A of the 1995 Act exceeds four years, but the custodial part is a "short-term" sentence, the sentencing judge is not presently obliged to furnish a report. In the overwhelming majority of cases, there is a trial judge's report, and the bulk of these go into detail as to the circumstances of the offence, whether the case was resolved by plea or by a verdict after trial, and what mitigation was adduced at the time.

The dossier next contains a series of staff reports, detailing the prisoner's progression through custody, dates of any changes in supervision status and location, any misconduct reports and the punishments awarded, plus current reports from the hall officers who come into contact with him most regularly. This section should offer some staff overview of his behaviour and progression within the prison system. Naturally, differences of opinion are not unknown, as not all staff members necessarily see the same side of the prisoner, and most of the comments are brief, consisting of a short paragraph. If there are suggestions that a prisoner with no history of drug test failures is involved in the prison drug culture, this should be specified so that the board is aware of it and the prisoner can answer the allegations. In the past some officers were guilty of simply writing "This prisoner tends to associate with Prisoner X and Prisoner Y", and expect parole board members to "join the dots", but it is now clear that any specific allegation should be made in a form in which it can be answered.

Reports from the prison chaplain and medical officer are also produced (in the case of the medical report consent is required), although these seldom impinge upon the issue of risk to the public, and their future usefulness for parole purposes must be somewhat questionable. If the prisoner has a history of mental health difficulties, or if he has spent a part of the sentence transferred to hospital in terms of s.71 of the Mental Health (Scotland) Act 1984, then psychiatric reports covering the period up to his return to prison (if that has taken place — it is not unknown for an offender still to be in hospital on his PQD) should be contained within the dossier.

Social Work Reports

7–11   Often the most crucial parts of the dossier are the two reports prepared by social workers — the Prison-based Social Worker's Report and the Home Background Report. The prison-based social worker should undertake an in-depth assessment of the prisoner's history of offending, substance misuse, whether he has any history of supervision failures within the community, his behaviour in custody, coursework undertaken and whether it was successfully completed, his current attitude to the offence, whether he has insight into its consequences for others, whether he demonstrates relevant victim empathy, his plans for release including his accommodation and employment prospects, and his attitude to any further offence-focussed work that may be required on release.

Based upon this, the report writer should be able to identify factors that are historically proven to increase risk, and those that are historically proven to decrease risk, and, using a recognised risk assessment tool, assess whether the prisoner presents a low, medium or high risk of reoffending. At present, most report writers use the Level of Service Inventory Revised Risk Assessment tool (LSI-R), an actuarially predictive scale in which factors relating to criminal history, education/employment, leisure/recreation, domestic/marital situation, alcohol/drug issues, emotional/personal issues and the offender's attitude to criminal activity are assessed and scored, out of a total possible mark of 54, with higher scores indicating greater risk. The other tool generally used these days is the RA3 Risk of Harm Assessment

The Home Background Report's function is somewhat different. Where the prisoner has indicated that he will be returning to a fixed address, this report will be written by a social worker from the appropriate local authority that will have responsibility for the prisoner's supervision. The writer should have made contact with the occupier of the intended release address, verified that the prisoner is welcome to stay there, and confirm whether the address is suitable. This will involve some assessment of the area itself in terms of its rates of unemployment, drug misuse and criminality, although these factors will not, in themselves, require the board to reach a decision unfavourable to parole. The quality of the accommodation may be an issue, as many prisoners require to return, albeit temporarily, to overcrowded family homes, and there may often be issues relative to the offence, such as the proximity of the address to that of the victim or their family, or in child sexual offence cases, proximity to schools, playparks or places where children congregate. Again, the board will expect these points to be addressed in detail. Secondly, the Home Background Report should provide details of relevant services available within the area. If the prisoner has no viable offer of employment, the availability of employment services should be addressed. Similarly, if there is a history of alcohol of drug misuse, details of local addiction services should be noted. In the case of sex offenders, local programmes designed to reduce reoffending should be identified.

Again, the writer of the Home Background Report should use all this information, combined with the historical factors already mentioned, to carry out their own risk assessment, which not uncommonly differs slightly from that of the prison-based social worker.

7–12 Since 2001, Scotland has had a Criminal Justice Social Work Development Centre, designed to assist in the development and implementation of evidence-based social work practice. It is based within the School of Social and Political Studies in the University of Edinburgh, and is run in partnership with the University of Stirling. National Objectives and Standards for various parts of social work practice, including the provision of throughcare services for released offenders, have been in existence since 1991. These are designed to produce clear objectives and targets for Criminal Justice Social Work staff to achieve in carrying out their duties, and further set out what is expected of an offender who is subject to a period of statutory post-release supervision. The Standards themselves are published by the Scottish Executive, and are now available online on the Scottish Executive Website. The Executive further established an accreditation panel in January 2003, whose function is to determine whether community-based supervision programmes should be accredited. At present, the panel meets to consider accreditation of programmes around three times per year.

Self-representations

7–13　　The Parole Dossier further contains the Prisoner's self-representations. Rule 7 (1) provides:

> "A person shall have the right to submit written representations with respect to his or her case together with any other information in writing or documents which he or she considers to be relevant to his or her case and wishes the Board to take into account, following receipt of the dossier under rule 5(1), any other information sent to him or her by the Scottish Ministers or the Board or any written notice under rule 6(2)."

Any representations a prisoner wishes to make must be sent to the board and the Scottish Ministers within four weeks of the date on which the Ministers or the board sent him the dossier, information or written notice, and, in a case where the person has a right to submit written representations following receipt of a written notice, the representations may include any representations about the non disclosure of any damaging information.

Prisoners are provided with a form on which to submit their representations. The form and content of them are as many and varied as the prisoners themselves, as this is, apart from the interview with a board member, the prisoner's only opportunity under the paper review system, to have his or her own say on whatever matters he or she considers relevant. The prisoner may of course submit other documents such as job offers or letters regarding the progress of a housing application, and these will likewise be placed in the dossier.

Notification of victims

Since the coming into force of the Criminal Justice (Scotland) Act 7–14
2003, victims of certain violent and sexual offences have had the
right to opt into the Victim Notification Scheme. After conviction,
the local Crown Office and Procurator Fiscal Service will contact
the victim (in the case of homicide the victim's family) and advise
them of their right to elect to join the scheme, which remains
entirely voluntary. In terms of s.16, victims are entitled to be
advised of the release, transfer, death, escape or abscond of a
prisoner who has offended against them, but they are not otherwise
involved. There are special provisions where the victim is a child or
an *incapax*, in which situations family members may assume the
rights and duties under the Act.

Where a victim elects to become involved in the scheme, they
have the right to be advised of the date upon which the offender is
eligible for parole and, in terms of s.17 of the Act, they are entitled
to make a written statement, known as a Victim Notification
Statement, which forms apart of the parole dossier. Such statement
will generally set out the victim's comments on the effect that the
offence has had on him and his family, and most victims attempt to
offer advice to the board. Generally the victim's statement (with
any identifying features excised) is inserted in the dossier, although
the provisions of r.6 may be invoked. A victim who has opted into
the scheme in terms of s.16 or s.17 is entitled to receive notification
of the board's decision, any licence conditions imposed (if appropriate), and whether any such conditions specifically relate to
contact between the offender and the victim. For the avoidance of
doubt, it is not necessary for the victim or their family to submit a
Victim Notification Statement to be advised of the decision of the
Board; any person who has requested notification under s.16 will be
advised of the Board's decision.

As stated before, in most cases the final item in the dossier is the
report of the interviewing member, which is accompanied by an
update by the prisoner's personal officer. This is usually completed
less than two weeks before the dossier is sent to board members,
who currently receive the dossiers eleven days before the meeting at
which the case is considered. The date of that meeting is not intimated to the prisoner.

However, in a small but significant minority of cases, an adverse 7–15
development occurs very shortly before the board meets to consider
the case, and this may be intimated to the board as late as the
morning of the meeting. These reports most commonly concern
very recent drug test failures, misbehaviour or breach of licence
conditions on home leaves, and occasionally failure to return from

home leaves. In any case where the interests of fairness require that the prisoner be given the chance to answer the allegations, the board will withdraw the case from that meeting to allow the prisoner time to make representations on the adverse development.

POWERS OF THE BOARD

7–16 The duties of the parole board in exercising their function under s.1 of the 1993 Act to direct release on licence or otherwise are, of necessity, expressed in a very broad manner. The matters to be taken into account are specified in r.8 of the 2001 Rules, which states:

> "In dealing with a case of a person, the Board may take into account any matter which it considers to be relevant, including, but without prejudice to the foregoing generality, any of the following matters:
>
> (a) the nature and circumstances of any offence of which that person has been convicted or found guilty by a court;
>
> (b) that person's conduct since the date of his or her current sentence or sentences;
>
> (c) the risk of that person committing any offence or causing harm to any other person if he or she were to be released on licence, remain on licence or be re released on licence as the case may be; and
>
> (d) what that person intends to do if he or she were to be released on licence, remain on licence or be re released on licence, as the case may be, and the likelihood of that person fulfilling those intentions."

7–17 From that it will be seen that there are no statutory criteria governing the grant or refusal of parole, nor is the system based upon any actuarial point-scoring system. Each case is considered wholly on the members' individual assessments of the prisoner's level of risk, and whether, in their view, he or she presents an acceptable risk to the public. The board must balance the prisoner's interests in regaining his or her liberty against the wider public interest in the prevention of further offending, and must release only those who are felt objectively to present an acceptable risk. It is not necessary for a prisoner to have pled guilty or to accept their guilt before parole can be granted. While those who deny their guilt may decline to engage in offence-focussed coursework, and express certain misgivings over supervision in the community, factors that may militate against the grant of parole, there is no hard and fast practice to state that only those who accept guilt and show remorse should be granted parole.

It therefore follows that denial of commission of the offence is not, in itself, sufficient reason for refusal of parole. It may often be a significant factor, and the Board of course cannot look behind the circumstances of a conviction, but is bound to assume its correctness. The Board must weigh the denial in the balance along with any other factors indicative of increased or decreased risk. For example, where the index offence was committed many years prior to conviction and there is no evidence of further offending in the period between the commission of the offence and eventual conviction, denial in itself may be far from determinative (see *R v Secretary of State for the Home Department, Ex P Lillycrop* [1996] EWHC Admin 281). Also, where an offender who denies guilt has taken steps in custody to learn new skills to enable him to modify behaviour (as was the case in *R v Parole Board and Secretary of State for the Home department, Ex P Oyston*, 2000 WL 191252). These matters were considered in Scotland in the recent, and as yet unreported case of *McBrearty, petitioner*, considered in the Outer House in January 2007.

Contrary to public perception, the board is not merely concerned with "good behaviour" in prison. While an absence of misconduct reports and drug test failures, combined with swift progression to low supervision status and thence to open conditions may seem encouraging, this may merely prove that an experienced inmate is "jail-wise", and knows how to work his way through the prison system. This in itself would not be enough to guarantee early release on parole licence. The board will be looking to see objective evidence of a reduced level of risk. Each individual case is presented at the meeting by a particular member of the board, who will summarise the dossier, note the prisoner's sentence, PQD and EDL, his or her offending history, their progress in custody, their release plans and any other relevant information, combine that information into an assessment of the risk factors, and recommend either for or against parole. All the other members of the board (save the interviewing member) may comment upon the recommendation, and may agree or disagree.

If there is no unanimity, the case proceeds to a vote, in which a simple majority suffices. Should the vote be tied, the chairman or presiding member holds a casting vote. It is obligatory for the board's minute of proceedings to record whether the decision was unanimous or by a majority. These matters are all governed by r.16. While it has recently been proposed by the Home Secretary that in respect of English board cases parole shall only be granted where the board (in England such cases are considered by three members) is unanimous, effectively granting a single member the right of veto, when similar proposals were made by Scottish Ministers, they were discontinued after initial consultation and consideration of the legal and ECHR implications.

7–18   In determining a case when it first comes before them at a case-work meeting, the Board effectively has four options available to it. These are:

1. To allow parole with effect from the earliest date available, namely the halfway point of the sentence.
2. To allow parole, but to grant it from a date between the PQD (halfway point) and the EDL (two-thirds point) — this is known as a "forward date"
3. To decline parole, but order that the case be returned to the Board for an earlier review than would normally be the case.
4. To decline parole and direct that the prisoner remain in custody until his EDL.

1. Granting parole at the halfway stage

7–19   Where board members are of the view that the prisoner presents an acceptable risk in terms of reoffending at the halfway stage of the sentence, then they shall direct that Ministers release him on his PQD, subject to the imposition of the seven standard licence conditions, and any other licence conditions they consider appropriate. He will then be subject to licence and liable to recall for the entire second half of his sentence. In the event that the parolee is a long-term prisoner serving an extended sentence, his licence will of course last from the date of his release on parole until the final expiry of the supervision period specified in terms of s.210A. In addition, the new Home Detention Curfew provisions discussed in Chapter 6 come into effect in terms of s.3AA(b). The reasons for the decision, and the fact that parole is to be granted on the PQD, together with the proposed licence conditions, must all be specified in the board's minute. It should be noted that while it is the board that decides upon whether parole should be granted, and upon what conditions, licences continue to be issued by, and in the name of, the Scottish Ministers. Alleged breaches of licence conditions are therefore also referred, at first instance to the Ministers who formally issued the licence.

As the decision to grant parole is normally made around twelve weeks before the PQD and ratified and issued in writing around ten weeks before, the prisoner has the option to elect for release on

Home Detention Curfew, and subject to the conditions for compliance therewith, for the period between the recommendation for parole being intimated to them and their PQD. At the time of writing it is unclear to what extent prisoners will elect to opt into the new system.

It should be noted that, in the event of any adverse development being reported to the parole board, whether in prison or on HDC, they have the power firstly to suspend the award of parole and then, after investigation and after giving the prisoner the opportunity to make representations on the allegations, if they no longer feel that he presents an acceptable risk, to withdraw the parole date altogether. In that situation they may direct no release until the prisoner's EDL, although it is not unknown for the Board to appoint a further review, or even a forward date, although the latter is extremely rare in practice.

2. Granting parole with a forward date

In some circumstances, the consensus of the board will be that a **7–20** prisoner presents as an acceptable risk for release, provided certain further conditions are satisfied — for example, he completes certain coursework or a college course he is undertaking, or he demonstrates a sustained drug-free period following a failed test, or he is able to resolve a difficulty in respect of his accommodation. In such situations the board may agree to recommend parole to commence on a date some time after his PQD but before his EDL. Such forward dates are normally of the order of one to four months, during which time the board will require him to be of good behaviour and free from reports, as stated above. The date upon which parole is to be granted must be minuted, as must the reasons for granting parole, *and* the reasons why a forward date is appropriate. This is a decision to grant parole, and must therefore be made on the grounds that the offender presents an acceptable risk to the public, provided he complies with the board's requirements. Therefore, the board will impose licence conditions as it sees fit at the time of making the decision.

Whether the prisoner is granted parole on the due date or a forward date, the licence conditions selected for the prisoner must be specified in full in the board's minute, which is sent to him on ratification. On his release, he will be given, and requested to sign, a copy of his release licence, which will specify the precise conditions upon which he is being released, the date of his release, and the date of expiry of his licence. It will also specify that breach of any of the licence conditions may result in his being recalled to custody to serve the whole balance of his sentence.

3. Declining parole but ordering an early review

7–21   Any prisoner serving eight years or more, who has a minimum of 16 months parole available, and who is not granted parole at the halfway stage, is entitled automatically to a further review in one years time. Where a sentence is of shorter duration and parole is not recommended, then the board may simply proceed to direct release on the EDL and impose non-parole licence conditions forthwith. However, there are many prisoners serving six or seven year sentences (and indeed some serving longer sentences) who have, after a difficult start to their sentences, begun to demonstrate an improvement in behaviour and attitude, that may indicate a diminution in their risk. The board may therefore be satisfied that, as at the date of consideration, they present as an unacceptable risk, but that a sustained period of good progress and onward progression might mean that a differently constituted board, presented with positive information at a future date still in advance of the EDL, might take a more positive view.

In such a situation, the board may refuse parole (the reasons for so refusing being duly minuted), but then proceed to specify the reasons for the early review, the progress they expect the prisoner to have made, and any specific additional information they wish to have in the next dossier. An early review means the preparation of a fresh dossier, with up-to-date reports from prison staff, internal and external social work personnel, a second interview by a board member, and additional self-representations. It must be submitted by Ministers to the board for consideration at a casework meeting. As the process of preparing for a review takes six months in virtually every case, early reviews are characteristically recommended for those serving five years and above, due to the impracticalities of further reviews for those serving shorter sentences, whose cases for parole might be considered a matter of weeks before they must be released by law.

4. Declining parole

7–22   There are of course a number of cases where, on consideration of the dossier at the halfway stage of the sentence, the board feels that the prisoner remains an unacceptable risk in terms of reoffending. The prisoner may have a history of supervision failures, may have offended when on licence, may still be involved with drugs, may remain at risk of further sexual offending, or may simply have done little or nothing to plan for release. As stated above, those sentenced to eight years and over who are declined parole at first review are entitled to a second review, but in the cases of those long-term prisoners sentenced to less than eight years, the board may direct that they remain in custody until their EDL, and simply proceed straight to the imposition of licence conditions. Once again, the reasons for the refusal of parole must be minuted, as must the fact of whether the decision was unanimous or by a majority. The licence conditions must be set out in detail in the board's minute.

A prisoner serving a determinate sentence will, in this situation, be on licence and thus liable to recall for the final one-third of their sentence, even, at present, when the board considers them to be an unacceptable risk at that stage, although current proposals to be placed before the Scottish Parliament are designed to address that particular situation.

Where the licensee has been sentenced to an extended sentence in terms of s.210A of the 1995 Act, and the custodial part is four years or more, he remains entitled to release at the two-thirds point of the custodial element of the sentence, whereupon he becomes liable to licence conditions for the entire period until the conclusion of the extension period. Therefore, in practice, supervision periods on licence in the community substantially longer than the period initially spelt in custody will not be uncommon.

On the prisoner's release he will be given a copy of his licence, **7–23** including the specified conditions, under exactly the same conditions as apply to those granted parole. Where someone released on non-parole licence refuses to sign the licence, this is noted on the licence itself. This does not preclude his release, nor does it invalidate the licence conditions themselves.

It is open to a prisoner who is unhappy with either the refusal of parole, or with the conditions imposed upon him, to seek to have the board's decision judicially reviewed. While many applications for Legal Aid are made in this regard, few seem to be granted, and there are very few examples of Scottish Parole Board decisions in respect of determinate sentence prisoners reaching the Court of Session. Two that did recently were *Baker v Parole board for Scotland and the Scottish Ministers* (unreported), 2006 CSOH 31 and *Gallagher v Parole board for Scotland* (unreported), 2005 CSOH 126.

In the *Baker* case, the petitioner had pled guilty to assault to injury and the danger of life, and been sentenced to five years imprisonment. The libel to which he pled guilty specified that he had pulled a dog lead round his partner's neck, and caused her to write a farewell letter to her daughter. He had a history of drug and alcohol abuse in the community, and had provided a positive drug test for heroin in prison. The Board's reason for declining to recommend parole was:

"He has a long history of serious alcohol misuse, and this is his second conviction for domestic violence. He demonstrates little in the way of victim empathy or relapse prevention. On release he will be homeless and he has no immediate prospects of employment. These factors increase the risk that he will revert to alcohol misuse. He therefore presents as an unacceptable risk in terms of re-offending."

7–24   The petitioner sought Judicial Review on the grounds that this was a decision that it was one that no reasonable parole board could have reached. In dismissing the petition, Lord Carloway reviewed the board's minute, including the paragraph above, noted the evidence from the dossier that supported each of the three conclusions in the foregoing paragraph, and observed:

"In summary, the first respondents had ample material upon which to base the decision they took. Indeed, it was perhaps the only reasonable decision open to them in the circumstances."

7–25   On the other hand, in the *Gallagher* case, the prisoner had been sentenced to four years for an offence not specified in the report. He had, shortly before his PQD, been downgraded from open conditions at Noranside to closed conditions for alleged "subversive activities", which were not specified in detail. The board then wrote to the early release liaison officer at Noranside explaining that it had been unable to decide whether the petitioner was a suitable candidate for release on parole without access to additional information. Despite a lengthy exchange of correspondence, intelligence scoring based on the system then in force was not produced to the board, which then, having deferred consideration of the case on a number of occasions, decided the case and issued a decision in the following, somewhat surprising terms:

"This was Mr Gallagher's first prison sentence. Until his downgrading the details of which are unknown he had been the subject of positive prison staff reports. Mr Gallagher had realistic plans for his release and considerable family support and commitment. The Board noted Mr Gallagher's progress but also the concerns of the Scottish Prison Service which had resulted in his downgrading. He, therefore, presents as an unacceptable risk."

7–26   Considering the whole history of the case, Lord Macphail then observed:

"The result, however, appears to be unsatisfactory. Because of the attitude of the Scottish Prison Service, the Board reached their decision in the absence of information which they had identified as essential. They did not know in any detail why the petitioner had been downgraded, but they nevertheless felt obliged to give decisive weight to the "concerns" of the Scottish Prison Service, the grounds for which they were unable to assess for themselves. It is difficult to see how that could be regarded as an acceptable method of reaching a decision as to the petitioner's possible entitlement to parole."

Following this decision, the case was swiftly placed before a board consisting of members who had not participated in the previous decision (and who were not provided with a copy of the above opinion), which reached a decision acceptable to all parties.

No doubt, however, future board minutes will continue to be challenged.

Standard and non-standard licence conditions

The granting of licence conditions is governed by s.22 of the 1989 **7–27** Act. While the formal issuing of the licence remains the function of Ministers, the conditions themselves are for the Board alone to determine. Section 22(7), as amended by the Criminal Justice (Scotland) Act 2003, states — "In a case where the Parole Board has recommended that a person be released on licence, no licence conditions shall be included in the licence, or subsequently inserted, varied or cancelled in it, except in accordance with recommendations of the Board."

There are seven conditions common to all parole licences. These **7–28** are known as the "Standard licence conditions" and are:

1. You shall report forthwith to the officer in charge of the office at [address].
2. You shall be under the supervision of such officer to be nominated for this purpose from time to time by the Director of Social Work of [local authority].
3. You shall comply with such requirements as that officer may specify for the purposes of supervision.
4. You shall keep in touch with your supervising officer in accordance with that officer's instructions.
5. You shall inform your supervising officer if you change your place of residence or gain employment or change or lose your job.
6. You shall be of good behaviour and keep the peace.

7. You shall not travel outside Great Britain without the prior permission of your supervising officer.

All these conditions seem self-explanatory. In terms of Condition 1, a released prisoner is under a duty to attend at the appropriate Social Work Department on his release date to meet his supervising officer, discuss his future needs in the community, and commence the reporting process, which must be undertaken in accordance with National Standards for Social Workers. In the initial stages after release it will be his obligation to be seen, either at the social worker's office or at his home, once a week, with this gradually reducing, depending on the offender's level of cooperation and perceived need for supervision, to fortnightly reporting and then to monthly reporting. It is open to the supervising officer, if he or she is satisfied that no further supervision is necessary, to apply to the board for early termination of supervision, but this is rarely requested in practice and even more rarely granted.

Condition 7 has, on occasions, proved controversial. It precludes travelling to Northern Ireland without permission, due to the differences between the respective legal systems, and the markedly different supervision system that has developed there over the past four decades, but it also means that foreign holidays and the like can only be undertaken by licensees with the express permission of the supervising officer. This has proved a source of grievance to a great many released prisoners, but it must be said that it is difficult to see why. Persons on licence are not free men and women, but rather they have been granted, by parliament, the right to serve the last part of their sentence within the community, *subject to such conditions as are felt necessary for protection of the public*. Once the licence period has expired, they are free to travel anywhere they wish, but when on licence they remain subject to the sanction of recall to serve the balance of their sentence, and it is frankly difficult, if not impossible, to see how a prisoner on licence can properly comply with conditions 3 and 4 as detailed above, whilst on holiday several hundred miles outside the United Kingdom.

Additional licence conditions

7–29   There are numerous situations in which the board will consider that the above seven conditions are insufficient to afford the public an appropriate level of protection. Over the years, a number of non-standard conditions have commonly been inserted into both parole and non-parole licences, and these are discussed below. Of course, the board may, in any case, impose a specific licence condition tailored to the particular circumstances of a case. Additional licence conditions may be mandatory (in which case a form of words including the phrase "as directed by your supervising officer" will be used) or discretionary (in which case the wording will be "if so directed by your supervising officer). In either case, the responsibility for ensuring compliance with the additional conditions rests upon the supervising officer, not the board or Scottish Ministers.

1. Accommodation

There are a great many situations in which a prisoner will not be **7–30** returning to a stable and permanent home on release. Often, the prisoner's family or a close friend will house him on a temporary basis for the initial few weeks after release, on the understanding that he will use this period to secure suitable accommodation of his own.

On the other hand, there may be serious concerns about a prisoner's proposed release address. He may be a drug user proposing to return to an address from which he offended in the past, in an area of significant criminality with a high transient population, and there may be concerns that he intends to "disappear" into the background. The licensee might be a predatory sex offender, in denial of his offending, seeking to identify an address where he is not known or recognised, but where he will have easy access to children.

Thirdly, the licensee may be a vulnerable individual, substantially damaged by years of alcohol or drug abuse, or with a long history of mental health difficulties, who would find it extremely difficult to cope with the sudden transition from the structured environment of prison or a mental hospital, and who will need a great deal of support and insistence if he is not to revert to past behaviours, and rapidly find himself returned to custody.

In order to assist supervising officers in dealing with persons in **7–31** these three discrete groups, the Parole board has developed three separate additional conditions in respect of accommodation, namely:

"You shall reside in accommodation as approved by your supervising officer"

"You shall reside only in accommodation as approved by your supervising officer",

and

"You shall reside initially in supported accommodation as directed by your supervising officer, and thereafter only in accommodation as approved".

7–32 Quite clearly each of these is designed to assist in a particular type of case. The first condition offers the supervising officer a modicum of control where the parolee is expected to move swiftly on from his initial address, but where his future address is unlikely, in itself, to create an objective concern. The second condition permits the supervising officer to refuse permission for a licensee to stay, even on a temporary basis, at an unsuitable address. It is commonly used as a non-parole licence condition in respect of sex offenders, who may seek to change addresses regularly, or stay overnight without permission with other sex offenders. Any residence other than as approved is a breach of this licence condition, and may be reported as such to Ministers or the board for consideration of recall.

Before the board can impose a condition of residence in supported accommodation, there must be evidence both that such accommodation is available and that local authority funding is in place. Sadly, even in the early 21st Century there are relatively few places in Scotland offering suitable supported accommodation for those with substance abuse or mental health difficulties, or learning difficulties, and pressure upon these places remains high. Community Throughcare Teams are aware of these difficulties, and when someone with particular needs is due for release efforts are usually made (not always successfully) to locate appropriate accommodation.

2. Employment

7–33 Given that a great many released prisoners have no history of gainful employment, may have limited literacy skills and no immediate prospects of obtaining employment on release, the Board has, for several years now, felt it extremely useful to ensure that supervising officers liase with appropriate local job search agencies. There is some evidence that suggests that those who access gainful employment are less likely to return to prison, and the board therefore has the option of inserting an additional licence condition to the effect that "You shall cooperate with an agency experienced in job search and advice for offenders if/as directed by your supervising officer". The "as" form of the clause is generally used when there is no offer of employment stated, or a limited history of employment, while the alternative phrasing, which leaves the matter at the discretion of the supervising officer, is more appropriate where there may be a possible job offer that may either fall through (or in some cases not be genuine).

3. Alcohol/drugs/addictions counselling

The majority of new prison inmates have a history of alcohol **7–34** abuse, drug abuse or both. Many in custody will indulge in whatever is available to enable them, as many put it, to cope with the boredom. While there is evidence that a significant number of prisoners use their time in prison to rid themselves of their addictions, not all succeed, and it remains a sad but true fact of life that, in most Scottish prisons, if you are determined to find drugs, you will find them. Therefore it must be recognised that many long term prisoners will leaves custody still addicted to drugs.

Similarly, it is a fact of life that a great many who leave prison filed with good intentions will return to the area where they first became involved in drug misuse, and to the same peer group. The board will scrutinise every dossier closely for evidence of any potential or actual drug or alcohol problem. Has the offender reverted to alcohol or drugs after previous sentences? Does he admit to being an alcoholic or a drug addict? Has he failed and drug tests in custody, and if so when? Even if his recent drug test history seems encouraging, is there any evidence of involvement within the prison drug culture?

Even if none of these can be demonstrably necessary, the Board may require the licensee to undertake an assessment for either drugs, alcohol or addictions counselling as directed by the supervising officer, and cooperate with any such counselling as may be recommended. Obviously, where no counselling is required, that is an end of the matter at that stage.

If counselling is found to be necessary, in selecting the appropriate licence condition for the individual's needs, the board will once again consider whether any counselling in the community should be on an "as directed" or an "if directed" basis, depending upon the licensee's perceived level of need for intervention. Once again, where it feels that substance counselling is necessary in reducing the level of risk an offender may post, the board has an unfettered discretion to select either drugs, alcohol or the catch-all of addictions counselling.

4. Specific conditions to protect individuals

A number of offenders have either targeted their victim, who may **7–35** have been known to him even peripherally, or have offended against spouses, partners and family members. Some, despite that nature of their offences, harbour a desire to resume contact with their victims, who may well have expressed a specific desire to have no contact with the offender. Sometimes, in cases of domestic abuse, children may not themselves be the victims of the offence, but have witnessed the incident, and, on release, the offender is seeking to resume contact, against the wishes of the children's mother.

In any situation in which there is a likelihood that an offender will seek to make contact with his victims, and such contact is objectively considered to be contrary to their interests, the board is often asked to insert specific conditions into the licence directly preventing any contact between the offender and the victim. While there are many situations in which the civil remedies of interdict or a non-harassment order may be available, the board may well, especially when victims are perceived as vulnerable, consider such conditions appropriate. Where the condition relates to no contact with children or step-children, the board may on occasions stop short of precluding all contact (in any event, it could be argued that to do so is usurping the functions of the civil court), but direct that an offender shall have no unsupervised contact with such children, other than as directed by the supervising officer.

5. The "Sex Offender" conditions

7–36   In addition to the above conditions, there are three conditions often inserted into the licences of sex offenders, that are almost never used otherwise. They are:

> "You shall not undertake paid, unpaid or voluntary work without the consent of your supervising officer"

> "You shall have no [unsupervised] contact with any child under the age of 17, without the express prior approval of your supervising officer"

> "You shall not enter parks, playgrounds, amusement arcades or similar places where children under 17 habitually resort, without the express prior approval of your supervising officer".

7–37 The first of these is specifically designed to ensure that no child sexual offender obtains unsuitable employment of a nature that would increase the likelihood of their coming into contact with children or "grooming" them. A significant percentage of those convicted of child sexual offences, particularly those who remain in denial, demonstrate entirely unrealistic ideas of the types of employment that are suitable given their status as convicted persons subject to the requirements of the Sex Offenders Register, and this condition affords the supervising officer both a measure of control and a mechanism for reporting breaches of the conditions to Ministers and two the board.

The second condition is broadly self-explanatory. It should be noted that the definition of "child" in s.307 of the 1995 Act is not, as commonly thought, a person under the age of 16, but the meaning assigned for the purposes of Chapters 2 and 3 of Part II of the Children (Scotland) Act 1995, which does include a number of persons over the age of 16. In addition, the age of 17 is specifically chosen as the cut-off point by Sch.1 of the 1995 Act, and thus the "special provisions" provided for under that schedule apply in respect of any offence committed against any person under the age of 17.

The third of these conditions is used somewhat more rarely, being specifically designed to impact upon the activities of predatory sexual offenders. As the vast majority of sexual offending takes place within a family setting, and as a great many such offenders are not convicted until many years after their last proven offence, and have no history of offending outwith the family setting (in its broadest sense), this condition is often not regarded as appropriate. Again, this is a condition that many offenders have sought to challenge, due in part to the breadth of the definition, but as at the time of writing the condition has not been successfully challenged by court action. It may perhaps be interesting to note that, despite its relative rarity as a licence condition, it is one where allegations of its being breached are not uncommon. While it is possible to argue that "similar places where children habitually resort" is inherently vague, in practice it offers supervising officers and those charged with the consideration of recall an extremely wide discretion, and everyday common sense is used in determining whether this condition has been breached. Thus, where an offender happens on a single occasion to be in a fast-food restaurant when a large group of children enter, and does not return, it would be surprising if the matter were reported for consideration of recall. However, returning to such a venue even once, after being advised that it is frequented by schoolchildren would be likely to result in consideration of recall, and perhaps, at the very least, a warning letter being issued.

In the recent past, a number of cases of persons using computers to access child pornography on the Internet have come before the board. The maximum sentence for transmission or distribution of images of child pornography currently stands at ten years, and a number of such offenders are now receiving extended sentences. A practice is therefore developing of inserting an additional condition into licences either forbidding altogether or severely restricting access to internet-linked computer equipment, including mobile phones with internet access. Where, for example, an offender has a physically disabled partner who is dependent on a computer link, a supervising officer may be given the power to attend the home at any time and scrutinise computer use by the licensee.

The future of parole and licence for determinate sentence prisoners

7–38   As stated in Chapters Two and Six, Ministers have published proposals that have formed the basis of the Custodial Sentences and Weapons (Scotland) Bill that is scheduled to complete its passage through the Scottish Parliament and pass into law in the course of 2007. It is proposed that sentences will be expressed in such a way as to include a minimum and maximum custodial term. The current definitions of "short-term" and "long-term" will be removed completely. The initial recommendation as to whether to release a person into the community subject to supervision will now revert to the Ministers, subject to review by the parole board.

In order to comply with the requirements of ECHR, and to avoid the suggestion that sentencing once more comes under political control, the functions currently undertaken by the board will alter radically. Instead of being the body at first instance that decides whether to recommend parole, the board is now to have an appellate function, effectively reviewing the information considered by Ministers, and determining whether the Ministers' recommendation was the correct one in respect of public protection. Periodic reviews of this decision are provided. In addition, it is proposed that the board have referred to it high risk cases, where the Ministers recommend that the offender should be detained beyond the minimum custodial part fixed by the court. These cases, in respect of all custody and community prisoners, will be considered by the parole board, whose statutory function is now to be defined as "advising Scottish Ministers in relation to any matter referred to it in relation to the release of prisoners".

As it is proposed that every sentence in excess of fifteen days will now comprise a "custody part" and a "community part", with the custody part being a minimum of one-half of the total combined sentence, and with Ministers having the right to recommend, in terms of cll 8 and 9, that the prisoner remain in custody until the three-quarters date on the grounds that he "would, if not confined, be likely to cause serious harm to members of the public", the work of the parole board is likely to increase massively. In any case where Ministers make such a determination, the case must be reviewed by the board in terms of cll 10 and 11 of the Bill, with the board retaining its right to direct release where they feel that the "serious harm" test has not been met. The new Bill places assessment of risk at the forefront of the entire custodial system, and will oblige prison staff to be engaged in a constant assessment of harm throughout any custody and community prisoner's sentence. A written risk assessment is expected to be available not only before the halfway point of such a sentence, but (at least in theory) to be available in time for Ministers to assess it, determine whether the prisoner is to be released at the halfway point, and if not to refer the case to the board for them to direct release or not. There are lengthy and complex new provisions for further review, which will not be addressed in detail in this volume.

Clause 14 proposes that the board will retain the duty to specify **7–39** licence conditions, except where release is directed by Ministers at the halfway point (cl.9) or is on compassionate grounds (cl.23).

As presently drafted, this Bill appears to create a role for the parole board in determining risk of harm in respect of a significant percentage of prisoners serving sentences of a few months duration. It will be some years before the full impact of this is known, although the first consideration of short sentences will manifestly occur within a few months of the commencement of the Act in its final form. The Bill completed its passage through the Scottish Parliament in March 2007, although at present no date has been identified for its provisions to come into effect. It is therefore clear that "split" sentences of the type favoured by the Executive will become the norm within the foreseeable future. There remains, of course, a degree of press support and public pressure for certain offenders to spend their "entire" sentences in custody, although this rather raises the question of what happens to these offenders on release. If they are not subject to any form of statutory supervision, then they have no entitlement to access housing, employment or addiction services at the time of greatest need. In addition, if they are not subject to supervision of any sort, there is no sanction available should they fail to access community support services. Unpalatable though it may be to some, evidence continues to show that provision of appropriate supports on release has some benefit in reducing the risk of reoffending in a number of cases, and there is no doubt that supervision in the community will remain a vital part of the sentencing process for the foreseeable future.

CHAPTER 8

LIFE PRISONERS AND PUNISHMENT PARTS

8–01 Prior to 1967, there was no system of parole for life prisoners as such. Those who were convicted of murder, and whose death sentences were commuted to life imprisonment, remained in custody until death or the intervention of the Secretary of State. Following the suspension, then abolition, of the death penalty the punishment for murder became mandatory life imprisonment, and it became clear that the previous *ad hoc* arrangements for release would not suffice within the new regime.

As seen in Chapter Seven, the Parole Board was set up in 1967, and a system of preliminary review by board members developed. In the light of the way in which life sentences have developed since the abolition of the death penalty, it may be interest to note certain observations of Lord Hunter in *HM Advocate v Fiddes*, 1967 SLT 2:

> "I have now been provided with more detailed information from which it is apparent that it has become very rare indeed, at any rate in the last 10 years, for the period of detention under a life sentence to exceed 9 years. Indeed the mathematical average from the detailed information, with which I have been provided, is a little under 8 years. These facts will, of course, come as no surprise to those who are familiar with the present situation, though they may perhaps surprise those who are not. The inference which I would draw from the information which has now been made available to me is that it is now the practice, except in special circumstances which appear to have occurred infrequently, if at all, to release persons sentenced to life imprisonment for murder after they have been under detention for 8 1/2 to 9 years, at any rate in an average case."

8–02 Between 1967 and 1993 it was, in practice, fairly rare for a trial judge to state, in open court, the minimum sentence that he recommended the offender should serve before being considered for parole. Such recommendations were characteristically given in around five per cent of cases, usually where there had been multiple murders, or the circumstances of the offence were demonstrably of an unusually heinous nature. While it was competent to impose life imprisonment for offences other than murder, this was, until recently, a fairly rare occurrence. Indeed, in the *Fiddes* case referred to above, the trial judge observed that life imprisonment had, at that time, been imposed in "one or two" cases of culpable homicide, as well as in at least one other case a number of years previously. It appears that the first instance in Scotland of the imposition of a life sentence for an offence other than murder was in 1963 for culpable homicide.

Over the past forty years, courts have become more willing to impose discretionary life sentences in cases involving serious violence not resulting in death, serious and violent sexual offending, and fireraising, particularly where the offender either has analogous previous convictions or where risk assessment reports disclose the existence of a personality disorder. With the High Court acquiring the further power, with effect from June 20, 2006, to impose an Order for Lifelong Restriction in terms of s.210F of the 1995 Act (as inserted by s.1 of the Criminal Justice (Scotland) Act 2003), it seems likely that the number of offenders receiving discretionary life sentences or their equivalent may well increase.

As at March 31, 2006, there were 658 persons serving life sentences (plus 24 recalled life sentence prisoners) within the Scottish prison system, of whom 69 (approximately ten per cent) are serving discretionary life sentences. The question of the appropriate length of the minimum custodial part of their sentence, and of the mechanism for deciding when they may safely be released back into society, has been a vexed one for many years, and one in which Scottish and English sentencing practice has varied.

Introduction of the "tariff" system in England

Until 1983 the English system was broadly similar to that in **8–03** Scotland. Under arrangements introduced in 1983, however, the Lord Chief Justice and the trial judge were consulted after the prisoner had served about three years, and were asked for their views on "the period of detention necessary to meet the requirements of retribution and general deterrence". It appears that, in the case of mandatory life prisoners, the "tariff" to be imposed was understood to mean "how long a prisoner should remain in custody as punishment for murdering someone" (*R v Secretary of State for the Home Department, Ex P Handscomb*, (1988) 86 Cr App R 59 at p79 *per* Watkins LJ). In the case of discretionary life prisoners, on the other hand, the expression was understood to mean "the appropriate fixed-term punishment for the crime in the absence of the mental element, the existence of which led to the life sentence". The first review was then fixed for a date after the expiry of the period recommended by the judges.

In the case of *Hanscomb* in 1987 this system, as applied to discretionary life prisoners, was criticised in two respects. First, the delay in consulting the judges until three years had passed (by which time a prisoner who was suitable for parole would have served the equivalent, under the system of parole calculation then in force, of a nine year sentence) was held to be unreasonable. Secondly, it was submitted that remission ought to be taken into account in determining the period to be served before the first review: since the date of the first review was fixed on the basis of a notional determinate sentence, allowance should be made for the remission which would have applied if a determinate sentence had in fact been imposed. In 1987, in the light of the *Handscomb* decision, the application of parole to discretionary life prisoners was altered.

Under the new system, the trial judge was to write to the Secretary of State at the time of passing the life sentence "giving his view on the period necessary to meet the requirements of retribution and deterrence. This view will be related to the determinate sentence that would have been passed but for the element of mental instability and/or public risk which led the judge to pass a life sentence and will also take account of the notional period of the sentence which a prisoner might expect to have been remitted for good behaviour had a determinate sentence been passed".

8–04   The date of the first review of the prisoner's case would then be fixed in accordance with the trial judge's view of the requirements of retribution and deterrence. The determination of the appropriate punishment part for any discretionary life prisoner has caused the courts some difficulty in recent years, both in Scotland and England. This matter was first considered by the Appeal Court in *O'Neill v HM Advocate*, 1999 S.C.C.R. 300, which was decided at the time that s.2 had been amended by Section 16 of the Crime and Punishment (Scotland) Act 1997.

Determination of "punishment parts"

8–05   In *O'Neill*, the appeal court prescribed the method for determining the designated part by taking guidance from relevant English authority. The court held that, in assessing the minimum period that the discretionary life sentence prisoner would actually serve as a punishment for his crime before he could be released, he should not be at a disadvantage when compared with a prisoner serving a determinate sentence for a similar offence. The court, in fixing the designated part, should therefore keep in view that the determinate sentence prisoner would be eligible for release on licence after one-half of his sentence, and entitled to it after two-thirds. Apart from the exceptional case where imprisonment for the whole of life would be the appropriate punishment period, comparative justice required that the designated part should bear a fair and reasonable relationship to the minimum period that a determinate sentence prisoner would have to serve in a comparable case, there being disregarded the special requirement of public protection that had led to the life sentence. Since every long-term prisoner could be released on licence after serving one-half of a determinate sentence, if the parole board so recommended, the court when specifying the designated part should normally decide what period of detention would be appropriate purely as a punishment for the crime and then designate one-half of that period. While there might be circumstances in which it would be appropriate for the court to assess the designated part at up to two-thirds of that period, that being the period after which a long-term prisoner was entitled to be released on licence, the court expressed no view about the circumstances in which that might be appropriate. In coming to this view, the court had regard to certain English authorities (including *R v Marklew and Lambert* [1999] 1 Cr App R (S) 6, which supported this view of the appropriate designated part.

However, following the coming into force of the Convention Rights (Compliance) (Scotland) Act 2001, which once more radically altered the terms of s.2 of the 1993 Act, the matter was reconsidered by a full bench in the case of *Ansari v HM Advocate*, 2003 S.C.C.R. 347. The appellant had had his punishment part fixed by the Appeal Court prior to the decision in *O'Neill*, and his case was referred back to the court by the Scottish Criminal Cases Review Commission. In *Ansari*, the majority of the court held that the court imposing a discretionary life sentence required to assess what determinate sentence it would have imposed, having regard to the general considerations set out in ss2(2)(a), (b) and (c), if a discretionary life sentence had not been available (the "notional determinate sentence"), and then deduct from the notional determinate sentence the element attributable to the protection of the public (the "risk element"), and finally fix a proportion of the notional determinate sentence as reduced in the light of the early release provisions that would be available to a prisoner sentenced to a determinate sentence for the same offence, and further that the sentencing judge will normally fix the appropriate proportion within the limits of one-half and two-thirds, but in a case of great gravity the proportion may be higher than two-thirds.

In a powerful dissenting opinion Lord Reed, after reviewing the history of parole and the development of the system of releasing life sentence prisoners, came to the opposite conclusion. He stated that in his view s.2(2) does not require the court to impose a sentence, but rather to decide the point at which the prisoner's case should be considered by the parole board, and the period specified should be the equivalent proportion of the notional sentence so as to ensure that the period before the parole board first starts to consider the possibility of releasing the prisoner on licence is no longer than it would have been had considerations of public safety not dictated the need for an indeterminate rather than a determinate sentence, and the appropriate proportion will generally be one-half, that the specified period is arrived at by deciding on an appropriate sentence to satisfy the requirements of retribution and deterrence, and then discounting the notional sentence so as to bring the specified period into line with the period which would be served by a determinate sentence prisoner prior to being considered by the parole board, that the court cannot take the gravity of the offence into account when deciding upon the proportion of the notional determinate sentence when the court has already taken account of the gravity of the offence when arriving at that notional sentence, but that situations may arise where a period longer than half of the notional sentence should be specified. The current sentencing practice in respect of discretionary life prisoners in England appears still to be more in line with the opinion of Lord Reed, than that of the majority.

Referral to Europe

8–06   By the time such designated parts first came to be imposed, of course, the case of *Thynne, Wilson and Gunnell v United Kingdom* (1990) 13 EHRR 666 had been referred to the European Court, and it was clear once that case was decided that a proper judicial system for the determination of whether the continued detention of discretionary life prisoners was necessary required to be put in place. In *Weeks v United Kingdom* (1988) 10 EHRR 293 it had been held that the parole board was a "court" for the purposes of Art.5(4), and, following these decisions and the coming into force of the Criminal Justice Act 1991 in England and Wales, the law of Scotland was reformed by the Prisoners and Criminal Proceedings (Scotland) Act 1993, which came into force on October 1, 1993.

Prisoners and Criminal Proceedings (Scotland) Act 1993

8–07   It may now be of little more than historical interest to note that, in *Rea v Parole Board for Scotland*, 1993 SLT 1074, an aggrieved life prisoner who had been recommended for release then downgraded to closed conditions following an alleged breach of prison rules, sought declarator that he was entitled to written notice of the grounds of the board's decision, a hearing on the evidence at which he might be present or represented, and reconsideration of the board's decision after the hearing. In dismissing the petition, the Lord Ordinary observed that there was no basis in statute for the rights contended for, and that it was not appropriate to introduce quasi-judicial hearings into an administrative structure.

Initially, s.2 of the Act governed only the release of discretionary life prisoners. As first enacted, it read:

"In this Part of this Act "discretionary life prisoner", subject to subsection (9)(a) below and except where the context otherwise requires, means a life prisoner—

(a) whose sentence was imposed for an offence the sentence for which is not fixed by law; and
(b) in respect of whom the court which sentenced him for that offence made the order mentioned in subsection (2) below."

Subsection (2) provided that the order referred to above is an order that:

"subsections (4) and (6) below shall apply to the life prisoner as soon as he has served such part of his sentence ("the relevant part") as is specified in the order, being such part as the court considers appropriate taking into account—

(a) the seriousness of the offence, or of the offence combined with other offences associated with it; and
(b) any previous conviction of the life prisoner."

It was not initially mandatory for the court to fix a "relevant part" **8–08** to a discretionary life sentence. Subsection (3) as initially enacted allowed the court not to make such an order, provided it stated its reasons for so doing (which could then be the subject of appeal). In cases that fell under s.2 of the Act, for the first time, the Secretary of State was obliged, if directed to do so by the parole board, to release a discretionary life prisoner on licence. However, the board's powers to make such an order were limited by subs.(5), which stated that the board shall not give a direction to release unless the Secretary of State had referred the prisoner's case to the board; and) the board was satisfied that it is no longer necessary for the protection of the public that the prisoner should be confined. This was the first time this now familiar formula found its way into the law of Scotland.

Under the terms of s.2, a discretionary life prisoner had the right, subject to subs.(7), at any time require the Secretary of State to refer his case to the parole board. However, no such requirement could be made:

> "(a) where the prisoner is also serving a sentence of imprisonment for a term, before he has served one-half of that sentence; and
>
> (b) where less than two years has elapsed since the disposal of any (or the most recent if more than one) previous reference of his case to the Board"

In determining for the purposes of the section whether a discretionary life prisoner had served the relevant part of his sentence, no account could be taken of any time during which he was unlawfully at large, and in the rare cases where a life prisoner was serving two or more sentences of imprisonment for life, he was treated as a discretionary life prisoner only if the requirements of subsection (1) were satisfied in respect of each of the sentences he was serving, and he had served the relevant part of each of the sentences. For the sake of completeness, it should perhaps also be noted that, where someone serving two life sentences was released, he or she was to be released on only one licence.

For the first time ever, the parole board, rather than Ministers, had the power to direct the release of a life sentence prisoner, and both the imposition of the sentence and the date of release from that sentence were dealt with by judicial process. For the first time, a quorum of three members of the parole board sat as a tribunal, with a chairman who held or had held office as a judge or sheriff, and two lay members, in the establishment where the prisoner was situated, to determine whether continued detention was necessary for the protection of the public.

8–09 Given the tiny proportion of life sentence prisoners serving discretionary life sentences, such tribunals were extremely rare, amounting to barely ten a year, in the early stages, until the category of prisoners eligible to have their cases was widened by the terms of s.16 of the Crime and Punishment (Scotland) Act 1997, which was itself amended by s.109 of the Crime and Disorder Act 1998. This altered the terminology, replacing the phrase "Discretionary life prisoner" with "designated life prisoner", to take account of the wider group that now found itself eligible to have cases decided by a Tribunal, rather than by Ministers. This change in the law followed the decision of the European Court of Human Rights in *Hussain v United Kingdom* (1996) 22 EHRR 1, which had held that the principles set out in *Thynne, Wilson and Gunnell* applied also to persons sentenced to detention without limit of time for murders committed by them when they were under the age of 18. A similar view was reached in *Curley v United Kingdom* [2000] Times Law Reports 270, in which the court further observed that Art.5(4) was violated by proceedings in which the "court" (i.e. the parole board) could not direct release, but merely recommend release to the Secretary of State.

With effect from October 20, 1997, s.2 further applied to a person sentenced, prior to the coming into force of the Act, to life imprisonment for murder committed by him before he attained the age of eighteen years, in respect of whom the Lord Justice General, whom failing the Lord Justice Clerk, after consultation with the trial judge, if available, certified his opinion that if s.2 of the Act had been in force at the time of his being sentenced, the court would have ordered that a certain period be served to satisfy the requirements of retribution and deterrence. Once the Lord Justice General issued his certified opinion, the life prisoner fell to be treated as a designated life prisoner, who became eligible for consideration for release on parole once he had served the length of sentence specified in the certificate. Where a prisoner sentenced prior to October 20, 1997, for a murder committed before he had attained the age of eighteen years had been released on licence, other than on compassionate grounds, he fell to be treated as a designated life prisoner, and his licence was treated as though it had been granted in terms of s.2(4) of the 1993 Act. Once again, the requirement that the conditions of the Act were satisfied in all cases was specified in respect of those serving two or more life sentences, and release could not be ordered until the offender had served the designated part of each sentence.

The result of this change in the law was to increase the number of tribunals held annually fourfold. The number of Life Prisoner Tribunals increased from nine in 1997 to thirty-eight in 1998, rising further to forty-four by 2001. However, matters were not to rest there. It was clear from the jurisprudence of the European Court of Human Rights that very few prisoners could ever be expected, at the time of their conviction, to receive a "tariff" that would cover the rest of their natural life. By 2001, the case of *Stafford v United Kingdom* (2002) 35 EHRR 32 was proceeding in the European Court of Human Rights. While that case was principally concerned with the circumstances of the offender's recall following release on life licence, he had been convicted of murder as an adult, sentenced to life imprisonment, then released on licence. With regard to Art.5(4), the court reminded itself that the tariff comprised the punishment element of a mandatory life sentence and the Secretary of State's role in fixing that tariff was a sentencing exercise. Upon the expiry of the tariff, continued detention depended upon assessment of elements of risk associated with the original sentence for murder. Those elements were liable to change over time and thus, new issues of lawfulness requiring determination by a body satisfying the requirement of Art.5(4) had arisen.

8–10   In anticipation of the decision of the court, and being mindful of the way in which European jurisprudence had developed since *Thynne, Wilson and Gunnell,* the Scottish Parliament passed the Convention Rights (Compliance) (Scotland) Act 2001. Part 1 of the Act substantially altered the 1993 Act, and Pt 2 amended the constitution of the parole board for Scotland, to take account of the obligations under s.57 of the Scotland Act 1998 for every public body to act in a manner compliant with the Convention.

Fixing of punishment parts

8–11   For the first time, the definition of "life prisoner" was widened to include every prisoner serving a sentence of life imprisonment. Section 2 now abolished the distinction between different categories of life imprisonment, and provided that subss.(4) and (6), which governed the parole board's power to direct release on life licence.

> "shall apply to the life prisoner as soon as he has served such part of his sentence ("the punishment part") as is specified in the order, being such part as the court considers appropriate to satisfy the requirements for retribution and deterrence (ignoring the period of confinement, if any, which may be necessary for the protection of the public), taking into account:
>
> (a) the seriousness of the offence, or of the offence combined with other offences of which the life prisoner is convicted on the same indictment as that offence;
>
> (aa) in the case of a life prisoner to whom paragraph (a) of subsection (1) above applies:
>
> > (i)   the period of imprisonment, if any, which the court considers would have been appropriate for the offence had the court not sentenced the prisoner to imprisonment for life;
> >
> > (ii) the part of that period of imprisonment which the court considers would satisfy the requirements of retribution and deterrence (ignoring the period of confinement, if any, which may be necessary for the protection of the public); and
> >
> > (iii) the proportion of the part mentioned in sub-paragraph (ii) above which a prisoner sentenced to it would or

          might serve before being released, whether uncondi-
          tionally or on licence, under section 1 of this Act;

(b) any previous conviction of the life prisoner; and
(c) where appropriate, the matters mentioned in paragraphs
    (a) and (b) of section 196(1) of the 1995 Act."

The effect of this was to ensure that every person then serving life **8–12**
imprisonment in Scotland (including the small number of prisoners
transferred from other jurisdictions) would be entitled to have a
punishment part fixed, at the end of which their case would be
referred to the parole board for consideration of whether they
presented an acceptable risk in terms of reoffending. It was necessary for there to be transitional provisions put in place for existing
life sentence prisoners, to ensure that such prisoners would be
neither better nor worse off than those sentenced after the Act came
into force. At the time, there were of course over 500 life sentence
prisoners in Scotland serving their sentences for murders committed
when they were aged eighteen or older, only a tiny number of whom
had had liberation dates fixed under the previous system, whereby
the parole board had recommended release on a future date and
Ministers had agreed to this. Schedule 1 of the 2001 Act set out
some fairly lengthy transitional provisions to ensure all that all
existing life sentence prisoners would be able to have punishment
parts fixed. These are now mainly of historical interest, and thus
will not require to be dealt with in detail. However, the effect
transitional provisions, especially in respect of those who had
already spent many years in prison, did give rise to a considerable
amount of debate, and a significant body of case law.

    Contrary to the popular myth that has grown up since the
coming into force of the Act, prisoners did not, *en masse,* and
without warning, apply to the court under the new legislation for
their cases to be referred for the fixing of punishment parts. Paragraph 3 of the Schedule provided that the "Scottish Ministers shall,
as soon as reasonably practicable after the relevant date, refer the
case of an existing life prisoner ... to the High Court of Justiciary
for a hearing [to fix a punishment part]." Prisoners were given the
opportunity under para.7 to state in writing that they did not wish
to participate. In practice, only the tiny minority of prisoners who
already had an agreed liberation date from Ministers under the
previous system did not elect to have punishment parts fixed.

    Between February 2002 and May 2003, virtually all life prisoners
appeared before a single judge of the High Court (where possible,
the original trial judge) to have their punishment parts fixed, and
such hearings briefly became a familiar fixture in the court calendar.

Ten such hearings were set down on the Monday at the start of each new sitting of the High Court, and within a relatively short time, all prisoners had received their punishment parts. Obviously, s.2 as amended having come into force on October 15, 2001, every prisoner sentenced to life after that date had his or her punishment part fixed at the time of sentencing. While in evidence before the Scottish Parliament it had been predicted that the average punishment part would be of the order of ten years, the courts tended to be much less lenient, and the final average punishment part for existing life prisoners was of the order of 13.4 years.

8–13   The imposition of the punishment part was expressly stated to be part of the sentencing process, and as such both prosecution and defence had the right of appeal against the sentence imposed, on the grounds that it was unduly lenient or excessive, as the case may be. Unsurprisingly, a number of appeals against punishment parts were marked, and the High Court issued its initial guidance in the cases of *McCreaddie v HM Advocate*, 2002 SCCR 912 and *Stewart v HM Advocate*, 2002 SCCR 915. In that case, Lord Justice General Cullen stated "It is plain that there can be a wide variation in the seriousness of a murder case according to the circumstances in which it took place and the circumstances of the offender. In the fixing of a punishment part it is necessary to take into account all known factors which are relevant to aggravation or mitigation. As regards aggravation, for example, conduct suggesting an intention to kill, the use of prolonged or savage violence and the use of a lethal weapon may well be of importance." The court did not see fit to enumerate factors that were relevant to mitigation.

Of greater importance, however, was the manner in which the court dealt with counsel's submissions in respect of the prisoner's expectation of release. In the course of her argument, counsel for the appellant submitted that it was open to a court which was concerned with the fixing of a punishment part to consider the practical effect of selecting a particular period, and in particular the effect which its selection would have on the expectation, prior to the coming into force of the 2001 Act, as to when the prisoner would be considered for release. In the present case one of the grounds of appeal specifically referred to the fact that the appellant had been advised that he was to be considered for release after 10 years, but that as a consequence of the fixing of the punishment part the parole board was unable to consider his release until he had served 14 years. It also states that the appellant had a "legitimate expectation" that he would be released after 10 years. It is probably more correct to state that the appellant had a legitimate expectation that release would be considered after ten years.

In rejecting this argument, the court stated "In considering this submission it is important to bear in mind that under paragraph 13 of the Schedule to the 2001 Act, the question is what would have been specified as the punishment part if the new statutory provisions had been in force at the time when the accused was sentenced. It follows that matters which were not known at that time cannot properly be taken into account (cf *Murray v HM Advocate*, 1999 SCCR p 956). Accordingly, in our view, the prior arrangements for considering whether the appellant should be released on licence should not be taken into account in the fixing of a punishment part."

This decision proved somewhat controversial. A considerable **8–14** number of prisoners who had spent several years in custody had been situated in open conditions on the date their punishment parts were to be fixed. They were taking home leaves, and could legitimately expect that, provided their behaviour continued to merit it, that their requests for release would receive a favourable hearing. However, some such prisoners received punishment parts of a length that required them, for operational reasons, to be returned to closed conditions, as they were now some two or three years away from the date upon which release could be considered by the parole board. These were prisoners who had progressed through the system, held low supervision status, and were considered by staff to be close to release. Despite this, the courts had held that they were to serve considerably longer in custody before their suitability for release could be considered.

An attempt by four prisoners, who had been in custody for many years, and who contended that they had, at the time their punishment parts were fixed, a legitimate expectation of release, given the terms of previous recommendations by the parole board, to restrict or quash punishment parts on the grounds that the conflicted with their pre-existing human rights under domestic law, on the basis that, prior to the coming into force of the 2001 Act they had a legitimate expectation of release, and that the imposition of punishment parts was incompatible with Art.7 of the ECHR, as it imposed a higher penalty than was available at the time of sentencing was unsuccessful (*Flynn v HM Advocate; Meek v HM Advocate; Nicol v HM Advocate; McMurray v HM Advocate* ,2003 SCCR 456), and the matter proceeded the following year to be heard before the Judicial Committee of the Privy Council (*Flynn v HM Advocate; Meek v HM Advocate; Nicol v HM Advocate; McMurray v HM Advocate (PC)* 2004 SCCR 281). While the matters raised before the Judicial Committee related to the competency of the procedure adopted by the Scottish Courts, and the appeals were unsuccessful on that point, in reaching its decision on the competency point, the Judicial Committee had to consider the soundness of the High Court's decision in *Stewart v HM Advocate*. The Judicial Committee accepted that the fixing of the punishment part in each case had deprived the appellant of the parole review that he had been led to expect. The majority of the Judicial Committee considered that Art.7 of the Convention was engaged, and it appears that they considered that if the interpretation in *Stewart v HM Advocate* were sound, the transitional provisions under the 2001 Act would not comply with the Convention. However, having regard to s.101 of the Scotland Act 1998 and s.3(1) of the Human Rights Act 1998, the committee concluded that the legislation could be read in a way that was compliant with the Convention if the court, when fixing the punishment part, took into account events relating to reviews of the sentence by the parole board. That, in the view of the Judicial Committee, was how these provisions should be construed. That approach was incompatible with *Stewart v HM Advocate*.

Following this guidance from the Judicial Committee, the four cases were referred back to the High Court of Justiciary, where they were considered by a bench of five judges, headed by the Lord Justice-Clerk, in *Flynn v HM Advocate; Meek v HM Advocate; Nicol v HM Advocate; McMurray v HM Advocate (No 2)* 2004 SCCR 702. In overruling *Stewart* and *McCreaddie*, the court held that the correct approach was to consider firstly what punishment part would have been set in each case if it had been set at the date of sentencing and secondly, having set the length of the punishment part, to consider subsequent events having a possible bearing on the appellant's prospects of release, in order to determine what weight (if any) should be given to them in all the circumstances by way of adjustment to the punishment part. In delivering the Opinion of the Court, Lord Justice-Clerk Gill stated:

> "In our view, the logical starting point is, in keeping with the hypothesis on which paragraph 13 is based, to consider what punishment part would have been set in each case if it had been set at the date of the sentence. We shall therefore first decide whether, on the criteria specified in sec 2(2) of the 1993 Act (as amended) and with all subsequent events being disregarded, the punishment part that has been set in each case was of appropriate length. If it was not, we shall vary it. Having thus decided what punishment part would have been appropriate if imposed at the date of the sentence, we shall then look at subsequent events having a possible bearing on the appellant's prospects of release and decide what weight, if any, to give to them in all the circumstances by way of adjustment to the punishment part."

In reaching this view, the court observed that, under the tribunal **8–15**
system that had by then been in force for almost three years, relatively few prisoners had been released on their first review. In dealing with the individual circumstances of the appellants, the court had regard, in selecting the appropriate punishment parts, to their recent behaviour in custody.

As time passes, the significance of the transitional provisions will diminish. Every prisoner who has been sentenced to life imprisonment since October 2001 has received a punishment part at the time of sentencing, and, with a tiny number of exceptions, every prisoner serving life imprisonment at the time the 2001 Act came into force has received their punishment part, and had the appropriateness of the sentence considered on appeal. With the passage of time, the importance of the transitional provisions will diminish, but at present there remain a number of prisoners who received "straight" life sentences prior to 2001, whose post-2001 punishment parts have not expired, and whose cases have not yet been considered by the parole board.

CHAPTER 9

THE LIFE PRISONER TRIBUNAL SYSTEM

9–01 Every prisoner currently serving life imprisonment has now received formal notification of the length of their punishment part, at the end of which their case will be considered by the parole board in terms of s.2 of the 1993 Act as amended. Section 2(5)(a) requires Ministers to refer such cases to the board, and in practice the prisoner's case will be assigned a hearing as soon as possible after the expiry of the punishment part, usually within one week or less. While there is at present no direct English equivalent to the 2001 Act, it may be interesting to note that, in *R (Noorkoiv) v Secretary of State for the Home Department* (2002) 1 WLR 3284, the English courts were concerned with the arrangements which led to the continued detention of a prisoner subject to an automatic life sentence after the expiry of the penal or tariff element of his sentence. The court held that the system for his release should have been designed to provide for the necessary assessment to be made before rather than after the expiry of the tariff period, or very rapidly indeed afterwards, in order to engage Art.5(4), noting that continued detention in custody after the expiry of the tariff must be justified. In Scotland, the assessment of course commences some months before the hearing, which takes place as soon as possible after the expiry of the punishment part. This is another area which is expected to be altered by the terms of the Custodial Sentences Bill; cl.16 of that now indicates that "Before the expiry of the punishment part of a life prisoner's sentence, the Scottish Ministers must, subject to Section 22, refer the prisoner's case to the Parole Board". Section 22 will cover the situation where the prisoner is serving another sentence as at the date of expiry of his punishment part.

The assignment of a tribunal of course presupposes that the prisoner is not, as at that date, serving any other sentence of imprisonment, and that he has not, during his sentence, at any time been unlawfully at large. Any days during which the prisoner is not in lawful custody fall to be added to the end date of the punishment part (s.2(8)), in order that the prisoner has spent the precise time in custody as directed by the sentencing judge.

If, as at the expiry date of the punishment part, the prisoner is concurrently serving another sentence, and he has not reached the half-way point (if short-term) or Parole Qualifying Date (if long-term), then his tribunal cannot proceed until he has served the appropriate proportion of the other sentence, in terms of s.2(7) and (7A) of the 1993 Act.

The procedure to be adopted at tribunals is set out in Pt IV of the **9–02** Parole Board (Scotland) Rules 2001. In terms of r.18(1), cases are dealt with by a tribunal consisting of three members of the parole board appointed by the chairman to deal with the case. In respect of life sentence cases, r.18(2) provides that no member of the board who took part in a recommendation to recall a prisoner to custody in terms of s.28(1) of the 1989 Act may sit on a tribunal convened to consider that person's re-release under s.28(4), while r.18(3) is to similar effect in respect of extended sentences, where recall and re-release are governed by s.17 of the 1993 Act. Rule 18(4) states that (4) the members of a tribunal shall include either a person who holds or who has held judicial office (whether as a Senator of the College of Justice or a sheriff), or a solicitor or advocate of not less than 10 years standing (this being the qualification necessary before one can hold the office of sheriff), and the chairman of the board shall appoint that person to be chairman of the tribunal. Until the 2001 Rules came into force, only those who held or had held judicial office could chair tribunals, but now several of the legal members of the board who chair tribunals have not held judicial office.

In the event of the death or incapacity or unavailability (for whatever reason) of any member of a tribunal before the hearing has commenced, r.18(5) provides that the chairman of the board shall, subject to paras(2), (3) and (4), appoint another member of the board in the place of the absent member. Where the hearing has commenced, the case may continue to be dealt with by the two remaining members of the tribunal, where the absent member is not the chairman of the tribunal and with the consent of the parties. If this does not occur, then the chairman of the board must, subject to paras (2), (3) and (4) appoint another member of the board in place of the absent member, in which circumstances the hearing must recommence. In practice, cases commenced by a quorum of three and concluded before two members are extremely rare.

Rule 19(1) states that "Subject to the provisions of these Rules, a tribunal may regulate its own procedure for dealing with a case." The chairman of the tribunal is afforded a wide discretion in respect of giving, varying or revoking directions for the conduct of the case, including directions in respect of the timetable for the proceedings, the varying of the time within which or by which an act is required, by these Rules, to be done, the service of documents, and the submission of evidence, and the chairman of the tribunal has a duty to consider whether such directions need to be given at any time. In practice, requests to adjourn tribunals, on the motion of either Ministers or the prisoner's representative are not rare, and it is by no means uncommon for vital evidence to be submitted to the tribunal very close to the date of the hearing. In that situation, the chairman of the tribunal has a very wide discretion whether to admit evidence or not, and if late evidence is to be admitted, whether the hearing can still proceed on the appointed date. Directions may be made either on the motion of the chairman, or, more commonly, following a written application made by one party to the chairman, in which case intimation must be made to the other party (r.19(3)(b)). Rule 19(7) provides that the chairman of the tribunal shall take a note of the giving, variation or revocation of a direction, and that this shall be intimated to the parties as soon as practicable. In general, decisions on adjournments, permission to allow witnesses to attend or the admission of late reports are made by the chairman, but are intimated to parties by the Parole Board Secretariat, as approved by the chairman.

9–03   Rules 19(4)–(6) provide that the chairman of the tribunal may hold a preliminary hearing, to be held in private, at which the chairman shall sit alone, upon giving the parties fourteen days notice of the date, place and time of the hearing. In practice, such hearings are extremely rare.

The hearing of a prisoner's case shall be an oral hearing unless both parties and the tribunal agree otherwise (r.20). Again, it is unknown in practice for any Life Prisoner Tribunal to consider a case on the basis of a paper review. While some prisoners exercise their right not to attend the hearing in person, even where a prisoner has expressed a clear wish not to attend or be legally represented, an oral hearing will take place, at which Ministers will be represented, and the strengths of their argument will be tested by questioning by the members of the tribunal.

Notice of the hearing is governed by r.21. This provides that the tribunal shall give the parties not less than three weeks' notice of the date, time and place of the hearing or such shorter notice to which the parties may consent. However, unless both parties otherwise agree, r.21(2) provides that the hearing shall not take place earlier than three weeks after the expiry of the period within which the prisoner may send written representations to the tribunal under r.7. As r.7(2) provides that the prisoner's representations shall be sent to Ministers and the board within four weeks of the date on which he received his dossier, this means that the period between the prisoner receiving his dossier and the hearing taking place must be seven weeks. The tribunal may, however, vary any notice given of the date and must give the parties not less than seven days' (or such shorter time as the parties may agree) notice of any such variation, provided that any altered hearing date shall not (unless the parties agree) be before the date notified under para.(1). It should perhaps be noted that these hearings take place in the prison where the prisoner is then situated. Scottish Ministers will generally be represented by a member of the Justice Department and by an officer from the establishment, who will generally be either a Lifer Liaison Officer or a Governor Grade. The Justice Department has a limited number of staff trained in the presentation of cases before tribunals, and the board itself comprises fewer than 25 members, all part-time, and it is generally extremely difficult to vary the date fixed for the hearing of a tribunal at short notice

The tribunal has the power in terms of r.21(4) to adjourn the **9–04** hearing and in the case where the date, time and place of the adjourned hearing are announced before the adjournment, no further notice to parties is required. Where the decision to adjourn is made outwith the presence of the parties, r.21(4)(b) obliges the tribunal to give the parties not less than seven days' (or such shorter time as the parties may agree) notice of the date, time and place of the adjourned hearing.

As with criminal trials, civil proofs and all other forms of court and tribunal procedure, the reasons for seeking adjournment are many and various, but usually cover the standard explanations of last-minute illnesses, late instructions, the need to obtain or consider a report received just before a tribunal, or the non-availability of an essential witness. Where the motion to adjourn is made at the outset of the hearing, the tribunal members will decide there and then whether to adjourn the hearing, and if so until what date. In considering the motion, the tribunal must have regard to common-law procedural fairness, and thus, if either party may be materially prejudiced either by the grant or refusal of an adjournment, this must be considered fully by the tribunal.

Occasionally, a situation may arise in which the decision to adjourn requires to be made either during the hearing of evidence, or occasionally after all evidence has been heard. In such situations, it is highly desirable that the three members who have heard the evidence thus far are the same members who hear the case to its conclusion, unlike the situation where a case is adjourned before evidence is led. Very occasionally, important new evidence comes to light after the tribunal has concluded its deliberations, but before its decision has been issued. Perhaps a prisoner with a history of recent negative drug tests, who has given evidence of his intention to remain drug-free on release, returns from home leave and provides a positive sample, or perhaps a prisoner may abscond. In such situation, the prisoner must be afforded the period of 21 days specified in r.7 to make representations on this adverse development, then the tribunal should reconvene to conclude its deliberations, taking into account the extent to which the new information impacts upon the question of risk.

Representation at tribunals

9–05   In terms of r.22, each party may be represented at the hearing by any person whom he or she has authorised for that purpose, although r.22(3) provides that the tribunal may refuse to permit a person to represent a party at the hearing, if it is satisfied that there are good and sufficient reasons for doing so. Where a prisoner intends to be represented, he must give the tribunal and the other party written notice of the name, address and occupation of any person authorised in accordance with this rule, not later than the expiry of the period within which he may send written representations to the tribunal under r.7, that is to say within four weeks of receiving his dossier. Despite the fact that there are now around three hundred tribunals and oral hearings per year conducted by the board, and despite the fact that the standard letter sent to the prisoner enclosing the dossier specifically refers to this rule, it still is far from unknown for legal representatives to attend the hearing without intimation of their interest being sent to the board.

In the vast majority of cases, prisoners choose to be legally represented, usually by solicitors, although it is not unknown for representation to be by counsel or a solicitor-advocate. Occasionally prisoners, particularly recalled prisoners, will indicate a wish to decline legal representation and to represent themselves. If, during the course of the hearing it becomes apparent to members of the tribunal that the prisoner does not understand the proceedings or is otherwise unable to present his or her case properly, the tribunal may, by using its duty under r.27(2) to "conduct the hearing in such manner as it considers most suitable to the clarification of the issues before it and generally to the just handling of the proceedings", adjourn the hearing and recommend that the prisoner be legally represented when the hearing reconvenes. While Legal Aid is not available for tribunal hearings before the parole board, para.3(g) of the Advice and Assistance (Assistance by Way of Representation) (Scotland) Regulations 2003 specifically provides that Assistance By Way Of Representation (ABWOR) is available in parole board cases, which are defined in para.1(2) as cases of a prisoner to which Pt IV of the Parole Board (Scotland) Rules 1993 applies. Regulation 11 of the ABWOR regulations states:

"The assistance by way of representation which may be provided under Part II of the Act in relation to a Parole Board case shall be for representation of the prisoner at all stages of the proceedings before a tribunal relating to that case."

Where a prisoner does not authorise a person to act as his or her representative, the tribunal may, with his or her agreement, appoint someone to act on his or her behalf. Again, in practice this is effectively unknown.

Persons authorised to attend tribunals

In terms of r.23, where a party wishes to call any person to attend **9–06** a tribunal hearing and to give evidence before the tribunal, or to produce documents which relate to any matter in question at the hearing, he or she must, not later than the expiry of the period within which he may send written representations to the tribunal under r.7 (i.e. four weeks from receipt of the dossier), make a written application to the tribunal to authorise that person to attend the hearing to give evidence or to produce documents. Any application under this paragraph must specify the name, address and occupation of each person in respect of whom the application is made, together with a brief statement of what the general nature of his or her evidence is expected to be. The party making such an application must, at the same time as the application is made, send a copy of that application to the other party.

The decision on whether to permit a party to attend as a witness falls, in terms of r.23(4), solely within the discretion of the chairman of the tribunal, who may grant or refuse an application made under this rule. The chairman must give each party written notice of his decision and, where the application is refused, of the reasons for that decision. This rule is probably, in everyday practice, more honoured in the breach than in the observance. It is not uncommon in practice for requests for witnesses to be received very close to the date of the tribunal, often with no specification at all of the expected evidence the witnesses may provide. Often the request is for someone to attend who can add virtually nothing to the question of risk, or the request is made for a witness to attend solely to speak to a report contained within the dossier. In every case, the chairman of the tribunal must consider whether to permit the witness to attend, and to advise parties accordingly.

The tribunal's powers to order the attendance of witnesses before it are, however, somewhat limited. As the tribunal is, by definition, not a court, failure to attend is not contempt of court, nor can the chairman issue a warrant to apprehend a witness who fails to attend. However, r.24 does afford the chairman of the tribunal the power to require a person to attend to give evidence or produce books or other documents, either on the application of a party or on the motion of the tribunal itself. Again, where a party wishes to ask the tribunal to cite a witness, the usual timescale in terms of r.7 applies, as does the requirement to specify the name and address of the witness, and to intimate to the other party. Again, it should perhaps be noted that it is, in practice, extremely rare for the tribunal to require to cite a witness under r.24, although there are some examples of this power being used where there is a clear factual dispute over the accuracy of information provided within the dossier.

9–07   Rule 25 further provides that where a party wishes to be accompanied at the hearing by another person or persons, in addition to their appointed representative, he or she shall, not later than the expiry of the period specified under r.7, make a written application to the tribunal to authorise that person or persons to accompany him or her at the hearing. The application must give the name, address and occupation of the person or persons whom the party wishes to accompany him or her and a statement of the reasons why he or she wishes to be so accompanied, and the party making the application must, at the same time as the application is made, send a copy of the application to the other party. This provision is quite often used in cases where the life prisoner has, subsequent to conviction and sentence, been found to be mentally ill. In that situation the Life Prisoner Tribunal must take place within a hospital, although the same procedural rules apply, and the tribunal is still applying the "protection of the public" test. In such cases, it is fairly common for the prisoner patient to request that, either in addition to a legal representative or instead of one, a mental health advocacy worker attend the hearing. Such requests are rarely refused. Where the prisoner is accompanied under r.25, but otherwise not represented, the tribunal will generally adopt a more inquisitorial role in questioning Ministers' representatives. It should also be observed in this context that, following representations from within the psychiatric profession, the medical practitioner most closely involved in the patient's care does not sit with Ministers' official from the outset of proceedings, as a prison officer does, but instead is called into proceedings as a witness on behalf of Ministers. It was felt that to adopt the same position as in prisons, where a member of prison staff employed indirectly by the Executive sat with a civil servant employed by the Executive from the outset of the hearing presented to the patient an impression that an independent NHS employee was attending the hearing on behalf of Ministers, giving rise to a perception of conflict of interest. That situation no longer arises in current practice. Again, the chairman of the tribunal is afforded an unfettered discretion to grant or refuse an application under this rule, although r.25(4) obliges him to give each party written notice of his decision and, where the application is refused, of the reasons for that decision.

The tribunal hearing

The hearing will almost always take place in the prison where the **9–08** offender is situated, although when two tribunals are set for the same date, and both prisoners are not within the same prison, one of the prisoners and his Lifer Liaison Officer will attend the selected venue. Where the prisoner has been found to be mentally ill since the imposition of his sentence, and remains in hospital at the time of the hearing, it will proceed within the hospital or other appropriate medical facility. For the avoidance of doubt, the sole criterion for the tribunal in that situation remains the same assessment of risk in terms of s.2 of the 1993 Act, and it therefore follows that a decision by a tribunal that the requirements of public protection, based upon criminal justice criteria, do not require the offender's continued detention is neither binding upon, nor persuasive, in respect of any decision that may be made by a Mental Health Tribunal exercising its powers under s.21 of the Mental Health (Care and Treatment) (Scotland) Act 2003.

Attendance at hearings of life prisoner tribunals is governed by r.26. The hearing takes place in private. While it has, on occasions, been suggested that this may not be in conformity with Art.6 of the ECHR, the sensitive nature of the matters to be discussed at the hearing would be likely to be compromised were the hearings to be open to the public. There has been little pressure from prisoners to have such hearings made public, although a petition to the Court of Session in 2001 by a life prisoner did raise this as one of the alleged grounds on which the tribunal system was not ECHR compliant. The petition was opposed by Ministers and the board, but sadly the prisoner died of natural causes before the case could be heard, and the matter was not pursued further. The board's view is that the requirement that hearings take place in private does not contravene any Convention Rights, and is objectively necessary. Occasionally, relatives of victims request permission to attend, and these requests are treated as though made under r.23. Given the often robust questioning to which Ministers and tribunal members subject the prisoner, it is generally felt that the presence of victims' relatives might not be conducive to a full and open discussion of the issues of risk, especially where sensitive matters relating to relapse prevention are under discussion, and to date the board has not granted permission for victims' relatives to attend.

Of course, victims and their relatives retain the right to submit written representations, in terms of the victim notification provisions of s.17 of the Criminal Justice (Scotland) Act 2003, and such statements are now fairly commonly seen in life prisoners' dossiers. The content of these statements will often be put to the prisoner by Ministers' representatives or tribunal members. While it may seem surprising to some that the relatives of victims have no automatic right to attend, the format of the hearings is such that, whether or not release is opposed by Ministers, the board does not lose sight of the existence of the victim. It must be borne in mind that the starting point both of the dossier and the decision letter is the circumstances of the index offence.

9–09   Rule 26 (2) specifies that the only persons entitled to attend the hearing are:

(a) a member of the tribunal;

(b) the clerk to the tribunal (it should be noted that since 2004 clerks to tribunals only attend hearings in hospitals, the Board having decided that they were surplus to requirements within prisons)

(c) a party;

(d) a representative of a party;

(e) any person who is authorised by the chairman of the tribunal to attend the hearing under or by virtue of rule 23 or 25 or paragraph (3) of this rule;

(f) any person who is required to attend by virtue of rule 24(2)(b) (i.e. a person cited by the tribunal itself);

(g) any person who is authorised by the tribunal to attend the hearing under paragraph (4) of this rule; or

(h) a member of the Council on Tribunals or of the Scottish Committee of that Council.

Paragraph (g) and r.26(4) authorise the attendance of observers at hearings under certain circumstances. Occasionally, the chairman of the tribunal is requested to authorise the attendance of an observer. This power is usually exercised to permit those persons who are going to become involved in the tribunal system, such as newly appointed Lifer Liaison Officers or new members of the parole board or the Scottish Executive Justice Department, who are permitted to observe the conduct of tribunals before themselves taking part in the procedure.

Where the Scottish Ministers, or any person responsible for the security of any prison, hospital or other building in which a hearing takes place, consider it desirable that any person or persons should attend the hearing so as to preserve the security of that building or to ensure the safety of any person attending that hearing, they may apply at any time to the chairman of the tribunal for authorisation for additional security to be put in place, in terms of r.26(3), and the chairman may grant or refuse such an application. The chairman must inform parties of his decision. Where the application under this rule is refused, the chairman must state the reasons for that decision.

Procedure at tribunal hearings

This is governed by r.27, which is specifically designed to allow a **9–10** degree of flexibility in the conduct of tribunals, and to ensure that the hearing is carried out in such a way as to clarify the issues before it, and be conducted in a manner consistent with the requirements of common-law procedural fairness. The tribunal has a duty to conduct the hearing in such manner as it considers most suitable to the clarification of the issues, and to avoid formality in the proceedings. At the beginning of the hearing, r.27(1) provides that the chairman of the tribunal shall explain the order of proceeding which the tribunal proposes to adopt at the hearing.

The prisoner will have received, approximately seven weeks before the hearing, two copies of the dossier to be presented, one for himself, and one for his legal representative. Where the prisoner has misplaced, destroyed or damaged any part of his dossier prior to the hearing, the Board will, on request, provide his authorised representative with copies of any missing papers. Each of the three members of the tribunal will be sent a copy of the dossier at the same time, and the Ministers' official (from the Justice Department) and representative (from the prison) will likewise have copies of the entire dossier. Each copy should be identical.

The dossier for a life prisoner tribunal will follow broadly the same pattern as that for a long-term prisoner as described in para.7–09. It should contain the original indictment, post-mortem report, usually the minute of proceedings before the High Court, and the trial judge report.

Where the prisoner appears for a first tribunal after spending **9–11** many years in the pre-2001 Act system, there will generally be a note of the circumstances of the offence as prepared for Ministers under the previous system (these are no longer prepared under the present system), plus notes of the outcomes of any previous parole reviews. Staff reports covering the whole sentence will be provided, as will details of any admissions to hospital under s.71 of the Mental Health (Scotland) Act 1984, if appropriate. If there have been any psychiatric or psychological reports prepared, including pre-trial reports, these should be included. In most current cases, a relatively recent psychological report will be produced. Staff reports should culminate with a Lifer Liaison Officer's overview, prepared shortly before the dossier is issued by Ministers. Details of any misconduct reports, their dates and the punishments awarded, should be included. The minutes of any recent Risk and Needs Assessment, if appropriate, should be included. Reports from a prison-based social worker and an up-to-date Home Background report are essential. As the tribunal has the power to direct release, even where the prisoner may be of no fixed abode, such a report should identify whether appropriate homeless accommodation may be available.

Given that the dossier is prepared by Scottish Ministers and issued to parties and the board some seven weeks before the hearing, it is extremely common for additional papers to be submitted, often up until the morning of the hearing. The prisoner may incur a misconduct report, or his domestic circumstances may change. His solicitors may obtain up-to-date reports whose conclusions differ from those relied upon by Ministers. Any report or other document obtained by any party, that may have even a peripheral bearing on risk, will be tabled and sent to all parties. A practice has grown up of some tribunal chairmen checking, in advance of the hearing, that all late tabled papers have been received by all parties, in order that copies may be made available of any documents not received. While the production of such documents is governed by r.23, general practice is to admit any relevant document before the hearing, even when its intimation has not fallen within the prescribed time period. This is particularly relevant where a misconduct report on the prisoner is made immediately before the hearing. Such a matter has an obvious bearing on the question of risk, and, provided the prisoner has an opportunity to make his own views known to the tribunal, the interests of fairness require the tribunal to consider the matter. On occasions the significant nature of an alleged recent adverse development may require the hearing to be adjourned. It should, however, be noted that tribunal cases are specifically excluded from the provisions of r.6, which governs non-disclosure of information, by the terms of r.6(3). This is considerably different from the procedure in England, most recently brought into sharp focus by *Roberts v The Parole Board* [2005] UKHL 45, in which the Home Secretary sought, and was granted, permission not to disclose certain sensitive information to the prisoner and his representatives, but in circumstances where an independent "special advocate" was permitted access to the information. This practice was held by the House of Lords to be lawful, and is now enshrined in r.6 of the Parole Board Rules for England and Wales. It appears that, were a similar situation to arise in Scotland, Ministers would require to make application to the chairman of the tribunal in terms of r.19(2)(c) to make an order directing that certain documents not be served. The situation has not, however, yet arisen before any Scottish tribunal.

Often the last paper sent to the tribunal is the one of greatest concern to the prisoner. While there is no specific duty on Ministers in terms of the Rules to provide the board with a position statement, setting out whether release is opposed and if so why, or, where release is not opposed, what additional licence conditions Ministers feel are necessary, such statements are now issued by Ministers in every tribunal case. These documents set out, in detail, the position that Ministers will take before the hearing, particularly where release is opposed, but they are very often not sent to parties and the board until a matter of days before the hearing. Thus, the prisoner, his representatives and the members of the tribunal are not aware until a very late stage in preparation whether Ministers oppose release or not.

Rule 27(3) states: **9–12**

"The parties shall be heard in such order as the tribunal may determine and shall be entitled at the hearing—

(a) to be heard either in person or through their representative;

(b) to hear each other's evidence and to put questions to each other (or in the case of the Scottish Ministers, their official or officials attending the hearing) and to any person called by the other party;

(c) to call any person whom the tribunal has authorised to give evidence or to produce any document in accordance with rule 23; and

(d) to make submissions to the tribunal,

and any member of the tribunal shall be entitled to put questions to any party or representative or any person giving evidence."

Rule 27(4) gives the tribunal the power to exclude any person, including witnesses or those accompanying the prisoner in terms of r.22 or r.25, from the hearing or any part of it, if their conduct either has disrupted or is likely, in the opinion of the tribunal, to disrupt the hearing. In a recent English case, *R (on the application of Gardner) v The Parole Board* [2006] EWCA Civ 1226, the Court of Appeal held that the tribunal was entitled, in terms of the analogous provision in the English rules, to exclude the prisoner from the hearing, but permit his legal representative to remain, when a witness who had expressed a fear of giving evidence in front of the prisoner (in this case due to serious allegations of domestic violence) was giving evidence at the tribunal hearing. At the conclusion of the witness's evidence in chief, the prisoner's counsel had been granted an adjournment to take instructions prior to cross-examining her. The court held that this procedure complied with accepted notions of fairness, both at common law and in terms of Art.5, and observed that the rules were deliberately designed to be flexible and permissive, in order to achieve a balance between the interests of the prisoner and those of society as a whole, and that the tribunal chairman had exercised his discretion appropriately.

At present, the standard format for Life Prisoner Tribunals is that, after the chairman has introduced the members of the tribunal, and the parties and observers, and made his introductory remarks, proceedings are opened by the Ministers' official (usually a civil servant from the Justice Department, but sometimes a senior prison officer) stating, in brief, whether Ministers will invite the tribunal to direct release or not. This is followed by the prisoner or his representative stating, in brief, whether the prisoner is inviting the tribunal to direct release.

9–13 The Ministers then present their case in detail. Where release is opposed, the reasons for opposition are generally enumerated in detail by the Ministers' official, based upon information in the dossier, and generally following the terms of the position statement referred to above, following which the Ministers' representative will set out the proposed prison management plan that has been devised for the prisoner, and the timescale that Ministers and prison staff regard as appropriate for the completion of this plan, and the coursework identified in it (if appropriate). Ministers almost inevitably propose a period, of either the maximum two years specified in terms of s.2(5A)(b) of the 1993 Act, or such lesser period as they consider appropriate, before which the next review should take place. The prisoner or his representative then has the opportunity to cross-examine both the Ministers' official and representative, in respect of any matter he considers relevant. The breadth of the provision of r.27 means that there is no bar, in the course of this, to the tribunal hearing briefly from the prisoner himself in respect of any matter where there may be a factual dispute. After the prisoner's cross-examination is concluded, it falls to the members of the tribunal to ask any question they consider relevant of Ministers. It is current practice for the two lay members to be given the opportunity to question Ministers first, with the chairman asking questions last. The Ministers may elect to call a witness, for example in the case of a prisoner downgraded from open conditions an officer from the previous establishment to speak to the circumstances of a downgrade, or someone who can speak directly to alleged misconduct on a placement.

Where release is unopposed, the Ministers' case is customarily presented by a prison officer. He or she will set out the proposed additional licence conditions Ministers regard as appropriate for management of risk, and again may be cross-examined by the prisoner or his representative, and may be questioned by the members of the tribunal. It should be noted that the decision whether to release or not is solely for the tribunal — even where both parties are in favour of release, the tribunal may not be satisfied that the "protection of the public" test has been made out in the prisoner's favour and may decline to direct release.

Where Ministers wish to call a witness or witnesses, and their attendance has been approved by the chairman under r.23, there is no set point within their presentation at which they must be called. This is entirely at the discretion of the chairman, and tends to depend on the particular evidence the witness may give, and whether it would fit logically before or after the other submissions. Witnesses are not put on oath, but are examined and cross-examined in a similar manner to that in a trial or proof. Again, all members of the tribunal may ask any questions they consider relevant of the witness.

The issue of hearsay evidence, particularly when it relates to **9–14** intelligence gathered from anonymous sources, was considered by the Court of Session in the recent case of *Alexander Birrell, Petitioner* (unreported, [2006] CSOH 181). In that case the petitioner had been convicted of the murder by fireraising of a grandmother and two young grandchildren. On the expiry of his punishment part, a Life Prisoner Tribunal was arranged. Shortly before it took place, Ministers presented written evidence to the effect that police had been advised, by an anonymous source, that the prisoner was seeking to source weapons for a specific criminal purpose. They called an officer to the hearing, who had not personally spoken to the anonymous source, but confirmed the outline of the information. Having considered this and other evidence, the Tribunal declined to direct release.

The prisoner submitted a petition for judicial review, contending that the procedure adopted by the Tribunal was procedurally flawed. It was observed that the evidence given was secondary hearsay, and the source was not identified, but it was further noted that the police officer who gave evidence was cross-examined by the solicitor-advocate for the prisoner.

In refusing the prayer of the petition, Lord McEwan observed "It is accepted that the Tribunal acted upon hearsay evidence. In my view on the authorities they were entitled and indeed bound to do so ... The prisoner had the right to have his case properly heard. I do not think, in the case of a life prisoner, there is any presumption that he has a right to liberty and indeed, in my view, there is a presumption that he remains a risk. The second interest is that of the informer. The relevant authorities have a duty to protect him. Thirdly, and most important of all, the Tribunal has a duty to protect the public. That must prevail over all other interests."

9–15   The court further held that it would not have been appropriate for the tribunal to seek to secure the attendance of the informant, that there was no rule precluding the admission of hearsay, and that the procedure adopted by the tribunal was fair to all.

Once Ministers have led all their evidence, they close their case, and it passes to the prisoner of his representative to make such submissions or lead such evidence as they wish. Again, there is no set formula for this — some agents begin by leading evidence from the prisoner immediately, while some prefer to develop a full oral submission before either questioning their client or inviting questions from the Ministers and the members of the tribunal. It should perhaps be noted that r.27(5) provides that — "The tribunal may consider any document or information notwithstanding that such document or information would be inadmissible in proceedings before a court of law but no person shall by virtue of these Rules be compelled to give any evidence or to produce any document which he or she could not be compelled to give or produce in proceedings before a court of law."

It may perhaps further be observed that r.9, which governs confidentiality in proceedings before the board and tribunals, and provides that any information in connection with the tribunal, or the information given to the tribunal, shall not be disclosed, either directly or indirectly to any person not involved in the proceedings or to the public, has two important exceptions. The chairman of the tribunal may, in terms of r.9(i), direct a waiver from the terms of this rule, and, perhaps more significantly, r.9(ii) provides that the rule does not apply in connection with court proceedings. Thus, where a prisoner has elected, having been advised of the terms of r.9, to provide the tribunal with an explanation of, for example, and outstanding criminal charge, members of the tribunal may subsequently be cited as witnesses at the trial for that offence. So far as I am aware, only one request has ever been made in terms of the former provision, and no member of the board has ever been called as a witness to speak to matters that took place during a tribunal. Given the clear terms of r.9, the chairman of the tribunal should always advise a prisoner who is facing outstanding charges that he is not obliged to answer any questions on these matters. With that exception, the tribunal may hear evidence in respect of any matter that has a bearing on the prisoner's potential level of risk. While it is of course possible for a prisoner to decline to take questions from Ministers or tribunal members, virtually all prisoners are willing to answer questions in the course of the hearing, although, as with court procedure, this is not always the most prudent move. The general perception remains that as the purpose of the hearing is to determine whether is remains necessary that the prisoner continue to be confined, he or she should be wiling to address any potential concerns directly, by giving evidence and answering questions.

Again, the prisoner or his representative may call a witness or **9–16** witnesses on exactly the same basis as Ministers. It is fairly common for prisoners to call family members or supervising officers to give evidence as to proposed release plans.

Once the prisoner has been questioned and his witnesses have given evidence, his case is closed. The tribunal then hears closing submissions as provided for in r.27(3), again in such format as parties or their agents consider appropriate. Ministers present their submissions first, so that the prisoner or his representative is permitted to speak last. Members of the tribunal then retire to consider their decision.

The decision of the tribunal

Unlike the cases of determinate sentence prisoners, where the **9–17** parole board is considering granting parole on some future date, the question for the tribunal is whether, *as at the date of the hearing,* it is no longer necessary for the protection of the public that the prisoner should be confined. If the board finds that confinement is no longer necessary, then they must direct release, in which situation the prisoner will be released into the community within 24 hours of receiving the board's decision. The decision rests with the board alone. They may direct release where it is opposed, and may decline so to direct even where both parties move them to direct release. Continued detention after the expiry of the punishment part has been analysed within the jurisprudence of the European Court of Human Rights as solely with a view to the protection of the public (*Weeks v United Kingdom*, (1988) 10 EHRR 293). Over time, it has long been recognised that a prisoner's level of risk is likely to change, and Art.5(4) of the ECHR specifically provides an entitlement to take proceedings by which the lawfulness of his detention shall be decided "speedily" by a court, and his release directed if the detention is not lawful. The wording of this Article is permissive, and presumptive in favour of liberty. In *Zamir v United Kingdom*,

(1983) 40 DR 42, a case concerning the lawfulness of detention of an illegal immigrant, the European Commission opined that "the state, as the detaining authority, should be required to prove that the individual is lawfully detained". At present, the test set by s.2(5)(b), however, creates, by its wording, a presumption in favour of continued detention "unless ... the Board is satisfied that it is no longer necessary for the protection of the public that the prisoner should be confined". While there is no specific onus on the prisoner to adduce sufficient evidence, the board's duty is to order continued detention where it is not satisfied, on the evidence produced, that the public would be adequately protected should he be released. In common with every other public body, the board is bound by the terms of statute law. At present, there appears to be no public or parliamentary pressure to alter the terms of the statute into a form that might create a presumption in favour of liberty. The petition for judicial review in 2001 referred to previously challenged the "reverse" burden as being incompatible with Art.5(4) of the ECHR, but the prisoner died before the matter was judicially determined, and, to my knowledge, no similar submission has been made to the court since. However, it is probably instructive to note that in *R v Lichniak*, [2002] UKHL 47, decided in November 2002, Lord Bingham of Cornhill stated:

> "I doubt whether there is in truth a burden on the prisoner to persuade the Parole Board that it is safe to recommend release, since this is an administrative process requiring the board to consider all the available material and form a judgment. There is, inevitably, a balance to be struck between the interest of the individual and the interest of society, and I do not think it objectionable, in the case of someone who has once taken life with the intent necessary for murder, to prefer the latter in case of doubt."

In the light of these comments, it may be doubted whether the matter will be re-raised in the Scottish Courts.

The board's power to release is found in s.2(4) of the 1993 Act, and their duties are specified in s.2(5). Where the board declines to direct that a prisoner be released on licence, in terms of s.2(5A) it shall:

> "(a) give the prisoner reasons in writing for the decision not to direct his release on licence; and
> (b) fix the date when it will next consider the prisoner's case under this section, being, subject to subsections (5AB) to (5AD) below, a date not later than two years after the date

of its decision to decline to direct the release of the prisoner."

Sections (5AB) to (5AD) referred to above cover the variety of **9–18** situations in which a prisoner may, either before the tribunal has been convened, or after a first tribunal has declined to direct his release and a date has been fixed for a review, have received a further custodial sentence that he will be serving as at the date fixed for the review. If he would not be eligible for release on the date previously fixed for the review, another date must be chosen. Such date must be either the date on which the prisoner would be eligible to be released, or considered for release, from all such other sentences (subject to any change to the date on which he would be so eligible, for example if he were to abscond or receive a further sentence), or a date as soon as practicable after that date, and the new date selected must replace any date previously fixed for considering the prisoner's case.

The precise format of the board's decision is governed by r.28, **9–19** which provides that:

"(1) A decision of a tribunal may be taken by a majority and the decision shall record whether it was unanimous or taken by a majority;

Provided that, where the tribunal is constituted by two members, the chairman of the tribunal shall have a second or casting vote.

(2) The decision of the tribunal shall be recorded in a document which shall—

(a) contain a statement of the reasons for the decision;
(b) be signed and dated by the chairman of the tribunal; and
(c) be sent to the parties not later than 14 days after the end of the hearing."

Where the tribunal members, or the majority thereof, are in favour of release, then they must determine the appropriate licence conditions before the decision letter can be issued. The process of determining conditions is effectively the same as that for long-term prisoners, as described in Chapter Seven. Generally, the seven "standard" conditions will be imposed, and the tribunal will then consider, in the same way as the board does in respect of a paper review, whether other conditions in respect of accommodation, job search, alcohol or drug counseling, or no contact with specific individuals are appropriate. Once again, in selecting the additional conditions, the tribunal must have regard to the question of risk, and the purpose of the additional conditions is to assist the prisoner in further reducing his or her level of risk.

9–20   It should once again be observed that, while the formal issuing of the licence is carried out by Ministers, they do not themselves determine the conditions in the licence itself. Section 12 of the 1993 Act states:

> "(3) The Scottish Ministers may under subsection (1) above include on release and from time to time insert, vary or cancel a condition in a licence granted under this Part of this Act; but—
>
> (a) in the case of a long-term or life prisoner released by the Scottish Ministers under subsection (1) of section 3 [i.e. a prisoner released on compassionate grounds] of this Act without consulting the Parole Board, no licence condition shall be inserted, varied or cancelled subsequent to the release except in accordance with the recommendations of the Parole Board; and
>
> (b) in the case of any other long-term or life prisoner, no licence condition shall be included on release, or subsequently inserted, varied or cancelled except in accordance with such recommendations."

As is widely known, a prisoner released on life licence remains subject to that licence for the remainder of his life. However, where a released prisoner has demonstrated a continuous period of good behaviour in the community for ten years, with no criminal charges or convictions, no recalls to custody or requests for recall, and where his cooperation with supervision has been acceptable throughout, the supervising officer may contact Ministers and request that they refer the case to the parole board for consideration of termination of supervision conditions. The board has a complete discretion whether to grant such a request and terminate the supervision requirement. In the event that the request is granted, the sole remaining licence condition will read:

> "You shall be of good behaviour and keep the peace".

Obviously, any involvement with the criminal courts after that remains the sole licence condition is likely to give rise to consideration of recall to custody.

9–21   Where the tribunal does not direct release, it must specify the reasons for its decision in writing. The letter is sent to the prisoner himself, with copies being issued to the prisoner's representative, those who appeared for Ministers, and the members of the tribunal. The format of the letter may vary from chairman to chairman, but the letter must specify reasons for the decision and the date of the next review. Where the case is heard within a hospital, a courtesy copy is sent to the Responsible Medical Officer, although he is not, as has been seen, a party to proceedings. Customarily the letter will contain a section headed "The degree of risk and the steps to be taken to address this", "The desirability of transfer to different conditions within the options available", and "The period before the next review". As such decision letters may be the subject of proceedings for judicial review, the letter must be fully detailed, and explain the reasoning whereby the tribunal has reached the view that the prisoner presents an unacceptable risk. Reference should be made to submissions made on behalf of Ministers and the prisoner, and where there is a dispute over the interpretation or significance of a passage of evidence, the tribunal's letter should give reasons why it preferred one witness to another. While it is preferable that the letter also be comprehensible to the prisoner, the number of prisoners with literacy problems and learning difficulties, combined with the requirement that the letter must stand alone as the sole record of proceedings before the tribunal, mean that very few decision letters will be fully understood by their prisoner recipients.

Further, the letter must specify the date upon which the case will next be considered. European jurisprudence is to the effect that, where automatic reviews of the lawfulness of detention have been established, in order to take account of the possible diminution in levels of risk, reviews should take place at reasonable intervals. Two years was considered to be the maximum acceptable period between reviews, and that has therefore been specified as the maximum period in terms of s.2(5A). Where the tribunal declines to direct release, it has manifestly concluded that his continued detention is necessary for the protection of the public, and it is therefore directing a further review on a future date, on which another tribunal will consider a fresh dossier. It should be noted that it takes around three to four months to complete all the reports necessary for a second or subsequent dossier. As r.28 requires that the decision letter be issued within fourteen days of the hearing, and as rr.7 and 21 read together require the prisoner to be given seven weeks notice of the hearing, it is impractical to fix a review date shorter than six months from the date of the hearing.

Within these parameters, the tribunal has a complete discretion **9–22** as to the length of review selected. In selecting the date of the next review, where the tribunal is of the view that there is a genuine prospect that the prisoner will progress through the system towards release, the date of the next tribunal should be selected for a period by which, if all has gone as expected, the prisoner will have made significant progress. There will of course be cases in which prisoners present as utterly resistant to the notion of onward progression, in which the tribunal may consider that the maximum length of review is its only option. While the tribunal system is generally geared towards encouraging prisoners to progress towards release, it is recognised that there will be some inmates who have little realistic prospect of release at the expiry of their punishment part, or for a great many years thereafter, if at all. The tribunal is not bound to accept proposed timescales from either party, although these may be persuasive. While the tribunal fixes the date of the next tribunal, any comments that it makes in its decision letter as to the proposed progression of the prisoner up until that date are not directive, but merely recommendatory. The tribunal may consider that a prisoner spend a longer or shorter period in certain conditions prior to the next hearing, and, while Ministers will generally pay heed to these recommendations, it is by no means unknown for them not to be accepted.

Where the board has fixed a review date and circumstances alter (for example, serious outstanding criminal charges are dropped or the prisoner is acquitted after trial, and the prisoner progresses to open conditions several months earlier than expected, therapeutic work recommended by the tribunal is no longer available, or accommodation suddenly becomes available), s.2(5C) of the 1993 Act permits the board, at the request of the prisoner, to direct Ministers to refer the case to the board before the date fixed. Such requests are not uncommon. They are made in writing, usually by the prisoner's legal representatives, and are considered by the board at a casework meeting. If the board is satisfied that cause has been shown for an earlier tribunal, then it selects a date for the hearing, and directs Ministers to prepare the dossier and conduct the hearing on the new date. If the board is not so satisfied, the previous review date stands.

Proposed changes to the tribunal system

9–23   At the time the 2001 Act came into force, it was estimated that there would be around 140–180 tribunals held in Scotland each year. This was based, to an extent, on the expectation that most tribunals would either direct release or order a two year review. In practice, review periods of nine to 18 months are the norm, and very often prisoners are not released on a second review due to adverse developments since the previous hearing. When the growing number of tribunals considering the cases of recalled life sentence and extended sentence prisoners, plus the 30 or so determinate sentence oral hearings are added to these, the number of Parole Board hearings now stands at around 300 per annum.

This has obviously created somewhat of a strain on the budget **9–24** allocated to the Board by the Executive, and, in the Financial Memorandum to the Custodial Sentences Bill, it was proposed that the cost of Tribunals be reduced by reducing the number of Board members hearing each case to two, one of whom would be legally qualified, and would act as chairman. The reasoning behind these proposals, other than on pure economic grounds, were not immediately apparent, and few were surprised when they were found to be absent from the draft Parole Board (Scotland) Rules 2007, designed to come into effect once the Custodial Sentences and Weapons (Scotland) Act 2007 came into force. Tribunals will continue to consist of three members, one of whom may dissent from the majority view.

CHAPTER 10

RECALL AND RE-RELEASE

10–01 Of all the subjects covered in this book, the one that is probably least known to the public yet best known to long-term prisoners, and that generates by far the largest amount of litigation, is that of recall of prisoners to custody, and the circumstances in which they may be re-released. As the operation of s.16 of the 1993 Act and its effect upon short-term sentences has been covered in detail earlier, this chapter will deal with the effect of recall on long-term, extended sentence and life prisoners. While the effect of recall is rarely reported in the press or on television, recent studies have shown that around one in six long-term prisoners subject to parole licence is referred for consideration of recall during their parole period, and that around one in three of those subject to non-parole licence conditions is likewise referred to the parole board. Where cases are referred to the board, it recommends recall in around 75-80 per cent of cases. The number of persons recommended for recall has been rising steadily, from 20 parole licensees and 96 non-parole licensees in 1998, to 49 and 236 respectively in 2005. Of these, 30 were recalled and re-released, 37 had warning letters issued, 34 were disposed of in another manner without returning to custody, and the remaining 184 were either not re-released, or their cases had not been determined by the end of the year. Thus in 2005, 75 per cent of all those recommended for consideration of recall spent some time in custody as a result.

The power to revoke licences and recall prisoners to custody originates in modern practice from s.28 of the 1989 Act. There are two separate powers under which a prisoner on licence, whether serving a determinate of a life sentence may be recalled. Section 28(4) provides a statutory power to direct re-release following recall, and that will be discussed later.

Section 28(1) provides that "Where the Parole Board recommends the recall of any person who is subject to a licence under section 22 or 26 of this Act, the Secretary of State shall revoke that person's licence and recall him to prison." When the Act first came into force, the word "may" appeared where "shall" now appears, but once again Ministers are now obliged to act as directed by the

Parole Board. In respect of prisoners sentenced for offences committed since October 1, 1993, recall is governed by the analogous provisions contained in s.17(1) of the 1993 Act, which governs recall of long-term and life prisoners.

A more urgent, and increasingly commonly used power is that **10–02** given to Ministers under s.28(2) of the 1989 Act (for pre-1993 Act prisoners) and s.17(1)(b) of the 1993 Act. The former provides that "The Secretary of State may revoke the licence of any such person and recall him as aforesaid without consulting the Board, where it appears to him that it is expedient in the public interest to recall that person before such consultation is practicable," while the latter provides that Ministers may revoke an offender's licence and recall him to prison if revocation and recall are, in the opinion of [Scottish Ministers], expedient in the public interest and it is not practicable to await the recommendation of the Parole Board. In 2005, of the 285 cases referred, 32 had been recalled by Ministers under this section.

Although it may seem somewhat obvious in practice, s.22A of the 1989 Act, as inserted by s.34(3) of the Criminal Justice (Scotland) Act 2003, provides that, where a prisoner who has been released on licence is detained in prison while the licence remains in force, his licence conditions are suspended for the duration of the period during which he is in custody, except the condition requiring him to be of good behaviour and keep the peace and (if such a condition has been inserted) any condition not to contact a named person or persons.

Rules 17(4) and (5) of the Parole Board (Scotland) Rules 2001 preclude any member of the Board who took part in making a recommendation to recall from participating in the Board that next considers his re-release. In order to facilitate this, on their appointment to the Board each member is assigned as either a member of the recall panel or the re-release panel, where they remain (other than in rare emergencies or on their duties being varied by the Chairman of the Board) throughout their term of office.

For the avoidance of doubt, it should be observed that recall, whether by Ministers or by the Parole Board is not, in itself, a sentence, merely an administrative decision taken on the grounds that a licensee presents as an unacceptable risk to the public. It is therefore not governed by the Crown's attitude to bail on any outstanding charge, and the fact of recall does not preclude the court from imposing an unexpired portion of any sentence in terms of s.16 of the 1993 Act, It should, however, be noted, that s.204 of the 1995 Act makes it incompetent for any court to impose or attempt to impose any sentence consecutive to recall; the logic behind this being that, as recall is based upon an assessment of risk (which is not, by its nature, a static factor), the Parole Board may competently direct re-release some considerable period before the statutory sentence end date of the long-term sentence, on which date the consecutive sentence would theoretically commence.

Grounds for Recall

10–03   It has long been recognised by the courts that the status of a released prisoner subject to licence conditions is not the same as that of a free citizen. A prisoner on licence is still serving his sentence. He is not at liberty, save by virtue of his good behaviour and compliance with licence conditions and therefore revocation of his licence and recall to prison does not amount to a "deprivation of liberty", in the sense that arrest and detention do. In *Weeks v United Kingdom*, (1988) 10 EHRR 333, the U.K. government sought to draw a distinction between liberty, properly understood, and a life prisoner being permitted to live on licence outside prison. The court accepted that the freedom enjoyed by a life prisoner, such as the applicant, when released on licence, was more circumscribed in law and more precarious than the freedom enjoyed by the ordinary citizen. In *R (on the application of Giles) v Parole Board*, [2004] 1 A.C. 1, the House of Lords, having reviewed the relevant European jurisprudence on the point, specifically rejected the argument that a custodial sentence (in this case a determinate sentence) could properly be divided into two parts, these being the punitive element and the preventive element. Whether within a prison or within the community, a prisoner continues to be subject to the obligations of their sentence until the statutory termination date thereof.

Recall may be ordered by the board or by Scottish Ministers whenever it is considered necessary and in the public interest. The prisoner need not be aware, and in many cases will not be aware that he is being considered for recall. Indeed, the grounds upon which his recall was ordered are not intimated to him until his readmission to prison (s.17(2)). Grounds for recall themselves are many and varied, but they may broadly be categorised as falling into three groups, which may of course overlap with each other, namely (1) non-cooperation with supervision and/or licence conditions, (2) proven reversion to criminal offending, and (3) alleged reversion to criminal offending. Unsurprisingly, the last of these is the most controversial.

The first of these cover the myriad situations in which supervision on licence breaks down. Many prisoners fail to grasp that the central purpose of the 1993 Act is to permit them to spend the last part of their sentence in the community under supervision and subject to conditions, and resent being supervised. Many other leave prison full of good intentions, but struggle to cope in the community. Common reasons for recommending recall include — failing to attend a number of supervision appointments and continuing to do so after receiving a written warning, failing to make oneself available for prearranged home visits, changing address without advising one's supervising officer, failing to attend for drug/alcohol counselling as directed, failing to comply with job advice, misleading supervising officers in respect of material and relevant factors (for example, a reversion to alcohol or drug abuse), or simply not making oneself available for supervision. As the board has to be satisfied that the offender's level of risk continues to be manageable in the community, any one or more of these may result in them considering that the public interest favours recall to custody.

Where a prisoner on licence has been convicted of a further **10–04** offence, this automatically constitutes a breach of licence condition 6 — "You shall be of good behaviour and keep the peace", and certain consequences may follow. He may be remitted to the High Court for consideration of the imposition of a further period in custody in terms of s.16(2)(b) of the 1993 Act, and may in addition receive a custodial sentence for the offence itself. In addition to both these sentences, he may be recalled to custody, recall not being itself a sentence, but merely an order for return to custody to serve the balance of the sentence previously imposed. The parole board has a discretion in such cases, and not every conviction, even those resulting in a custodial sentence, would be regarded as justifying recall. It may perhaps be worth noting that in a great many cases information about convictions may take some weeks to reach the supervising officer, who then prepares a written report to Scottish Ministers, who then send a full dossier to the parole board, which then assigns a date for consideration of the grounds for recall. It is therefore not uncommon for the prisoner to have served their sentence and returned to the community on licence before the parole board considers the case. If other factors indicate a cooperative attitude towards supervision, then the board may consider that the public interest does not require another period in custody.

Of greatest concern both to prisoners and the public are the cases of persons accused of committing serious crimes whilst on licence. Not surprisingly, the public are concerned when anybody who has, on the face of it, been released "early", commits a further offence. On the other hand, recall may competently be ordered by Ministers or the board long before guilt is established, at a time when the presumption of innocence still applies, and the effect of a recall order is to stop the 140-day "clock" running in terms of s.65 of the

Criminal Procedure (Scotland) Act, as the prisoner is no longer "detained by virtue of that committal", but is in custody serving the remainder of his previous sentence. A prisoner in that situation is treated by the prison service as a convicted, not a remand prisoner, and the Prison Rules 2006 apply to him accordingly.

It should perhaps be noted that, in consideration of grounds for recall, Ministers or the parole board have been provided with a police report, detailing not only the charges, but the circumstances of these charges as reported to the procurator fiscal, and they may thus be in a position to consider whether, on paper, there is evidence sufficient to justify the decision to charge the accused. At present, information is not automatically obtained from the procurator fiscal or the sheriff clerk of the court where the licensee appeared, although in more serious cases it is usual for information as to the date of the last court appearance and whether bail was granted or not. The granting or refusal of bail is not determinative of the board's decision, although it may be persuasive. There is, however, nothing to prevent the board, who have of course the advantage of seeing the full police report not shown to the court, from taking the view that a person who has been released on bail presents an unacceptable risk in terms of reoffending. The functions of the board (and of Ministers) in deciding cases under the 1989 Act and the procurator fiscal or the sheriff in deciding upon bail in terms of the 1995 Act are in no way analogous. It is not surprising, therefore, that many prisoners both north and south of the border have mounted legal challenges, both in the domestic courts and in Strasbourg.

Challenging the Decision to Revoke a Licence

10–05   In *McRae v Secretary of State for Scotland*, 1997 SLT 97, a recalled prisoner sought quashing of the decision to revoke his licence as unreasonable. He had been charged with an offence whilst on licence, but the case was deserted *pro loco et tempore*. In refusing the petition, the Lord Ordinary observed "I am also of opinion, as was conceded by counsel for the petitioner, that the fact that an individual's guilt has not been determined is not an obstacle for the board when considering whether an individual's conduct since the date of his last sentence merits revocation of his licence". He further stated "In challenging the reasonableness of a decision of the Parole Board which has anxious, difficult and heavy responsibilities to discharge, in my opinion, a very strong case has to be made out before intervention by judicial review is justified. The petitioner has failed to persuade me that this decision was other than reasonable and I shall sustain the board's first and third pleas in law and dismiss the petition."

In reaching this view, the Lord Ordinary referred to *Howden v Parole Board for Scotland,* unreported, (1992 GWD 20-1186), in which Lord McLean had stated "The respondents in making recommendations have of course a duty to act fairly to individuals affected by such recommendations. The statutory responsibilities they owe however are owed by them to the Secretary of State for Scotland and no one else (see *Payne v Lord Harris of Greenwich,* especially per Shaw LJ at [1981] 1 WLR, pp 762 and 763-764). Their discretion in reaching any particular decision is unfettered. Their principal concern is for the safety of the public and whether that safety would be endangered if the prisoner were to be released on licence. They must, however, balance that consideration against the legitimate interests of the prisoner even in cases of mandatory life imprisonment. They must, too, have regard to all material considerations and they must have material before them to justify their decision."

A similar view was taken in the unreported case of *Holmes v Secretary of State for Scotland,* OH July 14, 1998, where a recommendation for parole had been withdrawn following a breach of temporary licence conditions. While that case did not involve recall, the court once more deferred to the board's discretion.

In *Varey v The Scottish Ministers,* 2000 SLT 1432 the petitioner **10–06** was on licence in respect of a series of fixed sentences totaling 29 years when he was charged with offences under the Misuse of Drugs Act 1971. Ministers revoked his licence under s.28(2), and the parole board, on consideration of his case, did not order re-release. He then petitioned the court for judicial review of the decision by Ministers to recall him to custody, but the petition was dismissed, noting that the decision of Ministers had effectively been reviewed by the parole board's decision not to re-release him. A further argument in that case, to the effect that the actions of Ministers were *ultra vires,* in respect that there was insufficient causal connection between the original offences in 1984 and the deprivation of liberty in 1999, and that there should, in terms of Art.5(4), be further court-like review of the decision to revoke his licence. In rejecting this argument, the court held that considerations in respect of Art.5 did not apply to decisions relating to prisoners detained under determinate sentences, and that, *esto* a review was required, the "paper" consideration by the parole board was sufficient. It will be noted that *Varey* was decided before the 2001 Act came into force. The position in Scotland is markedly different today.

The English courts took a different view to the Lord Ordinary in *R v The Parole Board and the Secretary of State for the Home Department, Ex p Giles* [2002] 1 WLR 654, in which it was held that the requirements of Art.5(4) did apply to the continuing detention of persons during that period of a determinate sentence that was attributable not to punishment but was imposed to protect the public from serious harm from the offender. The court held that the question of whether someone in that situation was lawfully detained should be determined by an oral hearing of an adversarial nature. As will be seen later, within the Scottish system, any extended sentence prisoner recalled to custody is now entitled to have his case considered by a tribunal in terms of s.3A of the 1993 Act, and determinate sentence prisoners may apply to have their case for re-release considered at an oral hearing.

In the case of English life sentence prisoners, Collins J drew a distinction between their status and those of determinate sentence prisoners, in the case of *R v Secretary of State, Ex p Stafford*, [1998] 3 WLR 372, stating — "The power of recall of a lifer who has been released on licence is exercisable on somewhat different principles. A failure to comply with conditions will usually justify recall since it will be necessary to ascertain whether his failure is indicative of an attitude which may show dangerousness. Once the lifer is back in custody, the necessary reports will be obtained to see whether there is in fact a risk of danger to the public. If there is not, he should be released."

10–07   In *R (Smith) v Parole Board, (No. 2)* [2004] 1 WLR 421 the Court of Appeal had to consider whether recall, where breach of licence remained unproven, involved an infringement of a persons Art.5 right to liberty. LJ Kennedy stated:

> "In my judgment the decision to recall is not an infringement of the right to liberty in the case of a prisoner serving a determinate sentence who has been released on licence because his right to liberty for the period up to the end of his sentence was lost when he was sentenced. There being no right to liberty which has been infringed there can be no right to take proceedings to decide whether the detention is lawful. That has already been decided."

Prisoners continue to challenge the power of the board to recall them, again more often in England. Most recently, in *Hirst v Secretary of State for the Home Department and the Parole Board*, [2006] EWCA Civ 945, a prisoner sought to challenge the entire statutory process for recall of prisoners in terms of the provisions of s.32 of the Crime (Sentences) Act 1997, which are analogous to the Scottish provisions of the 1989 and 1993 Acts, as being incompatible with Art.5 of the ECHR. He sought to argue that the power of the Secretary of State to effect the immediate return of a life sentence prisoner to prison, by revocation of licence, either on his own initiative or on the basis of a recommendation to that effect by the parole board in terms of the statute was unlawful, arguing that, as the parole board is not at that stage acting in a judicial capacity, the decision is made by the executive. It therefore followed that the scheme provided for a return to custody upon an arbitrary decision by the executive, without the normal safeguards built in to the criminal justice process. In their grounds of appeal, his agents described the process as "systematic executive incarceration", and contended that it was therefore incompatible with Art.5 of the ECHR. It was further argued that once the prisoner was released on licence, the link between his conviction for manslaughter and any possible recall was broken. If he was to be recalled, he was entitled to the safeguard of a system whereby some kind of initial or pre-liminary judicial determination, similar to a bail hearing, should take place to decide whether the recall should or should not take effect pending the final determination. No provision for such a safeguard existed in statute or elsewhere.

In rejecting this argument, the Court of Appeal observed that the process of recall "is not even remotely related to the process by which an unconvicted citizen may be arrested and detained." While the precise allegations that led to his recall were not specified, the court, after reviewing the authorities, observed "In our judgment this appellant's recall was justified in law by the link between the discretionary sentence of life imprisonment imposed following his conviction for manslaughter and his behaviour during the short period while he was living in the community on licence. This gave rise to realistic concerns for public safety", and held, therefore, that his recall was lawful, there being nothing in either statute law or European jurisprudence that could require there to be a form of adversarial or quasi-adversarial hearing to determine whether recall was appropriate.

The circumstances in which recall may be sought

Other than cases of extreme emergency, where police reports are **10–08** sent to Ministers indicating that serious offending has either taken place or is imminent, in which case Ministers will avail themselves of their statutory power to recall without reference to the board, reports of proven or alleged non-compliance with licence are sent by supervising officers to Ministers. Where offending is alleged, the licensee is under a duty to report this to the supervising officer, although commonly the supervising officer only learns of an alleged offence through colleagues within the court. Whether the breach is due to alleged offending or non-compliance with supervision, the supervising officer must report the circumstances forthwith to the appropriate section of the Justice Department.

In a few cases, the Justice Department may regard the matter as relatively minor, and they may elect to issue a warning letter without referring the case to the board. In the majority of cases, the circumstances are reported to the board, which may, after consideration of the full dossier (including all papers presented at the time of release on licence) by a quorum, either (1) decide no action is necessary, (2) issue a warning letter, reminding the prisoner of their obligations and the fact that the licence remains in force until the last day of their sentence, or (3) direct that the licence be revoked and they be recalled to custody, to wait their representations anent re-release.

In the last situation, the recall order is usually issued by Ministers within 48 to 72 hours, and from that date until their apprehension, the licensee is deemed to be "unlawfully at large". Thus, where a licensee is not apprehended for four months after the issue of a recall order, their sentence end date is extended by the exact same period.

Consideration of re-release

10-09   Given that the decision to revoke a prisoner's licence and recall him to custody manifestly involves deprivation of liberty, Art.5(4) of the ECHR is engaged, and procedures must be in place whereby the lawfulness or otherwise of the prisoner's detention must be determined by an appropriate judicial body. In Scotland that function is exercised by the re-release panel of the parole board. The manner in which consideration of re-release is undertaken has developed rapidly in recent years, following a number of important court decisions.

Reference has been made earlier to the case of *Stafford*. In that case, the prisoner had been convicted of murder in 1967 and was released on licence in 1979. Following a breach of licence conditions, he was recalled to custody in 1989, and the following year the parole board recommended that he be re-released on life licence. Subsequently, in 1994, he was convicted of cheque fraud and received a six year sentence. The Secretary of State revoked his life licence. When he became eligible for release from the fraud sentence, the Secretary of State declined to follow the board's recommendations in favour of release and directed his continued detention on the ground that he presented a risk of committing further non-violent imprisonable offences. Collins J took the view that the Secretary of State should not make decisions on the release of mandatory life prisoners by reference to considerations of a broader public character, and should decide cases only on the basis of dangerousness. He allowed the application for judicial review and quashed the home Secretary's decision not to release him. The Court of Appeal disagreed, and, in affirming the decision of the Court of Appeal, the House of Lords found [1999] 2 A.C. 38 that the Secretary of State had acted within the wide discretion conferred by the Criminal Justice Act 1991 s.35(2). On application to the European Court of Human Rights, Mr. Stafford contended that the Secretary of State had breached his rights under Arts 5(1) and 5(4), as the continued detention was no longer justified by his original sentence for murder and that he had been deprived of the opportunity to review the lawfulness of the decision in court.

In granting his application, reported at (2002) 35 EHRR 32, the court held that Mr. Stafford must be regarded as having exhausted the punishment element of his offence of murder. When his sentence for the later fraud offence expired, his continued detention could not be regarded as justified by his punishment for the murder. The Secretary of State had not relied on any evidence of mental instability or a risk to the public of further violence. Instead he expressly relied on the risk of further non-violent offending. In so doing, the Secretary of State breached Mr. Stafford's rights under Art.5(1) as there was no sufficient causal connection, as required by the notion of lawfulness in Art.5(1)(a), between the possible commission of other non-violent offences and the original sentence for murder. With regard to Art.5(4), the court observed that the tariff comprised the punishment element of a mandatory life sentence and the Secretary of State's role in fixing that tariff was a sentencing exercise. Upon the expiry of the tariff, his continued detention depended upon assessment of elements of risk associated with the original life sentence for murder. Those elements were liable to change over time and thus, new issues of lawfulness requiring determination by a body satisfying the requirements of ECHR had arisen. The original trial and appeal could not satisfy issues pertaining to the compatibility with Art.5(1) of his continued detention. The lawfulness of his continued detention had not been reviewed by a body with the power to release or with a procedure containing the necessary judicial safeguards and thus, his rights under Art.5(4) had been breached.

It therefore follows that, in determining the level of risk a life **10–10** prisoner may pose to the public, the parole board (in this case the tribunal) must be able to refer the level of risk to the index offence. Further allegations of violence, or of potentially violent confrontation such as breach of the peace or possession of offensive weapons or firearms are unlikely to pose particular difficulty in this regard. Acquisitive property offences alone (fraud, embezzlement, theft by shoplifting, reset and the like) will seldom, if ever, be referable as risk factors in respect of a violent offender. Where the offender offended when under the influence of drink or drugs, and there is evidence of a reversion to alcohol and/or drug misuse within the community, this might be felt to be problematic, if there is no direct evidence of recent violence. This point arose in the unreported case of *Andrew Malone, Petitioner*, (Outer House December 18, 2002), where a prisoner who had been recalled for breaching the terms of his life licence in respect that he was facing charges under the Misuse Of Drugs Act, and not re-released, sought judicial review of the board's decision to recall him, and sought interim suspension and interim liberation. In refusing the motion, Lord Nimmo Smith, having considered the cases of *Waite* and *Stafford* above, observed that a tenuous causal connection may be sufficient to justify recall. He observed "The nature of controlled drugs is that they are harmful to those who consume them, and consumers very often become dealers as may be the case here. They are often associated with crimes of violence. That seems to bring the case much nearer the end of the spectrum represented by *Waite* rather than *Stafford*". Thus, a reversion to drug misuse, particularly accompanied by an allegation of supplying will often be sufficient to justify recall of a person on licence.

Life sentence prisoners

10–11   Where a prisoner has been recalled for an alleged breach of his or her life licence, the decision as to whether to re-release or not is taken by a tribunal of the board, constituted and convened in exactly the same manner as any Life Prisoner Tribunal considering release on life licence, and with exactly the same powers to direct a review, and to recommend progression. The statutory powers to order recall and subsequent re-release can be found in s.17 of the 1993 Act. Where re-release is ordered, the board may, in terms of s.17(4A) recommend that the Scottish Ministers insert, vary or cancel conditions in the prisoner's licence. While the subsection gives the board only a recommendatory power, the wording of s.12(3), which prohibits Ministers from inserting, varying or canceling a condition in the prisoner's licence without the prior approval of the parole board, effectively means that only the parole board may impose licence conditions (although Ministers may, of course, propose such conditions).

Where the board does not order re-release, it must specify a date, not less than two years from the date of its decision, on which the case will next be considered by a tribunal. In practice, it is fairly common for recalled life sentence prisoners to spend several more years in prison, and to be considered by a number of tribunals before their level of risk is deemed acceptable.

At this point it should be noted that, as presently drafted, cl.34 of the Custodial Sentences and Weapons (Scotland) Bill may preclude repeated reviews of the case of a recalled life prisoner. The test for re-release is to be amended so that the prisoner must only be confined in future if he presents a risk of *serious harm to the public* (cl.33(3), and the parole board retains its directive power in respect of re-release. Clause 34(2) currently reads: "Where a prisoner's life licence is revoked by virtue of Section 31 (1) or (4), the prisoner must be confined until the prisoner dies". This does appear to be contradicted by cl.33(6), which does provide for further reviews, and no doubt this apparent confusion will be resolved before the Bill becomes law.

Determinate and extended sentence prisoners

The courts have further considered the test to be applied in considering whether to re-release persons who have been recalled during the licence period of determinate sentences. The court's observations in *Stafford* in respect of the lawfulness or otherwise of continued detention could be applied with little difficulty to the situation of a recalled prisoner. In *R (Sim) v Parole Board*, [2003] 2 WLR 1374, Elias J considered the case of a prisoner serving an extended sentence imposed in England, who had been paroled but was recalled by the Secretary of State during the licence period following breaches of the conditions of his licence. The parole board issued a recommendation confirming that recall, and the case for re-release was referred to the board, which refused to direct the claimant's release on the ground that the risk of the claimant re-offending if he was released was high. The claimant applied for judicial review of the board's refusal to direct his release on the ground, *inter alia*, that the board wrongly took into consideration hearsay evidence, and made certain factual findings on the basis of that evidence, when both fairness and compliance with Art.5(4) required that it should have called relevant witnesses to establish the material facts in dispute. It was therefore argued that Art.5(4) was engaged by the prisoner's recall, even where he was sentenced to a determinate sentence, and, moreover, that Art.5(4) required evidence which might be relied on as a basis for the continued detention of the prisoner to be led at an oral hearing. It was held that the parole board's decision to continue the detention of the claimant was justifiable and involved no unfairness but this was only because the court considered that the procedure adopted by the board satisfied Art.5. He stated, having reviewed and considered the relevant English and European authorities then in force, "The decision to continue to detain a prisoner who has been subject to recall during

10–12

an extended licence period is a decision which attracts the safeguards of article 5; it is not a sufficient response to say the detention is justified by the original sentence. Accordingly, the detention must be consistent with the aims and objectives of the original sentence and must be subject to regular supervision by reviews which are compliant with article 5(4) (as indeed they currently are.)"

It was observed that the extended sentence was, by its nature, qualitatively different to the "longer than commensurate" sentence that may be imposed in England, due to the offender's perceived level of risk, in which situation the offender required to spend longer in custody before being released on licence. Instead, it was noted, an extended sentence provided for a longer period of supervision on licence. The case was appealed by both parties on a number of grounds. In dismissing the appeal and cross-appeal, reported as *R (Sim) v Parole Board*, [2004] Q.B. 1288 the Court held that, given its conventional construction, the relevant English legislation required the parole board to be satisfied that confinement of the offender was no longer necessary for the protection of the public before it directed his release and, if it were in any doubt, to decline to direct his release; that such a construction was incompatible with the Art.5 rights of offenders who were detained after recall during the extension period, given the presumption in favour of liberty contained therein; but that, applying s.3 of the Human Rights Act 1998, the Act could be read and given effect in a way which was compatible with Art.5(4) by requiring the board to direct the release of such an offender unless it was positively satisfied that it was necessary for the protection of the public that he be confined.

The court further observed (at page 1320) "Licence conditions are imposed for a purpose. The breach of a particular licence condition may not be such that one can credibly argue on the basis of that breach that a "high risk" of further sexual offending exists, still less that such offending would be of a kind to cause serious harm." It was observed that the imposition of an extended sentence was a measure designed to provide greater protection for the public from the commission of further offences by the offender. Where an offender had been recalled for breaching the conditions of an extended sentence licence, the nature of the breach had to be referable to the risk elements that gave rise to the imposition of the extended sentence. There requires to be a causal connection between the original conviction and the eventual deprivation of liberty. Further, to comply with the requirements of Art.5(4), the further detention had to be consistent with the aims and objectives of the original sentence and be subject to regular supervision by reviews by a court-like body.

10–13   As s.210A of the 1995 Act specifically provides that the court may only pass an extended sentence if it "considers that the period (if any) for which the offender would, apart from this section, be subject to a licence would not be adequate for the purpose of protecting the public from serious harm from the offender" it therefore follows that, where a prisoner is recalled for breach of an extended sentence licence, he is entitled to have his case considered by a tribunal, that the test to be applied by that tribunal is whether he presents a risk of serious harm, and that the tribunal must only direct release where it has considered whether it is necessary for the protection of the public from serious harm that the prisoner should continue to be confined, and has concluded it is not so necessary.

Thus, when the Crime and Disorder Act 1998 introduced extended sentences into Scots Law with effect from September 30, 1998, a fresh s.3A was inserted into the 1993 Act at the same time, governing the re-release of recalled prisoners serving extended sentences. Where an extended sentence prisoner is recalled to custody in terms of the provisions of s.17, whether by the parole board or Scottish Ministers, and they are not at the material time serving another sentence of imprisonment, they are entitled, in terms of s.3A(2) to require the Minister to refer their case to the board. A tribunal is then convened in the same manner as a Life Prisoner Tribunal, generally in the prison where the offender is situated, and heard by three members of the board with a legally qualified chair. The procedure at the hearing is governed by Pt IV of the 2001 rules, subject to the exceptions that the test to be applied is that of protection of the public from risk of serious harm, rather than the simple "protection of the public" test in s.2(5), and that the tribunal must be positively satisfied that the prisoner's level of risk of serious harm, if any, can be managed within the community.

The tribunal is conducted in the same manner as a Life Prisoner Tribunal, with the important exception that, where the tribunal does not direct re-release, it does not fix the date for the next consideration of the case. Section 3A(2) specifies that, where a prisoner's case has previously been referred to the parole board either under that section or s.17 of the 1993 Act, he may require Ministers to refer his case to the board not less than one year following the board's disposal of his case. In practice, Ministers refer such cases to the board automatically at the one year point after last consideration. Thus, where an extended sentence prisoner is recalled to custody, and his tribunal is fixed less than twelve months from his sentence end date, where the tribunal does not direct release he remains in custody until the last day of his sentence with no right to a further review, and is released subject to no licence conditions whatsoever. Where the prisoner has more than a year until his sentence end date an re-release is not directed,

Ministers must refer the case back to the board not less than one year later. The tribunal may recommend an earlier review on cause shown, but unlike the situation in Life Prisoner Tribunals, where such an order is directive, Ministers are not obliged to fix an earlier review. Where the tribunal is satisfied that the risk the offender poses can be managed by supervision in the community, it shall direct release, subject to the imposition of appropriate licence conditions, and Ministers shall give effect to this recommendation by virtue of s.3A(5).

10–14 As with Life Prisoner Tribunals, Scottish Ministers are customarily represented by an official from the Justice Department and a member of prison staff with knowledge of the prisoner, a position statement is generally issued, and at the conclusion of the tribunal a decision letter is issued, signed by the chairman, within fourteen days.

However, the existence of Extended Sentence Tribunals appeared on the face of it to create a disparity between the rights of those determinate sentence prisoners who had received extended sentences and those who had not, and the question arose whether determinate sentence prisoners recalled in terms of s.17, who wished to challenge the circumstances of their recall, could only do so by way of paper review, or whether oral hearings analogous to tribunals were appropriate and necessary. In Scotland, the matter was argued before the Outer House in respect of a determinate sentence prisoner in *Dempsey v Parole Board for Scotland*, 2004 SLT 1107. In that case, a prisoner released on parole licence in May 2002 at the halfway point of a five year sentence had returned to Northern Ireland, and within two weeks of his arrival there had appeared in court charged with offences of theft, abduction and demanding money with menaces, allegedly committed in the course of the preceding week. Ministers revoked his licence in August 2002, and the parole board did not direct his re-release in November 2002. He was not afforded the opportunity of presenting his case at an oral hearing, there being no provisions in either the 1989 Act or the 1993 Act providing for such hearings, and neither he nor his representatives having requested such a hearing.

In terms of the parole system, as a recalled prisoner, he was entitled to have a further (paper) review of his case by the board within one year of the decision of November 2002, but in May 2003 the court in Belfast consented to his being released on bail, subject to the deposit of a sum of money. The prisoner being willing and able to consign these sums, he remained in custody solely as result of the revocation of his licence, and his agents contacted Scottish Ministers requesting that they call on the board to review his case. When Ministers indicated in June 2003 their inability to comply with this request, he lodged a petition for judicial review of both the board's decision not to order his re-release and the Ministers' purported decision not to review his case.

In dismissing the petition, the court held that the prisoner's **10–15** deprivation of liberty flowed from the five year sentence imposed in 1999, and as a prisoner sentenced to a determinate sentence, his entitlement under Art.5(4) to have the lawfulness of his detention decided upon was satisfied by the paper review in November 2002, that it could not be said that the parole board were not entitled to have regard to its assessment of the risk it considered the petitioner to present at the time it did not direct his immediate release, where this was specified under r.8 of the 2001 Rules, and the board's focusing on that criterion when making their decision did not result in a failure to comply with Art.5; it did not mean that the causal connection with the original sentence had been broken or that the basis of the deprivation of liberty suffered by the petitioner had come to depend on circumstances liable to change with the passage of time.

The court, having observed that no request for an oral hearing of the prisoner's case had been made, further decided that, had it been necessary to consider whether the proceedings on and preceding November 4, 2002 (when re-release was not directed) complied with Art.5, a second hearing would have been ordered, at which the prisoner would have been required to provide further specification of the circumstances and factual matters in dispute which he founded upon as indicating that Art.5(4) required an oral hearing in the present case. As that matter did not fall to be decided in this case, the court expressed no view as to the remedy that might have been appropriate.

The Right to an Oral Hearing

Matters did not rest there for long. Two English cases on the **10–16** question of the right of recalled prisoners to an oral hearing of their cases had been referred from the Court of Appeal to the House of Lords, and the conjoined appeals were decided in January 2005, in *R v Parole Board Ex p Smith and R v Parole Board Ex p West*, [2005] UKHL 1. Both appeals concerned the procedure to be followed by the parole board where prisoners recalled after their release from determinate sentences sought to challenge the revocation of their licence. Each of the appellants had been recalled to custody for alleged breaches of licence, and sought to have the matter determined at an oral hearing, at which evidence could be led and witnesses called, relying on the provisions of Art 5 and 6 of the ECHR. Both submitted that there were relevant matters in respect of their apparent breaches of licence that, had they been made known to the board at an oral hearing, might have resulted in the board reaching a different decision.

In allowing the appeals, Lord Bingham of Cornhill observed that "procedural fairness called for more than consideration of his representations, on paper, as one of some 24 such applications routinely considered by a panel at a morning session" and further observed that "while the Board's task certainly is to assess risk, it may well be greatly assisted in discharging it (one way or the other) by exposure to the prisoner or the questioning of those who have dealt with him. It may often be very difficult to address effective representations without knowing the points which are troubling the decision-maker. The prisoner should have the benefit of a procedure which fairly reflects, on the facts of his particular case, the importance of what is at stake for him, as for society." He therefore concluded that the parole board had breached its duty of procedural fairness owed to the appellant, by failing to offer him an oral hearing of his representations against revocation of his licence, and was accordingly in breach of Art.5(4) of the Convention.

In his concurring judgment, Lord Hope of Craighead stated "Assumptions based on general knowledge and experience tend to favour the official version as against that which the prisoner wishes to put forward. Denying the prisoner of the opportunity to put forward his own case may lead to a lack of focus on him as an individual. This can result in unfairness to him, however much care panel members may take to avoid this." He therefore concluded "I agree therefore that the common law test of procedural fairness requires that the Board re-examine its approach. A screening system needs to be put in place which identifies those cases where the prisoner seeks to challenge the truth or accuracy of the allegations that led to his recall, or seeks to provide an explanation for them which was not taken into account or was disputed when his recall was recommended by his supervising probation officer. Consideration then needs to be given to the question whether it is necessary to resolve these issues before a final decision is made as to whether or not the prisoner is suitable for release. If it is, an oral hearing should be the norm rather than the exception."

10–17   Immediately following this decision, the parole board for Scotland altered its procedures for consideration of re-release of recalled prisoners. The initial paper review by a quorum of three members required to be chaired by a legal member of the board, who could act as a tribunal chairman. On consideration of the dossier, it was to be minuted whether the prisoner had requested an oral hearing, and further, even when such a hearing had not been requested, whether in the view of the board, the interests of fairness required that there be such a hearing. Where the panel felt that there were issued raised by the prisoner that could not be resolved without an oral hearing, such a hearing would be convened urgently within the prison where the offender was situated.

While it is my understanding that such hearings are considered by a single legal member of the board in England (apparently there are fifteen members of the English Board authorised to conduct such hearings), r.14 of the 2001 Rules provides that the quorum in Scotland remains three members. However, there are some significant differences between the way oral hearings are conducted and the conduct of tribunals. Scottish Ministers routinely do not send an official to present their case at such hearings, nor do they generally issue a position statement. However, prisoners are generally legally represented, and the Scottish Legal Aid Board makes ABWOR available for these hearings in the same manner as it does for tribunals. While witnesses may be invited to attend, as the hearings are not convened in terms of Pt IV of the 2001 Rules, the chairman of the tribunal's power to cite witnesses under r.24(2) does not apply. A decision letter in the standard form is not issued, signed by the chairman within fourteen days; instead, a longer and more detailed form of the re-release minute, summarizing the evidence and submissions, and explaining the reasons for the board's decision is issued by the Secretariat. The test in determinate sentence prisoners' cases is not that of "serious harm", but the standard test of "unacceptable risk" in terms of reoffending. Since 2005, these hearings have become relatively common, as desired by Lord Hope, with about 10 per cent of cases being resolved by way of an oral hearing. There is no doubt that oral hearings will become a fixture of the board's work, and fresh procedures will no doubt be set up when the board's rules are next amended.

The future of recall and re-release

In its 2006 report "Early release from prison and Supervision of **10–18** Prisoners on their Release", the Sentencing Commission observed that the present arrangement, where members of the board customarily recommend recall for breach of licence, and then other members of the board determine whether the prisoner should be released or not, gives rise to the possibility of an appearance of bias being alleged. While it recognised that such an allegation would in reality be ill-founded, it recommended that the power vested in the board to direct revocation of the licence be removed, and that that be the function of Ministers alone, with the board's function being to review the justification to recall, and to determine whether the prisoner should be re-released. In their White Paper "Release and

Post Custody Management of Offenders", Scottish Ministers endorsed this proposal, with the exception that they propose that only Scottish Ministers should be able to recall for "serious" breaches of licence. As yet, this term remains undefined, and it remains to be seen whether regular and flagrant breaches of the requirement to attend for supervision appointments or specialist counselling, or moving address without taking any steps to inform a supervising officer, will be regarded as more serious than, say, facing a summary prosecution for theft by shoplifting or vandalism.

In any event, it should perhaps be noted that the function of the re-release panel of the parole board is not to "review the justification to recall", but to determine whether the prisoner presents an acceptable risk in terms of reoffending. There are a great many cases in which the decision to recall was entirely justifiable on the basis of the information available to the board at the time, but that the circumstances as presented on consideration of recall indicate that the prisoner's level of risk can now be managed in the community. The prisoner may have been acquitted of outstanding charges; he may now be welcome back into the family home from which he had been ejected; he may have undertaken a drug detoxification and now be drug-free and willing to engage more fully with supervision. None of these matters could be known to the body that revoked the prisoner's licence, and it is to be hoped that the function of the board is not to be varied from one of having a wide discretion in determining the question of risk, to acting purely as an appellate body, charged only with the responsibility of determining whether the decision to recall was justifiable at the time.

CHAPTER 11

CONCLUSIONS, AND LOOKING TO THE FUTURE

According to the most recently published figures, recorded crime in **11–01** Scotland fell by five per cent in 2005–06, to the second-lowest figure recorded in the last decade. Crimes of violence, dishonesty and drug offences continue to fall. While reported crimes of indecency, including rape, indecent assault and lewd behaviour did show an increase, these still represent substantially less that two per cent of all reported offences. Indeed, were it not for the huge number of offences of vandalism reported in the last two years (representing around 30 per cent of all reported offences), the decrease in the level of recorded crime would be even more marked. This is at a time when increasing use of sophisticated scientific techniques, and the omnipresence of CCTV recording equipment in shops and town centres would be expected to have a material effect upon detection rates for many offences.

At the same time, the Executive plans the building of another mainstream prison in West Lothian. The press and broadcast media continue to fill their newspapers and airtime with sensational reporting of exceptional cases, and the Scottish Parliament continues to promote new legislation, much of it designed to create fresh criminal offences, to make bail more difficult to obtain, to increase the courts' powers of sentence, and to "streamline" court procedures by allowing fines of up to £500 to be imposed without a case even being prosecuted, and to permit trials in the absence of the accused. The Criminal Proceedings etc. (Reform) (Scotland) Act 2007, which is likely to increase the population of both remand and convicted prisoners, received the Royal Assent in January 2007.

The provision of specialised supported accommodation for released prisoners with identified needs, whether in the field of mental health, alcohol or drug problems, remains poor. Twenty-six years after the Criminal Justice (Scotland) Act 1980 authorised the provision of bail hostels as a halfway house between a remand in custody, and release into the community, no such establishments exist. It is often extremely difficult to identify suitable resources into

253

which released prisoners, at risk of relapse, can be placed, particularly at short notice.

11–02   The criminal law, particularly in the field of sentencing, continues to develop apace. Since this volume was commenced, the higher courts have acquired the power to make orders for lifelong restriction. The Risk Management Authority, set up in terms of the Criminal Justice (Scotland) Act 2003, is now in place to appoint accredited Risk Management Assessors, whose functions are to enable the courts to make informed decisions on whether to impose such an order. Thus a further sentencing tool, analogous but not identical to the discretionary life sentence, is now available where an offender shows a tendency to serious violent, sexual or life endangering (for example, fireraising) offending. There can be no doubt whatsoever that risk assessment, in a form that would have been utterly alien to a Senator of the College of Justice even fifteen years ago, is now, and will continue to be, a fixture of the Scottish criminal justice system. The High Court of Justiciary considered, then made its first Order for Lifelong Restriction in October 2006, the case of *HM Advocate v Colin Ross,* which involved a man with a history of serious violent offending against women, attacking an American tourist without warning on a Highland pathway.

In August 2006, the Sentencing Commission for Scotland published a further report, titled "The Scope to Improve Consistency in Sentencing". Having noted the High Court's general reluctance, when sitting as an appellate body, to avail itself of the right under ss.118(7) and 119(7) of the 1995 Act to issue guideline judgments as to appropriate sentences, the Commission recommends not only that the Appeal Court should consider making greater use of this power, but also that the court should be required, in its Opinion, to make reference to the fact that it regards the opinion as constituting a guideline judgment. It further recommends the creation of a Sentencing Advisory Body, whose members should be appointed by Ministers, and which will have similar powers to the Sentencing Advisory Panel currently operating in England and Wales. If, as seems likely, these proposals are accepted by Ministers and fall to be enacted in the future, Scotland will join Canada, New Zealand, England and Wales, parts of Australia and at present 22 of the states of the U.S.A. in having in place a system of sentencing guidelines. Once again, this will present as a radical change in the administration of Scottish criminal justice, although our relatively small population and thus smaller judiciary may ultimately mean that little practical change will be seen "on the ground".

Well-publicised cases of offenders committing further offences whilst subject to licence conditions have given rise to understandable calls for "honesty in sentencing". Those who are most vociferous in their criticisms of the current regime do not present as aware that, of those long-term prisoners who are considered an unacceptable risk in terms of reoffending, and are therefore not granted the privilege of release on parole, substantially more than half do not reoffend during their supervision period. In addition, reporting of issues relating to the punishment of repeat offenders tends seldom to focus on the positive benefits that accrue to many offenders who are able to access job search services, alcohol and drug counselling and a level of support and supervision on release. It is not often observed that those who are recalled to custody and remain in prison until the last day of their sentences (a small, but not insignificant group) are released with no access whatsoever to any form of supervision, counselling or employment advice.

Most importantly for the subject matter of this book, and as **11–03** referred to in earlier chapters, the Custodial Sentences and Weapons Bill 2007, proposing radical alterations to the way in which sentences are expressed, and providing for risk assessment for a far greater proportion of prisoners, completed its passage through parliament in March 2007. It is anticipated that the necessary Statutory Instruments and Acts of Adjournal necessary to put the new systems in place will be in force by summer 2008. Effectively, this Act sweeps away the terminology of the 1993 Act. Sentences in future are to be based upon a "combined structure" model, with the court imposing a "custodial part" and a "community part" in all sentences. The minimum "custodial part" is proposed to be 50 per cent of the length of the whole sentence, although the court will have a discretion to increase this up to a maximum of three quarters (although Ministers will retain the right to vary or amend these statutory maxima and minima). It is currently proposed that risk assessment be carried out in respect of all prisoners serving sentences in excess of fourteen days, although it should be noted that the Sentencing Commission's proposed threshold for this was twelve months. Those serving fourteen days and less will be expected to serve every day of their sentences in custody, although it may perhaps be observed that certain new proposals giving courts wider powers to deduct fines at source may reduce the otherwise enormous number of fine defaulters who would be caught by this provision. At this stage it seems too early to comment on whether the new risk assessment proposals are the most effective use of the limited resources available to the SPS.

Perhaps most controversially, Scottish Ministers propose to take back certain powers currently in the hands of the Parole Board for Scotland. It is, however, proposed that there shall still be a body known as the Parole Board for Scotland. The decision as to whether to recommend certain offenders for release on supervision into the community, jealously guarded by Ministers in the past, and gradually eroded by European jurisprudence and UK case law, will revert to their control, thus on the face of it restoring a political element to the sentencing process. In order to meet any anticipated challenges that the proposed new system is not ECHR compliant, the Parole Board, which will be transformed into something of an appellate body under this system, will have the right to direct Ministers to release prisoners, even when release is not proposed, and likewise, where Ministers elect to revoke a prisoner's licence (that power also being removed from the Parole Board), review of that decision will fall within the remit of the Board. As enacted, the Bill imposes an obligation on Ministers to refer the cases of "custody and community prisoners" not recommended for release at the halfway point of their total sentences to the Board (cl.10), and life prisoners to the Board before the expiry of their punishment parts (cl.17).

There seems little doubt that, in the immediate future, the effect of these new sentencing proposals will be to create a sudden and sharp increase in the number of prison admissions. Whether the new sentencing systems will ultimately lead to a decline in the number of persons sent to prison can only, at this time, be a matter for speculation. However, it might perhaps be said that Scotland can still take little pride in the number of its citizens, especially male citizens, who spend a part of their lives housed in custody at her Majesty's expense.

USEFUL INFORMATION ABOUT SCOTTISH PRISONS

Scottish Prison Service Headquarters
Calton House
5 Redheughs Rigg
Edinburgh
EH12 9HW

Tel: 0131 244 8745
Web: www.sps.gov.uk

HMP Aberdeen
Craiginches
4 Grampian Place
ABERDEEN
AB11 8FN

Tel: 01224 238300
Fax: 01224 896209

Governor: Audrey Mooney

Type of establishment: Short-term prison that holds prisoners of all supervision levels. The prison accommodates all remand prisoners and male adults serving sentences of up to 4 years.

Contractual Capacity: 225

HMP Barlinnie
81 Lee Avenue
Riddie
GLASGOW
G33 2QX

Tel: 0141 770 2000
Fax: 0141 770 2060

Governor: Bill McKinlay

Type of establishment: Male remand prisoners and prisoners serving less than 4 year sentences.

Contractual Capacity: 1222

HMP/YOI Cornton Vale
Cornton Road
STIRLING
FK9 5NU

Tel: 01786 832591
Fax: 01786 833597

Governor: Ian Gunn

Type of establishment: Cornton Vale provides custodial facilities and services for remanded and convicted females (including young offenders) in all sentence ranges and supervision levels.

Contractual Capacity: 330

HMP Dumfries
Terregles Street
DUMFRIES
DG2 9AX

Tel: 01387 261218
Fax: 01387 264144

Governor: Nigel Ironside

Type of Establishment: Dumfries Prison holds up to 80 male prisoners who are remanded in custody for trial and those convicted but remanded for reports. Short-term convicted male prisoners may be retained at Dumfries or transferred to another establishment according to their length of sentence and the availability of spaces.

Dumfries Prison also provides a national mainstream facility for holding up to 120 long-term and short-term prisoners who require to be separated from mainstream prisoners because of the nature of their offence, termed as offence related protection prisoners

Contractual Capacity: 189

HMP Edinburgh
33 Stenhouse Road
EDINBURGH
EH11 3LN

Tel: 0131 444 3000
Fax: 0131 444 3045

Governor: Dan Gunn

Type of establishment: Known locally as "Saughton" the prison holds adult male and under 21 prisoners who are on remand and also convicted prisoners serving less than 4 years. Long-term prisoners and Young Offenders when sentenced are held at Edinburgh awaiting transfer to their prison of allocation. Edinburgh also provides a national facility for prisoners at the pre-release stage of their sentence.

Contractual Capacity: 756

HMP Glenochil
King OMuir Road
TULLIBODY
FK10 3AD

Tel: 01259 760471
Fax: 01259 762003

Governor: Audrey Park

Type of establishment: Long-term adult male prisoners with high, medium and low supervision security classifications. Prisoners are not committed to HMP Glenochil direct from the courts but are admitted, following conviction, from other prisons. Glenochil provides a range of opportunities for addressing offending behaviour and for work and education.

Contractual Capacity: 440

HMP Greenock
Gateside
GREENOCK
PA16 9AH

Tel: 01475 787801
Fax: 01475 783154

Governor: Tony Simpson

Type of establishment: Male prisoners (both adult and under 21s) on remand, and short-term convicted prisoners. It provides a national facility for selected prisoners serving 12 years or over, affording them the opportunity for progression towards release.

Contractual Capacity: 300

HMP Inverness
Porterfield
INVERNESS
IV2 3HH

Tel: 01463 229000
Fax: 01463 229010

Acting Governor: Fraser Munro

Type of establishment: Known locally as "Porterfield", this prison provides secure custody for all remand prisoners and short-term adult prisoners, both male and female (segregated).

Contractual Capacity: 150

HMP Kilmarnock
Bowhouse
KILMARNOCK
KA1 5AA

Tel: 01563 548800
Fax: 01563 548845

Director: Wendy Sinclair

Type of establishment: The first prison in Scotland to be built under the private finance initiative became operational on the March 25, 1999. The prison is operated under a 25-year contract by Serco Group plc on behalf of the Scottish Prison Service.

The prison is a closed mainstream high security establishment. It accommodates male adult prisoners — remands, short-term and long-term — and male young offender remands. It does not have a national Top End facility but prisoners are able to apply through the normal procedures and gain the same access to national Top Ends as from other mainstream establishments.

Although Kilmarnock Prison is operated by Serco, it is part of the SPS estate and prisoners remain under the care of the Scottish Prison Service.

Contractual Capacity: 500

HMP Low Moss
Crosshill Road
Bishopbriggs
GLASGOW
G64 2QB

Tel: 0141 7624848
Fax: 0141 7726903

Governor: Stephen Coulter

Type of establishment: Provides accommodation for some 330 short-term, medium to low supervision category male adult prisoners sentenced to less than 48 months. The prison does not receive prisoners direct from court but takes selected medium to low supervision category prisoners from Barlinnie, Edinburgh, Greenock and occasionally Kilmarnock. It has a number of initiatives in place to provide for prisoner needs whether those are alcohol related, drug related, social or educational needs.

Contractual Capacity: 300

Scottish Prison Service Open Estate

HM Prison Noranside	**HM Prison Castle Huntly**
Fern By Forfar	**Longforgan**
ANGUS	**DUNDEE**
DD8 3QY	**DD2 5HL**
Tel: 01382 319333	**Tel:** 01382 319333
Fax: 01356 650245	**Fax:** 01382 360510
Deputy Governor: Jack Thomson	**Deputy Governor:** Jim McKay
Contractual Capacity: 140	**Contractual Capacity**: 285

Governor: Ian Whitehead

Type of establishment: HMPs Castle Huntly and Noranside jointly make up the SPS Open Estate. Both focus on providing employment training and transitional/through-care for prisoners working towards a structured reintegration into society. Both are open prisons holding low supervision adult male prisoners, including life sentence prisoners, who have been assessed as suitable to serve part of their sentence in open conditions. Noranside holds a small number of prisoners convicted of sexual offences, while Castle Huntly holds prisoners who require the support of the SPS methadone program.

HMP and YOI Perth
3 Edinburgh Road
PERTH
PH2 8AT

Tel: 01738 622293
Fax: 01738 630545

Governor: Kate Donegan

Type of establishment: Perth holds short-term (less than four years) local adult male prisoners, including fine defaulters, and those on remand. The establishment also accommodates in secure conditions long-term adult male prisoners including high supervision prisoners who are serving sentences of up to life imprisonment.

Contractual Capacity: 481

HMP Peterhead,
Peterhead
ABERDEENSHIRE
AB42 2YY

Tel: 01779 479101
Fax: 01779 470529

Acting Governor: Mike Hebden

Type of establishment: It can accommodate up to 306 prisoners including those requiring high supervision. It is a national resource for convicted, long-term sex offenders offering a range of programmes designed to challenge offending behaviour in order to reduce the risk of reoffending on return to the community.

Contractual Capacity: 306

HM YOI Polmont
FALKIRK
FK2 0AB

Tel: 01324 711558
Fax: 01324 714919

Governor: Bill Millar

Type of establishment: Scotland's only all male young offender institution.

Contractual Capacity: 570

HMP Shotts,
Canthill Rd,
SHOTTS
ML7 4LE

Tel: 01501 824000 (Main Prison)
Fax: 01501824001
Tel: 01501 824124 (NIC)

Governor: Rona Sweeney

Type of Establishment: HM Prison Shotts is a maximum-security prison for long-term adult male prisoners.

Contractual Capacity: 516

Parole Board for Scotland
Saughton House
Broomhouse Drive
Edinburgh
EH11 3XD

Tel: 0131 244 8373
Web: www.scottishparoleboard.gov.uk

SCOTTISH PRISON SERVICE: PRISONER POPULATION

Prisoner Population at February 2, 2007

Untried Male Adults	1,125
Untried Female Adults	82
Untried Male Young Offenders	292
Untried Female Young Offenders	11
Sentenced Male Adults	4,546
Sentenced Female Adults	183
Sentenced Male Young Offenders	582
Sentenced Female Young Offenders	33
Recalled Life Prisoners	65
Convicted Prisoners Awaiting Sentencing	209
Prisoners Awaiting Deportation	25
Under 16's	0
Civil Prisoners	0
All Scotland Total	**7,153**

INDEX